Tania Glyde is an author, journalist and broadcaster. She has written two novels to date, *Clever Girl* and *Junk DNA*. Her short stories have appeared in the *Disco 2000* and *Vox 'n' Roll* anthologies. She was *Time Out*'s sex columnist for two years, and produced and presented the groundbreaking chat show *Midnight Sex Talk* on Resonance 104.4 FM. She lives in London.

Praise for *Cleaning Up*

'What sets this book apart from other similar memoirs is that it is not only very well written, it's actually useful, both for the sober and not-so-sober. It is illuminating about the inner emotional damage that leads to wildly self-destructive behaviour; and also about the society that allows such behaviour to flourish...pretty much unputdownable' Nicholas Lezard, *Evening Standard*

'Depicts with bravery and a blazingly defiant wit an ongoing struggle...Glyde provides more than a harrowing account...she explores why women drink and puts her experience into the context of a culture that deems alcohol inseparable from fun' *Metro*

'A wonderfully candid insight into what could be any binge-drinker's life...Honest and educational without being preachy' *Scarlet*

'Compelling and starkly candid' *Herald*

'Insightful...the points raised are important. *Cleaning Up* is timely' *Guardian*

'Harrowing...unflinchingly honest...an absorbing personal account' *Time Out*

'Smart, funny an[...]   [...]*azine*

'A frank book, sometimes disarmingly so, and will worry many readers who may have a sneaking suspicion they drink a bit too much' *Attitude*

'Eminently practical and personal…one to recommend to the friend who needs to clean up' John Sutherland, *Financial Times*

CLEANING UP

HOW I GAVE UP DRINKING
AND LIVED

Tania Glyde

A complete catalogue record for this book can be
obtained from the British Library on request

The right of Tania Glyde to be identified as the author of this work has been
asserted by her in accordance with the Copyright, Designs and Patents Act 1988

First published in 2008 by Serpent's Tail
First published in this edition in 2009 by Serpent's Tail,
an imprint of Profile Books Ltd
3A Exmouth House
Pine Street
London EC1R 0JH
website: www.serpentstail.com

ISBN 978 1 84668 655 9

Designed and typeset at Neuadd Bwll, Llanwrtyd Wells

Printed in Great Britain by CPI Bookmarque,
Croydon, CR0 4TD

10 9 8 7 6 5 4 3 2 1

This book is printed on FSC certified paper

Mixed Sources
Product group from well-managed
forests and other controlled sources
www.fsc.org Cert no. TT-COC-002227
© 1996 Forest Stewardship Council
FSC

In memory of

James 'CountB' Savage
1972–2006

and

Michael Payne
1964–2006

contents

introduction

I'm cold. My hair's stuck to my face. I'm trying to open my eyes but the sun's too bright. I'm cold because the bathwater's cold. It wasn't like that earlier. It was dark then and the water was hot, as hot as I could stand it. My neck hurts from where I passed out with my head on the side. It's light outside. Shit. This wasn't supposed to happen. There's a dirty glass on the floor. Actually, my neck is really stiff. The light's too bright. I have to move. I'm cold. The water's cold. Get me out of here.

I stand in the living room. Ashtray. Tinfoil. Lighter. Nearly empty vodka bottle. Lights glow on the amp. Nick Cave. It's warm with the sun coming in. I walk around naked. Neighbours interested across the way. I go back into the bathroom and slump on the loo. Mission aborted.

I'm alive. This wasn't the plan, but I'm still alive. Although I don't know it quite yet, it's the end of a twenty-three-year love affair.

Imagine going out tonight, and not secreting a small plastic Evian bottle full of vodka about your person before leaving the house, most of which you'll polish off in the queue anyway. Imagine not feeling the need to drink a bottle of red wine before making a pass at the person you've fancied for months. Imagine not watching someone's body language as they stand at the bar, moving in like a starving cat as soon as they order a round. Imagine not grabbing unattended cocktails from tables as you walk past, nor panicking when your glass is empty, nor sweating when the wine bottle hasn't come your way yet. Imagine not following groups of people you hardly know back to the home of someone you've never met, because there's talk of beer in the fridge and the promise of so-and-so coming round later to drop something off. Imagine not having on-off group sexual relations with people you either don't know very well and don't especially like, or who are already perfectly close enough friends, but, after a long night and a few bottles, pills, tokes or snorts, become more intimate than is necessary for a friendship. Imagine not spending the whole of the next day apologising to people for something you don't really, truly, remember doing. Imagine not spending the whole of the next day, or the day after that, eating Mini Rolls in a darkened room, surrounded by crushed and stained newspapers that you've read twice because you forgot it all instantly the first time. Imagine not forgetting to brush your teeth and take off your make-up, both of which have become long-forgotten indulgences anyway.

Once upon a time, I couldn't imagine living any other way.

I used to be a proud participant in UK pisshead culture. I did the white wine thing and the vodka thing, and launched myself joyfully into the consequent, almost inevitable poly-drug use. To paraphrase Madame Lily Bollinger, I drank because it was Friday night, but also because it was Monday, Tuesday, Wednesday, and Thursday, and because it was the weekend. I drank because I was in despair, and because I was slightly annoyed. I drank when someone hadn't called for a few days, and I drank before going to meet them when they did. I drank when I was bored, and when I had too much to do. I drank because I was lonely, and because there were twenty people that I just had to see.

I was an ardent consumerist and a champion of quality: more times than I can remember, in more pubs than I can count, on returning from the bar, I would offer my glass, suspiciously, to a friend, for their verdict on whether the doubles were in fact singles, or whether the singles had been watered down, or whether there was any alcohol in my glass at all. If I hadn't had a drink before going out in the evening, and found myself caged and sober, in a bouncing, rumbling tube carriage on the way to Soho, I used to think I was going to have a panic attack. The feeling would not abate until I was happily tucked in at a bar with a glass in front of me. Seated before the start of a large event, I would become increasingly irritable, and then desperate, if no wine was immediately available.

At times, I used to wonder if I had a problem, but decided that, because so many people I knew seemed to be drinking far more than I was, I wasn't the one with the problem. And anyway, I was, most of the time, a strict, clock-watching 6 p.m.-er, and I almost never threw up, or passed out, in public. And I never lost a phone. Or a credit card. I sometimes did quizzes on websites, which told me I was *probably* an alcoholic, but by the general public definition – i.e. my friends – I was not. I never put vodka on my breakfast cereal. I never drank in the mornings, unless I was still up. I rarely blacked out and lost whole swathes of a night, searching back through my bag for clues as to where I had been, and how I got home. I rarely passed out on public transport, and never ended up in Birmingham. I rarely flaked out in anyone's front garden, unless I was an invited guest. I almost never had public crying jags, and was often congratulated on my pristine make-up at sunrise. In fact, my acting skills were second to none. I could be crying my eyes out, then answer the phone and sound absolutely fine. The more hung over I was when I went out, the more beautiful and sparkling people told me I looked. Perhaps I should have capitalised on this more – become a club hostess or escort perhaps – because I was, in fact, hung over nearly every single day of my life.

Like so many millions of others, I felt a powerful sense of entitlement to get pissed and have it large until I fell over. It was my inalienable right, as constitutional as the notion of the Free Country invoked by old-school greengrocers when ordered to use metric weights. As the years passed, I noticed a self-righteousness in myself, and in the other women I drank with, about our consumption of alcohol, that was bested only by our competitiveness when consuming it together. At their worst, women have a disturbing capacity to jump up like puppies at a proffered biscuit when there is an opportunity to compete with each other, for however shallow or short-term a goal, like a petty triumph at work, or a moment's one-upmanship around a man. I was no different. But you can't blame me, really. Alcohol doesn't answer back, tell you that you look fat, or loftily enquire after your position on the property ladder. Alcohol is easily, and legally, available to anyone who's got the money to pay for it, and it isn't a jealous lover, because it knows you'll always come back.

My relationship with alcohol was the longest of my life. It began on sofas at home, and ended over two decades later, after a long, inexorable downward spiral of life events, like a rock-fall in slow motion. Alcohol itself can't be blamed for what happened, but it had me firmly by the hand and helped me go – and more's the point, remain – where it was neither beneficial nor useful for me to be.

I gave up drinking on the 12th of September 2002. The earth did not crack open and give forth fire-breathing three-headed dogs. No trumpets sounded in the sky. I didn't get a telegram from the Queen. Perhaps I should have, because only a public declaration of pregnancy, or cancer, would have elicited a similar reaction from those around me. Of course, there are differences between pregnancy, cancer and sobriety. The pregnancy would eventually have ended, and the responses to the cancer would have changed over time, depending on the progress of the disease. It's only to the self-declared ex-boozer that people say, 'Wow! Still?'

I should say now that I didn't spend time in detox, or in a halfway house – although there were points in my life where a bed in a nice, secure clinic, with fresh flowers and group therapy and kind people looking out for me, would have helped me a lot. This means that I have no anecdotes about the recovering rock stars, models and famous comedians that I would have met 'in group', although I inevitably met a few before I decided to sober up. I also attended very few 12-step meetings. But, after six years, I have got a lot of new friends who have only known me as a sober person.

Living without alcohol is one of the strangest experiences I have ever had. And it goes on being strange. I've chosen to write about it because the world we are all exposed to through the media has become increasingly cartoonish. There's so much *stuff* out there vying for our attention, that only the biggest, nastiest, and loudest manage to get it. You'd think that you've got to have been a truckstop hooker at twelve, a heroin addict at fifteen, and twice imprisoned by the age of twenty-one, and, during that time, you've got to have been repeatedly raped by a multitude of uncles, priests and nuns, and slept rough for at least six months, or your experiences just aren't bad enough. Misery is too easily represented by checkboxes. If you haven't got enough horror points, the thinking goes then you really ought to keep quiet about it. I'm trusting that not everyone believes this, because your life can fall into misery without you ever ending up in a clinic. Because you don't have to be hitting on – or hitting – cab drivers, and waking up in a plaster cast, to be suffering at the hands of alcohol.

For more than twenty years I thought that alcohol was the only way to feel whole as a person. It was my passport to seeming, and acting, normal. Whether I was out with other people, or alone at home, it was the one friend I could rely on to be there for me, despite the fact that it bit back viciously every morning. To be able to give that up was about as likely as winning the lottery. But I did it.

Sobriety is still weird, even after six years. To understand living sober you need to understand living drunk. In my world, living drunk didn't mean I was drunk all day. That's just another stereotype. Just the anticipation of intoxication can be enough to get you through the day, or a whole week. Sometimes it's all you have.

Everyone has their own drinking story. Mine is – partly – about being an introvert in a world designed for and run by extroverts. I once saw a television documentary about an autistic woman who found going into supermarkets unbearable, because there were just too many colours and letters coming at her. So, someone designed a pair of glasses for her that had special pink lenses, so that when she went out, everything looked black and white with a rosy tint, and she was fine. When the world became too exhausting and frightening, alcohol had the same role for me as those glasses.

My drinking story is about being British in a world that hasn't forgiven us our empire, or its loss, and respects us even less for leading the world today in getting publicly hammered. (This state of affairs persists even in late 2008, despite the now well-documented increase in alcohol-related violence, the increase in cirrhosis of the liver in those traditionally seen as far too young to get it, and the abject failure of the new licensing laws that were supposed to turn us into paragons of self-restraint but, of course, did not.) My drinking story is about being female in a world that has not yet fully decided what to do about women. My drinking story is, above all, about looking for love, and finding it in all the wrong places.

a note on names and identities

I've changed some of these. While this is very much a book about me, it feels somehow wrong to call it my autobiography. It's a portrait of a state of mind, to try to explain what it's like to be someone who only feels complete, and safe, when they're boozed up – no matter how wonderful their friends and lovers are, nor how many opportunities come their way.

a note on memory loss

Although I rarely blacked out and lost whole chunks of a night, that doesn't mean my memory is crystal clear. There are times when I can remember a good time, when all we did was laugh, but when I try and remember what actually happened, and what actually made me laugh, it's all a blur, as if I'm reaching into a hologram. This, I guess, is the true freedom of drinking, the happy place that alcohol and drugs take you to – oblivion without loss of control. Ultimately, what I remember best of all are the days when reality bit back.

1.   the learning zone

From the age of about twelve until I am perhaps fifteen, every wall in my bedroom, including the ceiling, is covered with adverts cut out of magazines. They are mostly for alcohol, cigarettes or beauty products. They are all very glossy and all very designed. The trouble is, if I happen to look from an advert for sun cream, with two fit models gleaming Caramac brown in the sun by a violent blue pool, to my own pale unformed teenage reflection in the mirror, the difference is so striking as to be painful. During this time, I discover alcohol. Twenty years later I am still discovering it.

It is my mid-twenties by the time it occurs to me that I spent so much of my childhood in a state of fear, dread, or high anxiety, that living in perpetual discomfort has become normal. As a toddler, I wasn't like that. I was gregarious and fearless. But by the end of my time at primary school, just being accidentally left out when the exercise books are handed back in class takes me to the edge of crying. I am having panic attacks and I don't even realise. In my mid-teens, I say to my first boyfriend, 'You know that feeling when you feel like you're about to cry and you can't breathe and you make these funny noises when you try to?' 'Nope,' he says. End of discussion.

kindergarten

I got my first taste of alcohol from sipping the dregs out of my parents' wineglasses after dinner. I discover I love liqueurs, and later bite a chunk out of a fragile crystal heirloom, one of the few, after endlessly licking around it. My parents are not alcoholics. There are no clanking bin bags late at night. There are no secret stashes of Valium, Quaaludes, or barbiturates either.

I grow up feeling like an outsider in my own home. I am an only child with both biological parents, who remain together and live in the same house all the way through my childhood, on the edge of a small town in the middle of England. There are no step or half siblings in my world. I meet few other children, aside from my cousins once a year, and occasionally the neighbours, until I go to primary school aged five. Playschool is disapproved of by my parents, for reasons never made entirely clear, and I never work out whether it is to protect me from the rest of the world, or to protect the rest of the world from me. I learn to amuse myself, through painting or building things, and become very good at it.

At home, a lot of things are banned. A selection of television programmes, in case I pick up the characters' working-class accents, any mention of my father's family, and all discussion of my mother's past. All I am given to know about the latter is that bad things, unspecified, might have happened. What is and is not allowed to be discussed is a complex maze of triggers, which I never really learn to navigate. While there is plenty of chat, plenty of criticism and plenty of screaming, to speak about life's realities, or expose anything that might be uncomfortable, is taboo, and punishable with a good slap.

sibilants

In the countryside, small sounds get magnified. Some kinds of noise just won't merge with birdsong or distant tractors. All day, my mother talks to herself in a low, hissing voice, in endless looping monologues I can never quite hear. Life veers between silence, opera and violent rows – rows about shopping bags, the long past before I was born, small DIY jobs that would never be done, a tone of voice used in the previous conversation, my father's family if accidentally mentioned, holidays, the lack of them, something that happened at Christmas five years ago. From my earliest days, my parents fight loudly. Once, when I am out of the room, one attacks the other with a stool, leaving a hole in the bedroom door that remains there permanently. Car journeys, of which there are many, involve me sitting in the back while my parents scream at each other. I cry and cry to make them stop, but am silenced with sarcasm from my mother, and accusations of being a peacemaker. Then comes the silence. My mother sometimes takes to her bed for days, and a shroud falls over the house. As an adult I still catch myself turning off lights slowly and carefully, and watching TV at a low volume, even on my own. Walking-on-eggs habits die hard, and cause puzzlement among my various flatmates over the years.

terror

From a young age I am riddled with phobias – of heights, ladders, water, spiders, going fast on a bike. I become immobile and start crying, which is a source of exasperated amusement for my parents. Despite the ban on any mention of my father's mother and sister as individuals – this being due to some terrible incident or infraction that occurred before I was born, and which has never, to this day, been explained – my father's genetic make-up is regularly held up to scrutiny. I have, apparently, inherited his 'tainted blood', which is forever brought up as a reason for his – and my – inadequacies. When I am six, my mother succeeds in making me hate my father's mother for an entire year. She sits me down on the sofa and tells me over and over what a terrible, evil old woman my grandmother is. I believe her, and take to badmouthing granny with gusto, in my mother's presence at least. One day about a year later, however, I wake up and decide that my father's mother isn't horrible, and that I like her. I am very proud of what is, aged seven, my first conscious act of independence from my mother. I keep it to myself. Her own family she refuses to talk about beyond small, tantalising details that are sometimes contradictory.

Despite my mother's ongoing and relentless assessment of everything – be it other people's wealth relative to ours, other kinds of people and their various iniquities, and the state of the house – no actual plans are ever made to change any of it, or make it more pleasant. The future is a void, a mansion of the inevitable, and is spoken of with tired dread as if it has been imposed by some omniscient legal or moral entity. In this tight universe, other people are sub-human, far below animals in the pantheon of sentiment. My mother flies into terrible rages at the thought of cruelty to animals, at the same time declaiming against people who claim poverty while buying cigarettes and owning a television.

Being the only child, I am the key that might unlock a door to somewhere else, and the only immediately available thing that can be made to change, if I only try hard enough. I am also an ever-present listening ear and private repository for whatever mood my mother finds herself in, which varies between bitterness, envy, scorn, self-pity, and rage. It is instilled in me from a young age that, while seemingly bright and creative, and superior to working-class children, I am pretty much a born failure; that I am allowed to try things, but I should expect very little as the outcome. The world is an awful place, full of people who are both simultaneously out to get me, but also, after having got me in various ways, will drop me instantly. Almost inevitably, I am told that I was a surprise, not really wanted, and that I should never have children myself, or get married, the latter often in front of my father. Neither he nor I ever point out how rude this is. I learn not to argue back, because it is pointless. She anticipates everything I might say. If I show anger or pain at anything she says, she cuts me off in mid-sentence, laughing delightedly. 'Oh what fun! Now you're going to say you didn't ask to be born!' Almost any response other than agreement causes her to tell me she is just being ironic, or 'rhetorical', and how stupid and slow I am not to have worked it out. If she cannot claim irony, I am simply told off for answering back, or laughed at for being literal-minded. I learn not to react. It is safer to just absorb. She is charming, cultured and creative to outsiders, so no one ever thinks there is anything wrong at home. In fact, neither do I.

history lesson

I often wonder if there is a lost child somewhere in my mother's past, a botched backstreet abortion, or a baby given away, or forcibly removed. Something, certainly, was taken away from her. The portrait of her as a career woman ahead of her time is unusual. She possibly even met my father at a swingers party in the sixties, but this is gleaned from chance comments let drop at meals, or during rows, and may be a misunderstanding. Her student years had been all about semi-starvation, and turning her hems inside out and re-sewing them each winter. Work had been miserable, and one of her flatmates had stolen her jewellery. Or something. She denies things if questioned, or talks to me as if I am too stupid to understand. As the years pass, despite the bitter anecdotes, she takes to staying in bed on the morning of any trips to London, so that my father and I have to tiptoe around the breakfast table, and I dread having to sit with him on the long journey down the M1. All I can tell is, something very bad must have gone on for her to leave the bright lights behind, get married, and come to live in a suburb of Leicester, just as the sixties were properly kicking off, and from then on, give up all independent life entirely.

Inevitably, someone has to be responsible for this denial of her happiness. Next to my father, who did not actually drug her and toss her in the back of a van in the name of forcing her to undergo such a drastic change of postcode, there is me. And so begins the unifying theme, that I am second best to some nameless entity, which varies according to the nearest and most appropriate example. 'Oh, I wish we had a *boy*, a lovely clever *boy* with black

curly hair who was musical and good at sports!' She says this
to me one sunny morning in the garden, before I go to school,
apropos of nothing. These sentiments are always expressed
using the same taunting facial expression, tinged with theatrical
wistfulness. My hair is brown and straight, and I consider school
sports to be torture, but I am, sometimes, quite good at music:
my piano teacher has recently asked me if I wanted to enter a
competition. Once, after school, while watching *Boy Dominic*
and eating a peanut-butter sandwich, I foolishly let it drop that
there was an optional after-hours gym class that day. My mother
screams and screams and screams.

inevitability

My parents do not make friends in the village where they live
for forty years. Occasionally a colleague or boss of my father's
comes to the house for dinner with his – always his – wife. This
brings on screaming rows before and after, about obligation,
and other peoples' – and my – rudeness. The same applies when
my own friends come to play. The moment the car door shuts
to take them away, the shouting starts. My mother remarks
constantly on how tatty the house looks, which is not untrue,
but although she does not do a single day's paid work from
the day she marries my father, neither will she countenance a
cleaner, as she is too ashamed of the house to let anyone see it.
Despite this insularity, they have a need for me to represent the
right kind of upbringing to other people, whether those people
are seen as superior or inferior. Ballet is out of the question,
because my mother did it as a child and hated it, and because I
am, apparently, too tall, but there is always music. At seven, it
is decided that I should learn the violin. I have no aptitude for
it whatsoever, and it is only after three years of begging, and
ritual humiliations at the hands of the local junior orchestra,
that I am allowed to stop. With hindsight, it always strikes
me as odd that some middle-class children get packed off to
learn a classical instrument, or indeed classical ballet, instead

of, say, the drums, the guitar, or football. In the classical arts, one mistake, whether wrong note, brushstroke or the position of a foot, and the whole thing's ruined. Personal interpretation can only come when you've already learned it perfectly. Only the supremely talented can ever achieve this perfection, leaving the rest to struggle on a hamster wheel of supposed failure and snarly correction by the teacher, even if they chunk their way through the exams, as I did for a few years with the piano. Not long after my teacher mentions the competition, I find myself losing all interest in music.

The struggle to keep up appearances is a hard one. Funds are not available to send me to a private junior school, so I go to the local village primary, where I am labelled 'posh', one of a minority there. One of the symptoms of poshness is that my parents take broadsheets on a Sunday, enabling me to gain a little kudos by bringing colour supplements with pictures of naked African tribeswomen to school, which causes joyous consternation in the toilets. I make no money from this, as I am too desperate to be popular to charge anyone for a look. Nothing especially bad happens to me in those five years. I am teased about my nose, which is a bit pointy, am nicknamed 'Glider' because of my surname, and have Daddy Long Legs thrown at me by the school bully, but I only get beaten up once, after telling another school bully that the seat she has just sat in is taken. Her gang leaves a single small bruise. However, it is inevitable that I am going to bring my classmates' language home with me. And so, from the age of six, continuing into adulthood, my parents repeat back to me every other word I say, followed with the 'correct' form, with a disapproving, irritated sneer. At ten I am suddenly told one day that I am not allowed to play with Maureen from the council flats any more, because she is too northern and too working class, and I have been picking up undesirable words from her. My parents talk about me in the third person while I am in the room. I become incredibly self-conscious, and cannot – still – open my mouth without thinking very hard about what

I'm about to say. Even now, hearing the word 'pronunciation' makes me uncomfortable. Gradually, my parents' desire to exist through their child becomes my responsibility, and it is my fault if I mess it up.

It is memories like these that stick. They're the ones that pick away at me in the dark moments when I'm wondering where everything went wrong. And I might say to myself, well, how bad was it really? To myself I reply, wouldn't it be great if childhood pain existed on one single scale of magnitude, from violent beatings at one end, to being denied a bicycle at the other? The trouble is that pain physically manifested is immediately tangible. This is why, for example, heroin addicts get more awed respect than mere suicidal depressives. Bruises, defilements, violations, care homes – all these constitute something 'real' that can be made into a movie. Childhood, however, is one time when actions don't always speak louder than words.

Sitting in the Wendy house on my first day at school, I get slapped round the face by a teacher for saying 'I beg your pardon', a phrase we never normally use at home, but which suddenly jumps into my head. I swear like a trooper. One mother and father occasionally come to the school especially to tell me off for being bossy to their daughter. I never understand why, as she is my best friend. One day we are waiting in line to leave the sports centre after swimming. We have been expressly told not to buy chocolate from the machine, because that is only for the boys from the private school that owns the building. Without any prompting from anyone, I go and buy some, and then tell my friend what I have done. Instantly she runs to the teacher and I am exposed. I am speechless.

Language is exported out of my home as well as imported into it. It gets me into all sorts of trouble – 'This is a Christian school in a Christian country!' – which generates concerned phone calls to my home, where I have learned to swear in the first place. A few years later, having read a Sunday newspaper article on this very subject, my parents begin fining me for swearing, incorporating 'blimey', 'crikey' and 'innit' into the list of potential infractions. Quoting from home gets me singled out more than once. At the age of nine I go for interviews for the big school in the next town. As I sit alone in the back of my parents' car, with all the windows open, the housemaster approaches me. 'Do you like it here?' he asks. 'It seems really nice,' I say, 'I thought there would be people whipping me and rubbing salt in the wounds.' He looks surprised.

personal growth

I gradually become a hybrid, not able to fit in anywhere without acting a role and preparing for it, always weighing up the safest way to appear. I often speak in a strange way, too articulate and verbose for my age, my accent flipping back and forth to fit in with wherever I am. Even now, people ask me if I am Australian or Irish, or assume that I come from money.

I say that my parents aren't alcoholics, but there are alcoholic rituals. Endless pots of coffee are made throughout the day, which heightens the atmosphere of irritation and intolerance, and one glass of wine over lunch makes my father aggressive and full of political rants.

My age hits double figures. At the age of ten I go as a day pupil to the big boarding school in the nearest town and morph from 'posh' to 'local' in one swift movement. I haven't yet fully learned to keep my mouth shut, and within a few months, there is a universal groan every time my name is read out at roll call. I soon come to understand that there is a 'me', and then there is a 'them', the pretty girls, the small girls, the girls with little turned-up noses and nice hair that turns under naturally, and isn't long and matted underneath at the back. Gradually I start to want things. Some of them are things that I can eventually have and some are things that I can't. All I know is that other things are better, and other people are better, because that's the message that I'm being given, most days. At home, I haven't fully learned to switch off yet. I am still listening.

new shoots

Aged ten, when I have been at my new school six months or so, I go to the fair with a group of friends. One girl, Hannah, who is very well developed for her age, always seems to know a lot more about life than I do. This is not really surprising. Her parents are well-travelled Australians whose generous and open ways baffle the local parents, who treat their international background with suspicion, perhaps also because they are Jewish. Their house is full of laughter, music made more recently than the fifties, shag pile rugs, black leather chairs and big squashy sofas. Much drink is consumed and there always seems to be a party going on. Hannah has two older sisters, which means that older local boys, men really, often come round to their house. As I am so tall for my age, I am always taken for older. Whenever I stay over, there are drunken gropes and giggles; all very harmless, really. At the fair we walk around, swigging wine. Suddenly a hard thing is pushed into me from behind. 'Wahey! She'll be a right goer when she's older!' The giggling group expresses surprise that I don't move or say anything when he shoves the wine bottle between my legs. I didn't know you were supposed to react to things like that.

At twelve I discover my father's porn collection; the books anyway. It has not needed great detective work. He hides them by putting them spine backwards on the shelf. Tomes about management theory and obscure technical abstracts provide no camouflage whatsoever. There is other porn, magazines, graphical, gynaecological close-up stuff that my mother tells me she has found and hurled to the back of the loft. After I have read all the books, my mother and I decide to have a campaign, and we put them all in a box and show them to him, and demand that he throw them out. In fact, though, sex is discussed much more than in the homes of my contemporaries, but to my mother, the idea of me actually doing it is a source of fear and horror. I once make a joke about needing a double bed when I am older, which causes the by now expected screaming fit. Another time she suddenly becomes similarly enraged about my obsession with the Bay City

Rollers, tears all my posters down and declares them banned. In future years, her matter-of-fact response to any relationship I am having will be 'He'll drop you.'

learning to be

I am always being bothered by something about myself. I sit down to do one of those personality quizzes in *Jackie*. Quizzes like this are supposed to be nothing more than a diversion, but I take them incredibly seriously, as if they really mean something, and tell eternal truths. This one is called 'What Kind Of Animal Are You?' and, depending on your responses, you are a tiger, a koala bear, or one of a selection of others: a cat, an eagle, perhaps a horse. I do it again and again, but cannot decide which answers to give each time. I suspect I am not one of the magnificent ones; but then I don't feel entitled to be any of them. Finally I settle on the tiger, which still doesn't seem quite right. (Years later, one of the many therapists I will see likens me to 'a baby leopard'. Let's let that one lie where it fell.) I become frantic. I don't want to be the cuddly, sweet, dependent type that the koala bear seems to be summed up as, by a hassled young editor somewhere in King's Reach Tower circa 1978. So I turn to my mother. I ask her, my panic rising, which one she thinks I am. I show her the quiz, with its black text on a pink or purple and white background and my multiple crossings-out and hard-pressed biro marks. She takes one look over the quiz. 'Well, you're hardly the tiger are you? You're more like a koala bear.' I go back to my bedroom. Something in me starts to slide. The other children around me all seem to know who they are. I can try and pretend for a few hours that I do too. But it doesn't really work. I begin to feel that I am trapped inside myself.

It's fun to ask people if they were popular at school. The answer is that, without much pushing, quite a few people will rush to admit that they were, definitely, in with the in crowd. It's a bit harder to get anyone to say that actually, they weren't. On the one hand, I could say that I just didn't have the skills for popularity, particularly social camouflage. On the other, the criteria are, in a nutshell, being pretty, being good at sport, and tanning easily so that people ask where you went on holiday. But there is more to it than that. For a start, you have to smoke. As usual, I relentlessly refuse to get it, and, aged eleven, my friend Mary and I decide to have an anti-smoking campaign. She gets some posters from a health charity, with lurid images of tar deposits from lungs being poured out of test tubes. We are proto-nerds making a stand against the alphas, and we have meetings about it, where we talk of little else but the badness of smokers. Then, one day, I see a packet of cigarettes at her house, and she confesses. I feel a mixture of disapproval that she has abandoned the cause, and envy that she is doing something that makes people like her. I just carry on not smoking, and anyway, just the thought of the hostile silence when I appear in the alley behind the post office, packet of Players or not, is more than I can bear. As it happens, I don't smoke my first cigarette until I am twenty-eight. At school, a few years later, I declare drugs to be equally stupid and clique-driven. This phase lasts several years, and then abruptly ends.

Oddly enough, as at primary school, I am seen as a disruptive influence. Mary's mother constantly points out to me, whether overtly or by implication, that I have ideas above my station, that a lot of people's parents are richer than mine, and she makes me feel that I am somehow breaking a code when my hitherto secret desire to escape starts to bubble out. My problem is that I don't know how to hide anything. I have always assumed that anyone from a small town would want to get out of it.

all in the stars

Given the urgency of my search for an identity, it's not really surprising that I turn to astrology, with its quick-fit profiles and easily remembered categories. My father's birthday is the day before mine. We are both Taurus. My mother's is exactly a month after mine, making her a Gemini. For those who know astrology, this is obviously not an especially good call. For those who don't, or don't wish to, Taurus the Bull is an earth sign, said to be given to much sensuality, art, and lying around, as well as being very hard-working. Unfortunately earth signs, particularly Taurus, get some of the worst write-ups of the whole zodiac and we are also described as dull, a bit simple, practical, homebodies who won't leave the field. Gemini, the Twins, an air sign, always gets sexy write-ups: charming, sparkling, volatile social survivors; they can also be shallow and two-faced (so say the books). My mother loves to have little digs at us about this. 'You Taureans are so slow and stupid, so stuck in the mud. Gemini is far superior. We are much cleverer and more cultured than you stupid Bulls.' (For those who believe in all this, there is a QED factor to this interaction, as Taurus is very slow to anger and is often too strong in situations like this. And so we ignore her, or pretend to.) Sometimes anyway, I give as good as I get. Not only do I have the Taurean's iron will and persistence (again, for those who believe in any of that); I have a dose of her Gemini venom as well. 'It says here that Geminis can be real gold-diggers', I read out to her one day, risking a slap. Superficially, though, she always wins, because neither of us has the energy to shout her down. 'So dull! So stupid!' echoes regularly round the house.

Exactly who is at war with who changes with each day, but when it isn't personal, the rest of the world is a convenient, neutral enemy. Money, for example, is a monster to be feared. People who have it must have done something bad to get it, or just be bad people. We live with a kind of financial anorexia, a state of relentless self-induced deprivation, because it is easier to shrink into an ever-smaller space than to break out of it. 'What with?' my mother screams, if I muse aloud that it might be interesting to go to Thailand, or learn to race cars, or have a nice house, as if the idea of me ever having, or making, the money to go anywhere, or do anything, is absurd.

Other people's money is also brought in as another way to attack my father. As the years pass, my mother's wistful needling increases. 'You see, he's *worked* to get where he is. I do love people with *energy*,' she says, pointedly, when some random tycoon pops up on the telly. Privately, I listen to her talk for hours about what a failure my father is. 'Sometimes I go to bed with speeches in my head,' she says to me when we are alone together. To his face, she laments that she did not run off with Mario or Franco or some other rich older married man she knew when she was younger. Even the financier Jim Slater, who allegedly lived on the floor below her in early sixties Knightsbridge, is dragged into it. Then, in the early eighties, new neighbours move in next door. They are open, generous, hospitable northerners, bemused by the closed face of England as it segues from the Midlands to points south. Not long after they first move in, the father is made redundant, and the mother has to work as a receptionist at the village surgery. They are desperate. But can-do culture is bursting out everywhere, so he sets up in business with his son selling batteries. Within what seems like a very few years they are millionaires, with a private plane, a yacht and increasingly smart cars. They give many parties, to which they always invite us. I once get so drunk that I throw up all over their house, including filling a glass to overflowing with my vomit while being watched by a man in his twenties, who really shouldn't have been trying to chat up a fifteen-year-old, and am sent over the next day to apologise.

Back home, my parents watch their progress with increasing scorn on my mother's part, and resignation on my father's. The comparison is ever-present. At home one day, my mother makes one of her endless coffees and tells me about how she has listened to the woman excitedly telling her about their new yacht, which is moored in Spain. No expense has been spared. My mother describes the fittings. When she gets to the gold cutlery she suddenly stops. 'That sounds really nice,' I say, to fill the gap. 'Capital. Vulgar. Display,' says my mother. I begin to speak again, but she interrupts me. 'Capital. Vulgar. Display.' She does not allow me to continue. On November the fifth we have fireworks and a bonfire. It is decided that we should invite the neighbours. At the last minute they ask if they can bring a couple of friends, one of whom is blind. Our house is small, but the garden is large, so they will not be taking up sofa space. My mother spits fire at this imposition for several hours until they come, and for several days afterwards. I say, a propos of nothing, how much I like them all. 'No, Tania, they're not our sort of people,' she replies. To avoid a slap, I do not ask exactly who our sort of people actually are, because there do not seem to be many of them.

One evening, I actually run away from her when she turns on me, physically running out into the garden. I can hear her laughter at my fear. Gradually she reduces me to pre-verbal terror, and, observing her violent reaction when my father uses the word 'you' – to address her directly is seen as aggression – I sometimes find myself replying to her in a baby-like squeak, which she then imitates, laughing.

snowballs

My periods come, and I have a crying fit in the hairdresser's when my first grown-up haircut – or so I thought it would be from the magazine clipping I bring with me – goes disastrously wrong, and adulthood is on its way. I decide it is time to disappear. I stop talking in class, and instead blush heavily if my name is called out. 'We used to be proud of you!' my father hisses in my ear one day, just before dropping me off at school. At exactly which point during my short life they have felt this is not clear. He coaches me in maths for hours, screaming and screaming when I cannot work out how to do it. I begin to take my mind elsewhere. I am so tense that I associate all communication with aggression and float off into a dream world. At school I begin switching off so much that I have no idea what I think or feel about anything. Nowadays somebody would have carted me off to a therapist, but that isn't part of the culture in seventies Leicestershire. The concept of therapy of any kind is scorned as self-indulgent, the financial outlay being only part of the indulgence. Therapy is for the amusement of the rich Hampstead liberal and the spoiled, tanned Californian kid.

However, although behind the post office is – socially, at least – off limits to me, pubs are a different matter. I am tall enough to get served easily, and don't need to be reminded to get the snowballs in as soon as we all sit down. Suddenly I am less of a freak. Neither I nor my friends are ever thrown out of the pub, either for behavioural reasons, or age-related ones. The only time I am thrown out of anywhere is the town's main hotel, at tea-time.

settling in

In the evenings, the three of us sit on a park bench, each having brought a half bottle of our favourite spirit and a bottle of our favourite martini, a different colour each, which we pass back and forth, one as a chaser for the other. These are the days of no hangovers, in my case anyway. But Mary is often incredibly sick, and has to take several days off lessons. Her parents are both teachers at the school, and it is all a small shame. Another friend begins sniffing Brut aftershave with some boys from the park, but we don't join her. There is some shouting, and some snogging, but we remain, for the most part, under the radar.

My favourite time is, always, getting ready for a party. My two friends – usually two because the other one usually spends Saturday afternoons doing stuff with her horse – come over early, sometimes right after lunch, and we spend the next six hours washing our hair, and trying on each other's clothes. One of us always sneaks in a half bottle of gin, another a bottle of vodka, and I get a half bottle of rum, all of which we drink, neat, while putting our make-up on. Years later, in my saddest moments, I remember these days and feel, almost – nearly – nostalgia. It seems like an innocent time. None of us are nicking cars, robbing chemists, dealing tranquillisers, or cutting ourselves.

1980

I become friendly with the boys from the local public school that pretty much owns our village, and is the sister school to mine.

Through them I am introduced to higher levels of sophistication, such as sniffing Tippex from a plastic bag. I watch them do it, but decline, as it makes too much of a mess. I live next door to one of the boarding houses, providing easy access for both parties. I can meet boys, and they can escape for a smoke, all helped by the split-level house-on-the-hill we live in. My bedroom windows are at ground level, and I enjoy the attention. None of the boys at my own school, a car ride up the road, take any notice of me whatsoever.

Aged fourteen, I decide to lose my virginity; because I feel like it, and because everyone else has. Actually, they haven't, and I am one of the first in my lot, but by then I am tired of my status as perpetual misfit. It has already become clear that no one knows what to do with me. I am not a case for social services or conventional punishment, as I see stealing as a sheep activity, like smoking, and any bullying I indulge in is of the conceptual variety rather than pushing and shoving. However, I have the capacity to influence others, while never being the obvious ringleader, so I am tagged as irresponsible and a bad influence by various friends' parents, and branded a disappointment by my own. To add to the medley of labels, at school I am seen as a bit of a square, with a dodgy haircut and not enough clothes, who has swallowed too many dictionaries in the course of my short life. This despite the fact that I and my friends obsess quite openly about sex, and I have already done plenty of research. I have learned a great deal from *Cosmo* and *She*, with their extensive problem pages, and, naturally, from my father's porn collection.

It is nice to tell people at school that I am seeing someone. Nick is fifteen, and his parents are really big in frozen foods. He has seen the porn film *Animal Farm*, he says. We have smoky snogs in the dark outside my parents' garage. Although Nick claims a sexual past of some vastness, I suspect he wants to lose his virginity as much as I do.

My parents are at a concert in the village hall on the Saturday night. It is November, it is cold and we are, in fact, sober. I lie back on the brown candlewick bedspread and suddenly, in the dim light, see my body as not quite developed enough. Nick produces a condom and puts it on. He lies on top of me and we do it. It sort of hurts, and despite his requests to know whether I am 'there yet', I do not come and neither does he, I think. We get dressed and he goes back to the house. Not long after, John Lennon, who I never really liked, is shot.

When I tell her I've finally done it, one of my friends says, 'Don't tell anyone at school, because they won't believe you.' The repercussions, however, are predictable. I am whispered about in the street, and Nick's housemaster deems me a 'teenage nymphomaniac'. My father becomes so angry when I innocently repeat this to him that I have to pretend it is a joke. But, on long drives to London when it is just the two of us, he asks me questions about lesbian sex and lubricants.

Boys take to turning up at my window at night, pissed and hopeful. One of them has an absolutely enormous penis, which only a fool would have taken on. Another, a quite beautiful boy who I have my first oral sex with, is killed in a car crash a few years later. Subsequently, I am not really sure what to do with myself. I introduce some of my friends to the boys, and try not to be depressed when Nick cops off with one of them, a sweaty-handed girl who inevitably becomes a sworn enemy. They all come over one Saturday afternoon when my parents are out shopping. They sit around in the sun, listening to the Clash and flirting. One boy, now a famous television presenter, expresses mild scorn at the ordinariness of my parents' home. Finally reduced to silence, I go to my bedroom to read, where my parents find me a couple of hours later and demand to know what I was doing indoors, with all those people sitting in the garden.

politics lesson

Around this time I find myself learning something: that, if you are the only woman in a group of boys, they will never, ever laugh at your jokes. The realisation hits me one autumn day, as a group of us walk across the playing field. As the banter bounces between us, whenever I say anything, there is a silence. It is easier just to look down at the mud and giggle. I have become tired of people imitating me when I speak, so I learn to use shorter words, and less of them. It seems to work.

Life seems to be about lessons learned like slaps in the face. 'Don't take make-up on a camping trip,' for example. A whole lot of us are bussed up to Derbyshire for a Duke of Edinburgh Awards weekend. A day of tramping, supper outside and then into bed in the tent, in a grassy patch on a moor somewhere. I have already ripped my finger grabbing onto a gorse bush while we scramble up a steep slope. 'You must be a really heavy smoker,' someone observes as I gasp for breath. I have at that point never had a cigarette in my life, and cannot figure out why everyone else seems to be able to go uphill so much faster than me, even when I have tearfully asked my three group-mates to carry my share of pegs and saucepans on top of theirs. The following morning I walk, as nonchalantly as I can, crunching through the frosted-over campsite, to the loos at the edge. Silently I go in and shut the door, and pull out my mirror and eyeliner, and silently I rest the mirror on the little ledge against the glass panel in the door. And then someone pushes the door, and there are no locks, and I clap the little mirror back against the glass with a bang, and the cat is out of the bag. The girl who has caught me is a big and nasty one. She rushes back to tell everyone that I am putting make-up on, and I am not allowed to forget about it for the rest of the trip. The time-honoured sentiment about girls like this is that, years later, you pass through the town where you went to school, and there she is, overweight, skanky-looking, and pushing a buggy. I have no idea what became of her, in fact.

the beginning

The first day depression hits me, I am sitting in my bedroom one sunny day with yet another boy from the school, who has the palest eyes I have ever seen. Neither of us is probably entirely sure why he has come round, except that he has heard about me having sex with a couple of his classmates, and is perhaps, in a fifteen-year-old boy kind of way, thinking it might be available on this particular Sunday afternoon. 'What's wrong? You look really sad and you're not talking,' he says. He leaves soon after. 'You're so unpopular now that I wouldn't be surprised if you were drummed out of the school,' says Mary one day.

Gradually, I begin to feel as if my life is already over, that I have had my chance and I've blown it. I beg to leave the school, but there is no more money. It has all gone on my education already, and there is none spare for anywhere else. It's a cliché, but I cry myself to sleep every night. This feeling will hit me again at twenty-five, and again at thirty-five, and for years after, I have a horror of the summer. I associate it with being left behind, to pace in a room, waiting for people to come back, or stuck behind glass as the sun blasts outside, hearing the sounds of people playing, travelling, doing things together, that somehow I cannot join in with. It is only many years later, when sober, that a man I meet in a mental health support group on the Internet talks me out of this feeling, and it never comes back.

Around this time, my parents try, as any parents might, to persuade me to get a job in the local shop. But I already stand out from the locals as one of those who goes to the private school up the road. Among the boys, I am already being whispered about in the street. The idea of being further on show fills me with pure terror. I already hate my appearance, and sometimes smash mirrors. Shame begins to compete with fear. As I walk up to the village square, I dread either being pushed off the pavement by the local kids, or being whispered about and laughed at by the boys. Coming back from school, I time all eventualities to the minute, wishing and wishing that the car would pick me up, or drop me off, within a specific five-minute window, so that I might be able to get out and scuttle home just before, or just after, the majority of boys are coming past. Dread, shame, and fear obsess me from mid-afternoon lessons onwards. The shop job is just not going to happen. Neither I, nor my parents, have the vocabulary to articulate what is going on. But life is not much fun for them either. I am reminded frequently of the sacrifices they have made to pay for my education. At the time I do not fully appreciate either what they have gone without, nor the pressure I am under because of it. In later years, I wonder if it actually provided an excuse for the stasis in their lives.

At my grandmother's house in Sussex one day, I am sitting on the floor watching television in silence, listening through her single earphone, while the family has its yearly catch-up, which my mother suffers with her usual charm. Despite the screaming caused by any mention of my father's mother and sister when we are back home, she finds a face for them once a year. She and my aunt are sitting on the sofa, talking. Suddenly my mother says, loudly, 'Can you hear me, Tania?' I do not reply and continue to stare at the screen. She turns to my aunt and, lowering her voice, says, 'She's been such a disappointment to us.'

1982

Finally, I find a boyfriend who is neither from the school nor from the village; tall, nice, a bit older, messed up by his father's divorce and living with his Irish mother in Leicester. We get it together on some large cushions at a party. I am wearing as much lacy underwear as I can fit on, and we are drinking Southern Comfort. For a year we explore each other sexually, and write regularly to each other despite only living twenty miles apart. After a year, I feel somehow trapped and it ends.

Leicester life

A boy called Keith has a sixteenth birthday sleepover at his mother's house in a suburb of Leicester. Keith gets teased a lot, and makes up for it by inviting people to parties at the other house she keeps near the school. The basement has been painted black, and people willingly come over to drink for free and giggle at each other's ultraviolet teeth. He still gets teased though. We trek, as dressed up as we can, me in a white fur opera jacket borrowed from my friend Rachel's mother. Perhaps because we are off-manor, I manage to cop off with an attractive boy, one of the popular ones who boards at school, and there are photos of me in a gold dress, snogging him, my long red nails clutching at his back. This coup is astonishing, and unprecedented in my social history so far. At one point, a can of blue spray paint is produced. Halfway through the night, I retch over the large silver punch bowl. 'You didn't puke, you *spat*,' Rachel says later, scornfully. We wake up on Sunday morning, blue spray paint everywhere, including all over the opera jacket, and Keith's mother's Persian cat, who has been wandering around looking for treats. I continue to pull pieces of chicken out of my nose and hair for the rest of the day. Afterwards, there is a Scene With A Mother, Rachel's, claiming that the jacket is ruined. There is a lot of spitting behind closed doors. It is, as my mother points out, just a rotten little bit of rabbit fur, but there is an issue to do with the dry cleaning, the outcome of which I cannot remember. The boy I snog commits suicide ten years later.

So far, so innocent. We drink, we throw up, we do tongues and body parts with various people, we gossip, and we get on with it. I am gradually learning how to act, but I am starting to buckle under the weight of labels. To people I know from home, I am a bad girl with a bad reputation. At the same time, at school, I am weird, square, use long words and am laughably middle-aged. At home I am both stupid and too clever by half. I am ugly, and shunned by boys who know me, yet I am increasingly pursued in the street, chatted up, and complimented, by strange boys and men. I am aloof, yet utterly without boundaries.

By the sixth form, things are improving at school. People are starting to take things more seriously, and I am starting to feel more accepted. Then, one day, I am informed – by a boy who will subsequently lose his virginity to me while *Zoltan, Hound Of Dracula* is on the telly – that, actually, lots of the boys fancy me, but are just too embarrassed to admit it. One day I am walking round the house in my underwear when my father calls me into his study and shows me a magazine. 'I just wondered what you thought of this,' he says, and turns the pages, revealing a man with breasts, and a close-up of a girl wearing bloodstained knickers. I leave the room hurriedly.

nearly there

A boy called Giles has his eighteenth birthday toga party at his parents' nice country farmhouse. I spend hours, literally, designing a toga that will be flattering. I begin with an old sheet, which I dye pink. The conventional baggy origami style I feel is too sack-like, so I gather every safety pin I can find in the house and set to work. After a long, long time, I have wrapped myself in a column of material – I am extremely thin at the time – which is held together with about twenty-five safety pins about an inch apart.

Alex, a boy I have already slept with, who I also have a not-so-secret crush on, is there. Because his mother is a famous actress, I have been informed by my mother that he will never want anything to do with me beyond sex. I drink a lot of wine and, I think, sherry, and I dance, kind of on my own. I start to lose it a bit on the dance floor, and all of a sudden I get a sense of ripping, and one of my tits falls out. Everything starts to twist. I can remember is the agony of Alex not really being interested in talking to me, and him chatting with the pretty, popular girls, all that stuff. But he does come and talk to me eventually, and we sit in my car and have sex, and then I start crying and can't stop. Back inside the house, later, I must have started acting up, because I remember screaming 'leave me alone' to anyone who comes near me. Then I really, really need to be sick. I find my way through the old stone doorway, negotiate the steps down to the gravel, and barf. When I am done, I go straight back to the party, except that I manage to get lost in the five-foot distance between the car I've been sick on and the front steps. So I head in the opposite direction, and end up at the bottom of the garden, where

I stagger into a flowerbed and fall over. Suddenly I am in terrible pain. I am straddling a low stone wall. It is, in country parlance, a ha-ha, a ditch with a wall on one side of it to keep animals out. It also has something very sharp running along it, which is now tearing into my flesh. I shout for help and an obliging man comes and gets me out. He takes me back inside, and there are cries of horror at the blood running down my legs. 'Ruined your career there, love,' says someone. After being cleaned up, I spend the rest of the night walking around crying, wearing a huge pair of sunglasses. As it gets lighter outside, Alex is nowhere to be seen, except in rooms with closed doors, which are shut rapidly after I have peered around them. I spend the rest of the night sobbing at the kitchen table, being talked to by Giles's mother, a cardigan over my despoiled toga.

Someone calls my parents the next morning, and my father comes to drive me home. By then, the bruises have come out. My mother thinks I have been gang raped. I have to laugh at that – very few of them would have come near me. On the insides of both my thighs, right near the panty line, are huge turquoise formations, like Monet water lilies, from where I slipped down onto the wall. Both my legs are gashed, and turning blue. My nose, which has swollen up around the sunglasses I have been wearing all night, is twice its normal width and purplish brown. I still have a tiny lump on the bridge of my nose to this day, and faint scars on my legs. When my mother calls her, Giles's mother is outraged that I've said it is barbed wire that I fell on. 'We don't have barbed wire on our land!' she says. It was, apparently, a rose bush. I take the next day off school.

I am never bulimic, mind.

a Brit abroad

After school I go to Paris, where I study, and eventually get a job working for a French family, as a cook. The plan is to spend five weeks with them in Ibiza, where they are renting their friends' villa. My culinary skills extend no further than boiling an egg, if that, although I claim at the interview that I am OK using a grill. I have, it soon becomes clear, been chosen by the mother because she wants her youngest son, a brutish thirteen-year-old, to pick up my accent. Social climbing proves to be their downfall, as it always does, and they spend their summer dining on soggy rice and relentlessly burnt meat.

There is no need to elaborate on my fling with André, the middle one of the three sons, our drunken games of naked poker round the pool, the polite suggestion that I cover up a bit more for the sake of the thirteen-year-old, the German woman who sunbathes naked on the patio down the hill from us, and the middle son's cute but fucked-up friend who will, in the ensuing couple of years, become a full-on heroin addict and end up selling his father's Mercedes – nor the conversation I overhear between André and his friend the morning after I've slept with him for the first time. My French is pretty good by then.

Most days we go to the beach in a little bay, with a bar and café. There is sand, and rocks, and lots of Europeans with sailboards, and children. One regular, a lady pushing sixty, suddenly looms from behind a car, baked like leather in a red thong bikini with rhinestones all over it, and lots of make-up and miniature gold jewellery. Generally, though, it is a pretty normal, peaceful place, until about eleven in the morning. You can set your watch by the puffs of smoke coming over the horizon, like those drawings in old children's encyclopedias that teach you how to tell that the world is round, as two or three passenger boats chug towards us. As the boats get closer, you realise they are, all three of them, crammed with people, very pale people, with bright red marks on their shoulders. The boats arrive, and their sweating cargo disembarks. Already barely able to stand, they let their beer bottles smash on the rocks in the water, and stagger through the sunbathers already there, mashing up their towels. I do not offer to translate for my employers. After the boats have exhaled their cargo and left, and when the newcomers have settled into a routine of screaming and smashing more beer bottles, one of them suggests a game. I forget the rules, but it involves the women taking their tops off and racing each other up and down. It's a bit like British Bulldogs, but without the delicacy or cunning. The winner is drenched in Pomagne, and then it starts all over again. I feel especially sorry for one very short chubby girl, whose breasts rival human heads in size, and who always seems to get picked for the next round. When the games become too much in the eighty-five-degree heat, they all stop and rest, which involves more beer and more screeching, and attempts to cool off by passing out in the sea, bellies upwards. One girl suddenly turns a pale jade colour, and her friends put her to bed in the full midday sunlight, on one of the rare empty parts of the beach, and leave her there, like a prisoner about to undergo torture, *Merry Christmas Mr Lawrence* style. In the evenings we go into Ibiza Town, and watch as the same people fight each other, kicking taxi doors in and smashing yet more beer bottles. San Antonio is worse.

I make it clear to my host family that I am nothing like these people, and apologise heavily for my countryfolk. All my own drinking in the previous months, adrift in Paris, going from one bout of crying to another, screwing and getting screwed, drinking the vilest, cheapest rum in my room from lunchtime onwards, one time sobbing so loudly on a bus at some inspectors, who catch me with an out-of-date travel pass during the rush hour, that they apologise, getting caught trying to do a runner from the Café Costes, passing out on the mat outside my front door, and once spending ninety minutes with a bread knife trying to cut myself in the shower – is kept strictly to myself.

a note on life choices

In Ibiza in 1985, clubs like Pasha are filling up with emergent freaks, the like of which I have never seen before. I dance in a green jersey dress that I got in the Joseph sale, with big holes cut out of the sides and my tits showing. Even now I sometimes try to stop myself wondering what might have happened if I'd stayed in what would soon turn out to be, in pop-cultural terms, the Right Place At The Right Time, and not taken up a place at the Top University that was waiting for me back home. In the event, I barely touch drugs until the following decade.

the two-minute Hamlet

At the end of my first year at university Olivia Channon, scion of a rich, aristocratic family, dies of a heroin overdose. Heroin, scary. Tabloid reporters roam the streets and lanes, nets spread wide, for youngsters that might talk. One morning I snarl at one who approaches me, feeling pleased with myself that I haven't got caught up by this man's snaky little eyes. I have not seen passing stories on to the nationals as a potential career move. Others are quicker to catch on.

I don't do drugs at all, all the time I am there, aside from the odd spliff. My social payoff is that I am tall, I am thin, I have long hair, I have a tan from the Ibiza summer, I have lots of Parisian clothing, and I am still in pieces from my first proper length of time away from home. In other words, I am a sitting duck.

absolute beginner

Before arriving, I am a mass of paranoia and fear. I am concerned about the mixed lodging that I will be moving into, and think that nobody will like me if they see me without make-up. All at once I am plunged into a world of people who talk like adults, and seem incredibly worldly. Everybody seems to be socialising madly, every single one of them like a nascent MP trying to get a seat. You have to know people, as many of them as possible, and if you don't, you must meet them in as short a length of time as you can possibly manage. Many of my contemporaries miss this step out, as they all seem to know each other already. I never understand this total self-assurance and self-confidence, although I am occasionally accused of having it myself. For students doing arts subjects, lectures are no more than an option, especially as they often occur in the morning. Suddenly there are thousands of parties, partly to promote an organisation, and partly to check out the new totty, although we aren't called that then, I don't think.

University is where a lot of people *really* learn to drink. Despite the social differences between them, every student group has its own very similar relationship with alcohol. Dining society members drop-kick bottles of port across ancient panelled halls, and sportsmen pass out in armchairs, pausing only to turn their heads to the side to allow safe passage to a stream of vomit. Me, I only get sick from food poisoning. I play grown-ups by having a drinks tray, but it soon becomes pointless because it all gets used up so quickly. I make a new friend whose mother isn't supposed to have even one sip of champagne, because she is an alcoholic. I have never met one of those before, and am fascinated by the stories, the like of which I have only read in magazines. It seems like a medical problem, far, far away.

I begin to encounter more cocktails than I have ever seen in one room. There is champagne and brandy with a sugar lump in the bottom, which appears frequently and causes the volume in the room to double within half an hour. There is something else mixed with blue curaçao that stains my tongue for days. The event where the latter is served may well have had a Tory connection; aged nineteen I am resolutely anti-political, and never go on a demo. My consciousness doesn't awaken in that way until I leave. A drink is a drink, and large numbers of men are large numbers of men. I sleep with a couple of people and start wearing black. At the end of the first term, my college holds a slave auction, where various of us are to be lined up as lots, to be bid upon for charity. I duck out at the last minute.

While I am sitting in the ancient dark-panelled college hall one lunchtime, it occurs to me that I will never really make anything of my life until I am forty. I am not sure what this means at the time, but it is comforting.

It isn't until ten years after I leave that a friend of mine who I met there, who would give up drinking eight years before I did, admits that she too hated pretty much every minute of it. Not that you'd have noticed, in either case. But perhaps I should have listened to all the people around me when I took the exams. My schoolteachers were very concerned that I would let the school down by failing to get in, and if I insisted on going ahead with this scheme, I should go for one of the women's colleges because they were desperate for people. My mother expressed concern that I wouldn't be able to manage it. After a few months there, I am so depressed that I cannot finish an essay, and my tutor suggests that I might have 'surpassed myself' at the interview, helpfully dropping in an anecdote about the sad fate of a famous playwright's son, and various others who didn't fit in, who have plummeted far down in life and disappeared. This genial man, on my arrival in his rooms for a pre-lunch tutorial, always pours me a double whisky and we sit out the hour, chatting, with most of my attention going on trying to catch sight of his watch.

dreaming

Hangovers just weren't so bad then. In fact I hardly remember ever having one. In my first year, I fall in with a group of public schoolboys eagerly playing out the Brideshead fantasy, with oyster lunches, champagne, and lighting Amaretto biscuit wrappers. It is never clear who is paying for all this. I learn to speak the language of whoever is around me. 'The third bottle is always a mistake,' is my pronouncement on champagne, which garners a raised eyebrow from those less impressed by it all. In the summer, I visit one of them at the house he is renting a room in over the summer vacation. The living room contains very little more than a fish tank, the water grey with cigarette ash and filthy, that contains nothing but a single goldfish, which is the subject of some humour, and whose unfed state is part of some revenge plan against its owner, who is away. Another one reputedly takes beaver shots of his sister, but this is never verified.

One day, a friend who has been playing several men off against each other decides to take an overdose of aspirin. Luckily, her door is unlocked. I and a friend find her, the bottle and pills scattered. We bundle her into my car and drive her to hospital. I take the wrong route and we have to shamble her down the hill over the hospital grounds to A&E, where she has her stomach pumped. She gets loads of attention and I am sort of envious that she has had the guts to do that. I always think people would shun me if I did it.

I take up drama, and am given the part of Atahuallpa in *The Royal Hunt of the Sun* at the Playhouse, as the director has decided to depict the Incas as women. I am sprayed gold, wear a gold breastplate, and have my hair put up in a six-inch vertical knot. The guy playing Pissarro has about fifty lines to my one, but I get to stand up and pontificate in most of the scenes. I get great reviews, and a terrible bruise on my elbow from the final scene, when I am dead and Pissarro gives a final speech, shaking my corpse in rage and sadness. Looking back, this has more significance than I would ever have given it at the time.

Oh yes, sex. A gay American friend of mine says that he hardly had any in the four years he spent there. It is clearly happening somewhere, as epidemics of warts occasionally pass through, but generally we are all so drunk that it is brief and messy followed by snoring, and then a staggered escape down ancient stone staircases. Pre-bed, it is all hysterical groping, laced with a raging misogynist undercurrent. I have a scrapbook memory of unwashed dressing gowns, a permanently nasty taste in the back of my throat from the vast amount of Elnett hairspray needed to sustain an eighties hairdo, and occasional bouts of cystitis.

In my third year I go to Greenham Common to interview the Yellow Gate women for one of the student magazines. I take two friends with me who take the piss out of me on the way because I have absolutely no idea how I am going to relate to the situation. We drive through a dank November day to a muddy encampment and sit on a swollen sofa, chatting to people who I have been brought up to see as figures of fun or outrage in equal measure.

It is the first time in my entire life that I have met anyone who actually believes in something, and does something about it.

dead pig

I go to one of those May balls that get featured in newspapers, with marquees, bands, DJs, dinners, and secret places. I am thin as a rake. My earrings are long enough to touch my shoulders, as is de rigueur at the time. I am wearing a black taffeta dress, which is skin tight and zipped to the knee, and flares out into a big frill around my feet. Fuchsia stilettos finish off the look. I look pretty good, but I kind of know it isn't going to be a good night. Rule of thumb: the more you pay in advance for a ticket, the more uncertain the outcome. Various men I've slept with are there, and various men I've been hanging around with and who I've subjected myself to socially, if not sexually. But I am still full of hope, that someone will take me aside, kiss me, want to be with me, all that alien fantasy stuff.

I go on my own, having not found a group to go with, and I get there way too early. The prospect of a night when something *might* happen always makes me very itchy-footed, eager to both prolong and finish the task of getting ready. Time passes as I walk around and around, catching glimpses of groups of people I know. They see me too, but no one beckons. As I get more plastered, I see a sign saying 'Pig Roast'. I follow the directions and climb up a grassy bank, to where a young man is tending to a huge object on a spit. 'Is it ready yet?' I ask, alone on the grassy knoll in the semi-darkness. I receive a tirade in return. Does it look like the pig is ready? He hasn't even lit the fucking fire yet and it will be several hours before it is cooked, and why don't I go away and come back then. I turn and go back down the bank. The ex-shags all take one look at me and pass by quickly with barely a nod. I am too naive to see it, but there is a lot of cocaine going around. I don't remember the next few hours – perhaps I fall asleep – but then it is dawn, and the sun is making everything look the way it looks in press photos: decadent, brown-ringed eyes, calling mouths, staggering over paper plates, ball gowns swishing and wobbling, couples holding hands, flowers and lawns bright with overturned champagne bottles in the morning sun.

My feet are in agony from the fuchsia heels. I take them off, and then run into someone I know, and begin to cry. 'You're crying, aren't you?' he says, blind drunk and shouting. Barefoot, carrying the shoes, I walk to the perimeter gate. It is only when I get to the street that I realise my feet are embedded with broken glass. I get back to my room about 6 a.m., but am woken two hours later by a glue sniffer with a spider's web tattooed on his face, singing 'Tutti Frutti' over and over again beneath my window.

Alas, none of my attempts to belong really work, as I am to discover a decade or so later, when a drunken, indiscreet friend repeats back to me the words of one of my contemporaries, 'She was so desperate to be *one of us*.'

I get quite a good degree, but never return to collect it.

2. Brits at the bar

safety in numbers

By the time I was legally old enough to drink, the world was informing me, on a regular basis, that I come from the booziest nation in the entire world. I'm not exactly sure what engendered this attitude. Perhaps it was the advent of cheap package holidays abroad in the sixties, or even the gin years in the first half of the eighteenth century – which made crack in the late twentieth look like a tea party – that created the meme of the arch-waster Brit. Perhaps smarting from the association with our now deceased empire, we still resolutely take pride in the fact that a gang of Brits out on the piss is about the only thing of ours left that the sun never sets on.

On my gap year Ibiza trip, in my eagerness to dissociate myself from my fellow British pissheads, I was just replaying an old argument. For every seasoned traveller, or ex-pat, who inveighs against the invasion of their pet Mediterranean island by the oiled-up, beer-swilling hordes, there are hundreds who will reply that, once upon a time, the less well off could never have even dreamed of going abroad until package tourism finally allowed them to do so. Actually, that argument rings a little hollow after forty years. Just about everyone takes cheap foreign travel for granted now, and there is a neo-colonial flavour to the systematic invasion of other cultures in the name of The Holiday.

When the number of tourists to a particular area reaches critical mass, whether in Corfu or as far away as Thailand, the regulation fish and chip shops, Irish theme bars and football pubs will soon follow, and the UK punters that frequent them are, in general, not a pretty sight. One parliamentary committee actually suggested that Brits who get in a mess abroad due to boozing should pay the Foreign and Commonwealth Office for bailing them out.[1] This followed a survey undertaken by the Foreign Office, which found that about a quarter of pre-nuptial tourists were getting into some form of trouble that needed consular assistance.[2] At the time of writing, an update on the report names the ancient historic town of Prague as top of the stag horror hit-list, for the sheer number of lost passports, arrests, and hospitalisations.[3]

a legal intervention

Back home in the UK, the heart-searching reached critical mass and, late in 2005 – after a long consultation period, which brought on many horrified and self-flagellating newspaper features and news items about battle-strewn high streets from Basingstoke to Newcastle – there was a change in the law on British drinking. For too long, the mad rush to get them in at closing time had been encouraging rapid, intensive drinking, which in turn caused endless fights and sick on the high street. In an attempt to break our Anglo-Saxon down-it-in-one tendencies and create a more 'Mediterranean' ambience – in other words, a single small glass of wine cradled in the hand for hours at a time – pubs and clubs were invited to apply for later licences.

A couple of years later, nothing has actually improved, and in many ways things have got a lot worse. Brits do not now quaff their vino until two o'clock in the morning, followed by a gentle promenade home to the sound of nightingales. On the contrary, in the middle of 2006, the police reported that there was now an alcohol-related assault every thirteen seconds,[4] and attacks on hospital emergency staff alone increased to one every seven minutes, according to one newspaper in early 2007.[5] But the effects are not purely physical. In-patient care for people with alcohol-related mental health disorders increased by 75 per cent in the ten years to 2005, when there were 126,300 admissions.[6] By the middle of 2007, a study reported that alcohol-related visits to the casualty department at one London hospital had trebled in a year.[7]

binge terror

For almost a decade, binge-drinking has been entrenched as one of Great Britain's chief national panics. Around the turn of the century, medical researchers announced that a person who didn't drink every single day, but partied heavily on just one or two days a week, was actually in more danger of liver damage than anyone who just drank half a bottle of wine every night of the week. The media grabbed hold of this, and a trend was born. The maximum number of 'units' allowed per week often seemed to vary from one public information leaflet to another, but the figure was always laughably small, especially for women, and represented most people's consumption during a single evening. Even more laughably, an American definition, dating from the early nineties, defines binge-drinking for a man as having had five or more drinks in a row *in the previous two weeks*, and for a woman, four. Four!

welcome to happy week

The last fifteen years have seen an expansion in British boozing. There are more places to drink than ever before. As rents rise and small businesses go down the pan, the resulting empty properties get snapped up by big chain bars, who can afford them, and who then pave the way for other bars to come along and join in. The days when happy hour really was literally just the one hour seem like a distant memory. Happy hour has become happy teatime, or happy whole evening, and you wonder what they're trying to get rid of. New forms of entitlement are always being introduced, such as the 'mashed voucher'. But, as in the case of food, cars and property, the Great British Rip-Off abounds, particularly in the price of soft drinks. In clubs it's worse, and a small bottle of water can cost five pounds or more. There there's the 'pitcher'. A big jug of something alcoholic and fruity seems like it should be a bargain, and the word 'pitcher' gives it all a rustic, wholesome feel, until you realise that it is 40 per cent ice, which will melt and thereby top itself up, giving an impression of magical alcoholic bounty that is utterly false. Club drink prices are ridiculous, and it's no wonder that people try and sneak in their own. Unfortunately, it is inevitably consumed on top of what you buy, rather than instead of it. In fact, you usually end up paying far more, because you're already so far gone.

Not only have people been drinking more, but they've also learned to drink for far longer. Once upon a time, your average night out used to end at about three in the morning. As Ecstasy began to appear in the late eighties, the clubs began to open until breakfast time. But who wants to go to bed when the sun's only just coming up? So, helped by the increasing availability, and relative cheapness, of cocaine as well as pills, we all carried on, work permitting – or sometimes not – until suppertime the next day. The habit, in many cases, has stuck.

us and them – cult of the guest list

With clubbing becoming an increasing staple of weekend entertainment, and on week nights if you could get away with it, a whole generation became accustomed to the concept of the guest list. Anyone connected with the music industry would have been well aware of it, but now millions more began to understand the value of knowing someone who could get you in for free. And some of these parties weren't cheap, especially weekenders and festivals. Queuing, and paying, was for wimps. Promoters of crappy nights could always rely on the guest-list crowd, even though they might all be standing around all night saying 'Christ, glad I didn't pay to get in here.' The end result was that you'd turn up at a venue and find that the guest-list queue was actually longer and far slower-moving than the ordinary Joe's ticket queue round the other side. And the guest list, more often than not, would be a paying one anyway.

Emblematic of something much larger, guest lists fostered a bogus sense of entitlement, which was only enhanced by the presence of 'security'. Bouncers are key figures in UK partyland, and are at times closer to the violence than is comfortable. Nominally employed to promote some sort of sense of safety, they are the last vestige of the exclusiveness that secret raves might once have provided. They may play a useful role at big venues, but their presence is less understandable in cocktail bars. There is something not entirely comfortable about being in a middle-class drinking establishment, whose clientele is probably eighty-plus per cent white, but whose door is guarded by a huge black man. In these sorts of places, most of the punters will be pretty drunk, and some are undoubtedly doing drugs, but no one is fighting or glassing each other, and if they are going to be sick they have probably managed to get outside first. The presence of the huge black man promotes age-old racial stereotypes, that black men are really scary, with an ever-present potential for violence, and that the mere presence of just one should strike terror into the mass of weedy whites. One particular private drinking club in west London, exclusive for a while in the mid-nineties, but which soon went inexorably downhill in a cocaine blizzard, was patrolled by typical 'security', which was peculiarly at odds with the image of haven for champagne-quaffing media and film industry movers and shakers that the club was trying to associate itself with. I was once thrown out of the toilets there for doing coke, but despite this, I had a strong suspicion, as with many places, that the 'security' was more involved in the supply of drugs than their apparent role appeared to ask of them. In recent years, both public and members-only clubs have made a huge show of making it more difficult to take cocaine in them, such as putting sloped surfaces in cubicles, and even covering entire bathroom interiors with Vaseline. The days of joyously discovering a line's worth of charlie scattered over the cistern may be numbered, but it doesn't stop anyone.

If you weren't staying out all weekend at first, you were hearing about people who were, and many wanted a piece of it. Whatever used to be 'normal' began to be seen as the behaviour of a *lightweight*. With the internet and endless TV channels keeping us informed, the stakes have got much higher. When you hear about someone who does half a gramme of cocaine before going to work, finishes the rest off during the day, and downs two bottles of champagne with vodka chasers after, goes to bed at 4 a.m., and still pulls in a six-figure salary, you might wonder why you're worrying about your silly little hangovers. You may even think there's something wrong with you if you're not doing as much as they're doing, and only managing twenty grand at the same time. It feels as if everyone else is always doing something cooler and wilder than you, and making more money while doing it. 'Wild' lifestyle stories can be read twenty-four hours a day, and are frequently updated. And when you've read about so-and-so's vanished septum, stomach pumping episodes, and collapses due to 'exhaustion', necessitating a month or two in an Arizona clinic, anything that's happened to you can't be that bad, can it?

misery loves company

Whenever I catch myself loftily dissociating from my fellow countrymen, the thought crosses my mind that they – as I on thousands of occasions – are only trying to have a good time, even if it doesn't look like one. In fact, I think that the only logical response to the pressures of today's society is self-administered oblivion. In case we ever thought we could relax, our media ensures we are kept on our toes by a solid diet of aspirational journalism. If you become tired of reading about abused children, suicide bombers and the destruction of the planet, you can turn to a literal wealth of lifestyle pages for escape from the horrors of today. But gone are the days of articles about saving money – unless it's on something already very expensive – or,

God help us, actually mending anything. Turn to the homes, travel or women-related pages and you will find an endless range of things to buy, stuff that most of the journalists who write the articles cannot possibly afford themselves. The irony is that the people who actually can afford £8,000 dining tables, third homes in France – mere second homes being passé – and shoes at £300 a pair will already know about them, be on the designer or agent's mailing list, and have no need to read about them in a national newspaper. Stir celebrities into the mix, and you have a nation of people living almost entirely through the lives of others, sinking slowly into debt as we attempt to emulate public figures whose lifestyles are already exaggerated for the purpose of publicity. And when we get out of bed and get in the car to go to work, to do pointlessly long hours in jobs we don't much like, to earn money that is already earmarked for mortgages and bills, we really ought to realise we've been had.

hangover nation

Although we are told, endlessly, that we British are far more miserable now than we have ever been, our standard of living has in fact become ever higher. My theory is that we are such a grim, whiny – yet so passive – lot because an alarming number of us are hung over – every single day of the week.

enter the ladettes

It's long been known that women don't process alcohol as well as men, but it's only recently that the concern at the genuinely serious physical effects of heavy boozing have caught up with the general moral opprobrium at women having a good time. The mid-nineties gave birth to an explosion of stories about high-profile people getting trashed, and women caught up with men very fast. It wasn't long before ordinary, non-famous people wanted a piece of the action, and magazines and newspapers were making it easier and easier for ordinary people to find out what their famous counterparts were doing. There was, and is, a secret admiration for the celeb girl waster, unless pregnancy or motherhood is in the frame. As much as any man, the ladette had fame and money, and so what if she wanted to have a good time? The rest of the population followed suit. At the same time as the media expanded and exposed the famous in all their ordinariness – where they lived, what they drank, and which brand of tampons they preferred – ordinary people began to express a growing sense of entitlement, reflected in a personal debt that, by the mid-noughties, hit £1 *trillion* – all racked up to pay for all the things that made them feel more like the people they read about every day.

Women getting hammered in public wasn't new, but the way binge-drinking has been documented, you would have thought that some time in 2000 or thereabouts a group of women sat down and said, 'Hey, why don't we go out all together, just us girls, get really drunk and see what happens. No one's ever done that before.' 'Nice one! I'm going to stand on a table in Wetherspoons and pretend to do a blowjob on a salami!' 'And I'm going to sit on the bar, pour Sambuca down me fanny and then light it!' 'And then we'll take a waiter each, go home, and be sick again!' Nearly a decade later, there is only one social group more held up to censure than a pissed Brit on the rampage, and that's a pissed *female* Brit doing the same.

3. eighteen warning signs

LIST NATION

Women are supposed to love lists. This, according to psychologists, is because we are 'task-orientated', which means that we have an inbuilt need to finish things and then cross them off to give ourselves a sense of achievement, however minuscule. We are also supposed to be good at simple repetitive tasks, like shelling peas or operating a stamping machine in a factory. Thus we are supposedly good at housework, with its Forth Bridge-painting element writ small. And thus much of our sex lives within marriage, so I've heard.

When it comes to drinking, you will find many hundreds of lists, some in the form of quizzes, that are designed to help the concerned drinker, or their loved ones, discover whether they have a problem or not. And, as with any pastime that has the potential for destruction, there are many signs to watch out for that indicate that your booze intake may be getting out of hand. But then, one person's problem is another one's ordinary day. And if you are shivering with potential shame at your own consumption, you only have to read the history books, or a tabloid newspaper, to find justification in the excesses of others. Once you've seen enough model-actress-singers with their legs behind their ears being sick in a taxi, whatever you're up to feels much more normal.

1 varying your sources

This one's a bit, cough, middle class, as who cares if you're a regular? What's the difference between you and the shouty old guy and his Tennant's? Well, one must keep up appearances, so I still walked longer and longer distances to get my wine and vodka, telling myself it was for the exercise. Thank God for supermarkets; so large, so impersonal. But despite the best efforts at cluster marketing by Tesco et al., not everyone has one round the corner. So thank God for Throatcutter et al.

2 secrecy

I once went to visit some friends in France. On the way, I bought them a great big litre bottle of Absolut red label as a gift, imagining that they would be as overjoyed as any English host would be on receiving such a prize. They were as polite as any well-mannered English person would have been on receiving decorative soaps, and placed it in their freezer, where it didn't remain for long, as I coyly asked for a shot as soon as I'd unpacked my bags. Cut to six months or so later, when I came back for another visit. This time, it was they who volunteered a glass before I'd even had time to hint. My joyful anticipation, as we stood around the freezer and pulled the bottle out, soon turned to disappointment. Nothing came out of the upturned bottle – it was frozen solid. My first response was total embarrassment – my gift was crap. Frozen vodka is an oily delight, but this was pure shame. As her husband crunched away at it down the neck with a sharp knife, tipping the bottle every few minutes to allay my concern, my friend and I discussed the stage at which the manufacturers, or sellers, could have diluted it. Or perhaps, I asserted, in the way of all products, it had just gone to the dogs, like Pimm's. It was only when I told a friend about it, who for family reasons was far better attuned to the habits of alcoholics than I, that I twigged. I have only ever lived alone, or with other drinkers, so the idea of topping anything up was unheard of. There are, of course, no limits to the ingenuity of the determined secret drinker.

3 not giving a toss

The opposite of the above. A friend of mine was on the tube at ten in the morning, drinking a can of beer, when one of her bosses got on and saw her. When you're past caring who sees that, you have reached a kind of social nirvana usually only available to the very rich, or the homeless.

4 rituals

Perhaps my country childhood had something to do with this. We used to watch the clock on top of the fridge, and listen for the six o'clock beeps on Radio Four. You can white-knuckle it until the 'cocktail hour', but when the bell tolls, it's damburst time. And, as long as you have your last drink before you go to bed, you're not an alcoholic, even if it's nine in the morning. Other rituals might involve what you drink and when. Only ever beer at lunchtime, only ever whisky after a meal, and repeating, over and over, that you 'shouldn't mix grape and grain'. I never understood this.

5 drinking on your own

A few desperate, late-onset mini-wagons aside, no day of my life passed without alcohol. Evening in, the telly, and a bottle of wine go together like horse, carriage and street cleaner. I would sink into it with utter relief that the official part of my day was over, and I could take off whatever mask had got me through the previous eight hours, even if I'd just stayed at home sending emails.

6 panic (pre-party)

Being sober after 6 p.m. was an unknown world to me. It just didn't feel right to be dressed up and on my way out somewhere, which would inevitably involve playing the part of somebody, without a decent dose of wine inside me. Public transport invoked fresh suspicions every time. Was that guy looking at me? What about those bitches over there? What's their problem? What if we get stuck in a tunnel and I start to die? It might have been pride that prevented me from regularly putting vodka in a small water bottle as a Linus blanket, unless I was going to a club, or the fact that for a while I was cultivating small handbags.

7 panic (pre-date)

Like a lot of Brits, you might have learned to relate to your favoured sex through drinking. You might not feel real, nor even particularly safe, going to meet them sober. Let's be honest, what's there to say? This habit frequently lasts an entire relationship. I had to remember not to get too much wine down me before a date, because sure as anything I'd cut my knee shaving, and miss the tiny but growing bead of blood until it had swiped itself on my clothing. Urgently replacing tiny soaked squares of toilet paper five minutes before you're due to leave is no fun.

8 lateness

I knew a woman who was never less than five hours late for a party, and her time of arrival could be anything up to twenty-four hours after the stated time, depending on the event. Sooner or later, everyone gets used to this kind of behaviour, and it becomes just one of a number of cute little ways, whatever they say behind the person's back.

9 panic (arrival)

If I arrived at a party and couldn't immediately find the source of booze, I would begin to flap crossly and hang around any doorway that looked as if it might lead to the kitchen, hoping desperately that someone with a tray of glasses might be about to come through it. I'd frantically check other people's glasses to see if they'd already had theirs filled, and feel a twinge of sympathetic outrage if they were waiting too, or one of envy if they were already sorted out. I talk about flapping crossly as a sign of desperation, but of course I probably hid it quite well, by laughing a lot. I had no idea how to start a conversation sober. Sometimes it's best to psych up in the loo first. For art or book launches, 'Are you going to buy one, then?' usually sufficed. It may not work so well at a children's birthday party.

10 somnolence

Something I almost never did was pass out at parties. It seems somehow pointless, but there's always one who'll get so loaded at the start that they'll have to slump off to a spare bedroom and snore for four hours before returning to the fray as if nothing has happened.

11 drinker's face

Others will notice this, way before the drinker does. Some long-term alcoholics and drug users have their habits etched into their faces, in lines that are not truly wrinkles but are dug deeper, right to the bone. Before that stage, the face begins to adapt to what is going on in your head. I knew one woman whose upper lip would get stuck on her teeth in a snarl, and remain that way for the rest of the night.

12 going into character

God forbid I be judgmental, but drinking can turn you into a number of gruesome characters which may amuse others, or at least give them something to talk about later. There is the woman who is kept at arm's length by everyone because she turns into a satanic trouble-making bitch after a couple of vodkas. Then there's the one who, after half an evening, will always be discovered straddling someone else's husband or boyfriend in the spare room. Her sister-lite is the one who always has to get her tits out, wherever she is.

13 indiscretions

You have a close friend who drinks. You chat to them about various people you know. You then go to a party with them and introduce them to one of these other friends. 'Oh, *you're* the one who had the really nasty divorce and then one of your kids was in hospital and then you lost your house!' This said while looking at you for verification. Or 'Oh yes, I've heard a lot about *you!*' OK, I've done this myself – booze and drug memories have their own specific aspects – but after a certain number of evenings spent with every body part clenched in sheer terror, as you desperately rack your memory for what you might have said that will be repeated, things will reach critical mass and you will have to get rid of a friend like this. But what if it's you?

14 crying

Like the spare bedroom sleeper, there's often a crier, especially if cocaine has entered the equation. After a certain number of hours, and everyone is laughing, there'll suddenly be an abrupt change of gear as people notice the small group gathering around the sobbing boozer. 'The world – it just hurts so much!' Sympathetic struggles to understand will follow from those nearest, while those slightly further away go on cackling and rolling about. Teenage years aside, I almost never cried, as it would have spoiled my make-up.

15 being sick

Only in Britain could two people go on a first date, drink so much that one or both of them throws up, and then continue to see each other, to the point of marriage and beyond. I have a vague and distant memory of when throwing up due to alcohol was something almost serious, a reason to go straight home and then blush a bit the next day. The entry into the mainstream of poly-drug use on top of alcohol heralded a new age far more accepting of the less predictable bodily functions. The ancient Romans would have nodded and smiled. The upper classes, it is said, vomited up one course to make way for the next, and there were public bogs where you all sat in a row, but twenty-first century toilet facilities have not yet evolved to keep up with this revival.

16 fights

I used to be a miserable cow. A few glasses of wine and I'd start digging at people, goading them, and screaming at taxi drivers. I got myself slapped a few times, and would, as evenings progressed, find myself bemused as the expressions on people's faces changed from basically friendly to basically cold and hostile. After doing this with a smartly dressed man in a private club, I was rewarded with the words 'I'll deal with you later.' I never remembered what it was all about. Back then, I was unlikely to get actual fist fights in the kind of places I was going to. As life went on, things got more colourful, culminating at one point in me being attacked in a pub by a woman so high on beer, coke and Prozac that she ended up slumped in a doorway down the road.

17 blackouts

How did I get home? Did I pay for dinner? Who put me in a cab? And how did I get those bruises? You look at the money you've got left and count backwards.

18 hangovers

The hangover has become such a cultural norm that it is barely worth mentioning in the context of a 'problem', unless you designate it alongside air pollution or the common cold.

...ticularly foul period of full-time employment, I
...ne whole time that I used to forget my own name,
...ainly the name of the organisation I was working for,
...I cold-called people. Forget networking and sucking up
the boss, daily life became a matter of dodging the worst of
what my body could throw at me. In fact, of course, getting
fewer hangovers is a far more ominous sign, as your body
adapts to its chemical spouse.

Even if you only drink one glass per week, your relationship
with alcohol is probably the longest you've ever had, aside from
with your parents and close siblings. It's outlasted relationships,
friendships, and even family. It's helped you through adolescent
angst, college blues, workplace anxiety, long-term affairs and
short-term burnouts, and it's been there for you in every single
crisis without fail. But is this a good thing? If you applied these
warning signs to a relationship with a human instead of a
fermented or distilled beverage, you'd worry.

4. the decade I would like back

Asserting the differences between men and women, beyond the purely physical, is a risky enterprise. Inevitably, I can only take what I've heard from many years of talking to people and reading. One thing I've noticed is that men seem to love their pasts, and speak wistfully of their twenties, university, and even school – school! – as the most fun they've ever had, and have strived to emulate ever since. From most women I've heard the opposite. Apart from the fact that to idolise the past would slow the process of reinvention that we all appear to love, women, if pushed, will shake their heads in dismay at the things that happened to them before they knew what they were doing.

For me, my twenties are a time of distended, damaging friendships, go-nowhere relationships, peculiar health problems, and laughably wrong career paths, all played out under the backdrop of a depression and rage that does not really begin to explain itself until I am nearly thirty. There's a photograph of me, on holiday in the US, at the Saguaro National Park in Arizona. I'm leaning on a car, with a huge cactus silhouetted behind me against the setting sun. What I find remarkable about this picture is that although I am only twenty-five at the time, I actually look older than I do now. I don't mean wrinkles and lines, but inside.

Even my bone structure looks different, as if I have stepped out of an old painting.

I get my first job in London, from which I am fired nine months later. I have a rotten work ethic. In fact I have none at all. Add this to my residual lack of interpersonal skills, my shell of not caring, and my now ingrained avoidance of reality, and I am a pretty rubbish employee. I make long personal phone calls, drop things on the floor and do not pick them up, and file flaky work because I can't be arsed to correct my own mistakes. Worse is the fact that, politically, I am barely out of kindergarten. The less nice of the two bosses lives in the shadow of his father, an ex-big cheese ad-man, who occasionally rings up and imperiously leaves messages for his son, private jokes which are apparently hilarious. One day, when everyone else is out at a meeting, I arrive at the office to find myself locked out. He then arrives and we puzzle over how to get in. Finally, he finds a solution. He is going to kick the door in. The lower handle of the door is very close to the lock so, not wishing to damage it, he asks me to hold it down so he can get a good aim. This involves me kneeling on the floor in front of him. I can still remember the scent of his baseball boot near my face.

During this period, I decide to get help for the first time in my life. All I can feel is blank. Going to an office every day seems like a terrible burden, seeing the same people, doing the same things. I have no idea who I am supposed to be or what I am supposed to do. I have no work ethic whatsoever. Perhaps I thought that I would leave college and walk into life and that would be it. I drink wine a lot, and spirits. The turning point comes when I am on a skiing holiday in France, God help me, with a bunch of people, one of whom is a vicious alcoholic who does not ski, but sits in the chalet drinking gin and lime until he has metamorphosed from affable, intelligent man to spiteful monster. I also do not ski. Somewhere during that week, the ground seems to shift and I begin to feel totally cut off from the others. They sense it too and slowly turn on me. I get so fed up with the teasing that one night, while they are playing charades, I quietly leave the room without a word and sit upstairs, racking my brain for friends in Europe that I can run to. As I listen to their game in the room below, I realise I am guessing the name of the film or book correctly before anyone else does, and I am not even in the room. The next morning I get up early and take the bubble lift down to the town. Shuffling along the sleety, sunny pavements I find a payphone in the town post office and call a friend whose mother is a psychoanalyst.

antiques roadshow

Through her, I visit analysts in Hampstead and Notting Hill, but I cannot really afford it. How can lying on my back counting someone's extensive antiques collection ever be of help? I then find a man who is still in training, and therefore cheaper than the rest. His revelations include asking me if I think I am a greedy person, describing some of my desires as childish, telling me I have 'no values', and asking what I think about while I am having sex. Sitting, or rather lying – ha – through an hour of this, before having to wait at least a week to hear more of it, is not really going to make me feel better. I do not mention any of this to my parents. Unfortunately, the cat comes tumbling out of the bag a few months later when I am away, and he rings them to look for his final payment. In fact, it would not have surprised them. On one of my visits home, I go to my wardrobe and notice that my copy of Dorothy Rowe's *Depression – The Way Out Of Your Prison*, previously hidden deep down in a box, has been taken out and pointedly placed where it can be very easily seen.

cherry red

Later the same year, I get a job in Istanbul, working on an English language newspaper. There is a sense of the Foreign Legion, with a very mixed bag of British, and north American runaways and nascent bureau chiefs. I have a fling with a Canadian trustafarian-and-lothario, who freely admits to modelling himself on Tomas from *The Incredible Lightness of Being* (the movie, natch). 'Of *course* I don't like my own sperm!' he shrieks at me one night. I forget why.

For my drinking, my move abroad is a turning point. Up till then in London, I have had a car, and am often the party driver while my friends experiment with Ecstasy. I still drink, mind, but take care of myself and my passengers, and only get breathalised once. Abroad, however, my care of myself ceases. Naturally, our drinking is soon remarked upon by the locals. Mostly eschewing the more expensive 'international' bars, we take occupation of a local men's drinking hole, where we make a lot of noise. The presence of women is, of course, commented on, but they hold back from bothering us too much because of the amount we are spending. Out in the street, the relentless groping and pursuit by locals puts me in a political rage that would have graced any demo of the seventies. At times, I narrowly avoid fist fights. Once, staggering home, drunk, down my lethally steep little street, I fall among the rusty needles and gash up my knee. It leaves a scab in the shape of Turkey, and a lump, which I have to have surgically removed, three years later.

It isn't a comfortable time. In the office, I don't really fit in, and there is a ripple of hostility when I enter the room. There is certain amount of not inviting me to group events, which I pick up on, and joyously attend anyway, pushing back front doors with a flourish. One night I travel halfway across the city to gatecrash someone's goodbye dinner, just to make a point. One of my least favourite colleagues, a bully who himself ends up in recovery in later years, throws a party, which I attend with gusto, and dive into the local brew with my usual smile. Later on, I must be feeling a bit funny, because I find myself in his bathroom. All I can remember is bending over the sink, and then being upside down on the floor, a sharp pain somewhere in me. Perhaps I black out, because when I finally manage to get up, the sink is overflowing, blocked by a pinkish swirl of tomato bits and frothy, dark red stringy matter. Figuring correctly that everyone else will be too drunk to notice, I carry on partying and then go home. A couple of weeks later, it gives me immense, visceral pleasure to hear that, due to Turkish plumbing not being adapted for British habits, my cherry-red bits of tomato barf, now rotting, are still bubbling up through his bathtub.

light brown

I occasionally hang around with a group of Africans, mainly Sudanese, who share a flat round the corner. They need guts to live in this town, as the Turkish police are openly racist, and whenever they raid one of our parties – as is usual at around 2 a.m. when the phone calls from neighbours reach a peak – they pick out any African in the room for a special public lecture. One afternoon I go to visit them and sit down for a beer. As we talk in a ragged mixture of English and French, I notice that they are all huddled over little bits of paper. One of them sucks something up, and then leaves the room to be sick, judging by the noises. Concerned, I ask the remaining group on the sofa if he is all right. There is a silence. 'Do you know what this is?' one of them asks, showing me the light brown powder. I don't want to appear naive, so I just look blank. '*C'est du hashish, ça*,' says another. There is another silence. The man being sick comes back into the room and picks up his bit of paper again.

the scarlet letter

It takes me a month to discover what is behind people's attitude to me. One of the Brits has seemed familiar from the start. I rack my brain to work out where we might have met before. He seems like a nice bloke, but he has been quite withdrawn from me from the day I arrive. His wife is openly hostile, however, like a raw little dog, snatching things out of my hand without even looking at me. One night, when we are all in the bar after work, it comes to me. 'Hey! I remember you,' I say enthusiastically. 'We were at primary school together!' I continue my eureka moment with genuine candour. 'Why didn't you say something? Did you realise?' His reaction is as unexpected as it is powerful. He turns crimson – in fact, really *purple* – and looks down into his beer. Judging by the silence around the table, it is clear that everyone else was informed of this a long time previously. As usual, I just smile, but, though I hate to admit it, I am hurt. Later on I am told that 'village bike' is the basic story. Aged nine, my besmircher had been a charming, lively boy. He'd then gone to the boys' school in the village, my fate was sealed, and thus, municipal two-wheeler I inevitably became. Unicycle, perhaps – I wasn't *that* easy.

Towards the end of my time in Turkey, when the paper has lost so much money that most of us have been sacked, I make a half-hearted attempt at employment – selling computers, underwear modelling – but none of it really floats my boat. The Canadian has begun to do my head in, coming on to me one minute, and disappearing the next. There is a slightly dismaying unerotic roughness about him in bed, which doesn't sit right with his neurotic rich-boy routine. I occasionally share anecdotes with the increasing queue of his disgruntled exes. The night before I am due to leave the country for good, he comes to my goodbye drinks, but leaves very quickly. I am, in spite of myself, furious. I go back to the flat. The people I've been living with are away. I scream and kick a wall. My rage unabated, I turn to the collection of a hundred or so used beer bottles ranged on the kitchen floor, carefully amassed by my flatmates with the intention of taking them back to the shop in return for a couple of lire each. I am wearing steel-capped army boots, with which I kick the bottles to smithereens. I then go into the bedroom and kick several holes in the door that leads onto the balcony. A few hours later, with my hangover encroaching, I am overcome by paranoia that, after I have flown home, a burglar will somehow get in via the new holes and rob my flatmates. So I find a ball of string and loop it, like a giant cat's cradle, between the holes in the door, the handle and a nearby ceiling light. I also tie a couple of the remaining beer bottles to the contraption, leaving them hanging down like dull, brown Christmas decorations. Overcome by guilt, I clean up the mess in the kitchen, naked. The stench of stale beer is unbearable.

somebody else's decade begins

I have come of age during a brave new wave of overt self-actualisation, the late eighties, when the younger you are, the more important you are, and the papers are full of stories of vast starting salaries. 'Everybody else' seems to be getting traineeships on national newspapers, so I do the same. If ever a person were unsuited to such a job, it is me. Once I've made a cup of tea, I like to sit and enjoy it. It is yet another in a now familiar line of attempts at fitting in. It would have been a kindness not to take me on. The moment I get the phone call telling me I've got the job, my flatmate's older boyfriend, a publisher, waits until she has left the room and then says to me with smug certainty, 'Oh, they won't let you actually *write* anything.'

Just before starting, I go to Rome to stay with some beautiful people. Someone's father has a huge mansion with a sculpture garden. I am taking weapons-grade antibiotics for a gynae problem, the kind you can't drink with, and I am lost. I am exhausted from the moment I arrive. I've gone deaf, and spots have broken out on my chest. I cannot even have one sip of wine, even the tiny glasses that they have one or two of during a several hours-long meal. One Italian woman, about to marry a society designer, is tall, statuesque and blonde, and, due to a back injury, walks around wearing little more than a highly tailored orthopaedic corset. I decide the spots are something to do with the sun, and wrap myself in silk scarves, even on the beach. 'Now I have actually met someone whiter than me!' she calls out, in everyone's earshot. It takes me three years to discover that this reaction is in fact an allergy. Back home, an old lover finds me and comes round with a bottle of champagne. I am in a dressing gown, with no make-up and my hair scraped back. I tell him about the antibiotics and explain that I cannot drink alcohol. As he leaves, he scoops up the bottle. 'No sense in wasting it.'

I know the moment I walk in the door that this place isn't going to be good for me, and soon every white corpuscle in the place is doing its best to get me out of there. Around this time,

I get into Retsina, which is £3.19 at Sainsbury's; sometimes with Ribena. I rarely fetishise what I drink. I never learn the names of fine wines, nor endlessly quote whichever French avant-gardist it was who said that the proper way to make a martini is by putting the two bottles together and sitting them in the sun. The only drink I ever invent is a carrot juice Bloody Mary, and it is horrible.

life rage

Everything starts to slip. I start to share a flat with a friend who, it turns out, seems determined to stick a knife in me at every opportunity. The flat is owned by another friend who seems determined to do the same. I become the go-between during their stand-offs. It never even occurs to me to get up, ditch the cheap office clothing, dump these cows and get the hell out. If I had actually managed to do that, I could have left the whole festering mess behind, found myself a nice squat somewhere, crashed in front of a bass bin and got myself shagged by a bloke with the sides of his head shaved, beaded plaits, and a napkin ring stuck through his ear, while pointing at the pretty lights on the ceiling. Somewhere out there is a word or phrase for what I am, and it isn't anything cool.

I am twenty-four, and every day is the same. Two alarm clocks because I have done the usual thing of waking up at 4 a.m. with a banging head, and a sense of impending doom, and then fallen back to sleep again half an hour before it's time to get up. I get to work and have a huge, stagnant coffee before rushing to the loo. Then I steel myself to make phone calls. At times I can barely remember my own name, let alone the name of the newspaper I am working for. At work I sweat and sweat onto my silk shirt, and therefore keep my leather jacket on, which I have already been told off about, to hide the sweat patches, which makes me sweat more.

I have only one decent work jacket. One hot summer morning, dressed in my shirt and skirt, I leave home a bit earlier than usual to go to Sketchley's to get this jacket before work. I get a blank, rude look from the girl. It isn't ready. I shout at her. It still isn't ready, and I demand loudly, my voice ringing in my ears, that they get it ready. The other customers look away. It is going to take a few minutes, apparently. Stress rising, I run to a phone box and call the office, thanking Christ when someone junior, and nice, picks up the phone. 'I've had a run-in with the neighbours. I might be a bit late.' Finally, I get the jacket, and get on the tube. I arrive on time. No one would have known a thing. Every day ends the same way. Sod presenteeism – leave as early as possible to get wine. One day, when it is summer, and boiling, I leave work hardly able to breathe with fury. On the way home I am stuck in the back of a crowded tube carriage. All I want is a drink, and I want it now. As the doors open at my stop, I begin to shove. The much smaller woman in front of me remonstrates with me but I just swear at her until I am off the train. I storm through the station, and when a white van drives in front of me on a zebra crossing, I bang violently on the bonnet and scream abuse. I grab a bottle of wine from the off licence. Once home, in the urgency to get a drink, I would have bitten the top off if I could.

Feigning illness to get the day off is a delight. However, I feel so ill most of the time that the muffled assertion that my 'glands are up', spoken from a lying-down position under a pillow for extra effect, seems highly superfluous. One day I find myself crying and cannot stop. I find a local GP, a posh blonde, who looks bemused as I sob about feeling bullied and victimised and not fitting in anywhere, and she helpfully explains that she has a friend who went to the same university as me, and it had all been exactly the same for her.

I am amazed I have any friends left, as all I ever do is rant at them, either about the situation at work or the situation at home. The bottle-of-wine phone call becomes a nightly habit, often to several people. My love life goes from nought to sixty and then back to the swamps, without a warning. If a man does not return my call, or says something slightly off, I again drink a bottle of

wine and phone up to five friends, for an hour each, to discuss it.
One night I make someone I have picked up take me to his house
in Chesham. I am so drunk that I tell him, over and over again,
about how I just really like him and just want to go home and sit
with him and he doesn't have to do anything. During the twelve
hours or so that I am there, he showers five times, and when I get
into his bed, he turns his teddy bear to face the wall.

That year, my mother destroys Christmas, as many others,
with a screaming fit, and rips down all the decorations. Instead
of telling her what I really think of her – because I as yet only
half understand what I feel – I actually call her when I get back
to London and ask if she is all right. Even as I speak the words
aloud, I wonder where on earth they are coming from. She
answers with theatrical faintness. The word 'sorry' is not in the
vocabulary of our home.

hospital trip

Another day off, and I am suicidal. I have nowhere to put my
feelings. I hurl a mug of herbal tea across the room and the teabag
bursts, sending splats of greenish brown compost over everything.
It is time to demand help, rather than just ask for it. I pick up the
phone to call the doctor again, but the line is dead. I go out to a
phone box and queue behind a group of Italian tourists, crying.
After some persuasion, I am sent for an assessment at a mental
hospital in Kensington. An attractive, thin, vulnerable, educated
young woman. Would you like fries with that, sir?

There should be a ban on youngish good-looking people
being doctors, especially doctors who resemble the various
emotional nemeses of your past. How can anyone talk about
their innermost problems to someone who they'd otherwise be
chatting up in the pub? This is just before Prozac is introduced
in this country, and drugs for mental illness are still seen as
taboo, heavy hitters that make you fall off your bike and slump
over at work, if you are even capable of working at all. I am
more scared of the taboo than the side effects. This will only

drive me even further down in everyone's estimation. My pride is damaging me more than anything. I am unbelievably relieved when one of the young good-looking men says 'We're not going to give you drugs.' 'Oh, oh, I don't *want* drugs!' I say, gratefully. If only, if only, if only, if I knew then what I know now, I would have got down on my knees and begged them – fellated them, even. I am referred to a social worker, name of Roger, bearded, lovely guy. I've subsequently often found that the fewer letters after a person's name, the more understanding they are. Of course, I tell no one that I am seeing a social worker. I am up to my neck in shame.

I am booked in to see one of the good-looking doctors alone. I turn up, hung over, on a chilly, sunny January morning. I sit in the chair, as you do, and launch into my usual thousand words a minute, about work and relationships, and sex. It is only after a few minutes that I realise the man is rubbing his crotch, very fast. Maybe it is just his crotch *area*. Maybe it's just a tic. We all know that frozen feeling, when a man's doing something that's just wrong, but too many of us have been taught not to believe our own eyes from a young age. However, when discussing such situations, women have a tendency to talk tough – especially when they're not the one it happened to. 'I wouldn't take that crap from anyone!' 'Bloody hell, you let him carry on? I'd have thumped him!' Yeah right. He tells me he will refer me to group therapy. The letter never comes. A couple of years later, another therapist tells me, with a look that says it all, that the hospital has closed down. The building is subsequently demolished to make way for high-end apartments.

Throughout most of this, no one mentions alcohol. And neither do I. Not really. This is probably because there is no outward drama in my situation, the drama of deprivation that gets people off so much. I am, as I've said, quite a good drinker. I rarely fall over in public. I confine my nutter outbursts to boyfriends, or cab drivers who expect tips. My attitude does get me slapped a couple of times, though; once at a society wedding at Claridge's, and once at a party, by a now well-known journalist. But there are no stories about me waking up in a bush fifty miles away with my skirt over my head; or taking on the rugby team or some squaddies; or bottling someone at closing time; or pissing my jeans. None of this is me. Mostly I just laugh along at the back. Or just go totally silent. Like at school, I keep watching, to make sure people think I am OK to spend time with.

expanding skillset

Every time I invite friends to dinner, no one ever dresses up, apart from me, and no one ever brings any drugs with them, looking bemused when I ask them if they have. Something has to be done so, aged twenty-four, I try my first cocaine, with some people who are living the Portobello dream, in a basement with antique French furniture, bits of cracked mirror everywhere, and verdigris candlesticks overflowing with old wax. To my everlasting shame, not long after my first couple of lines, I begin speaking in French. (It hurts to read that back.) Later on, as we are all walking down the road, the guy from the flat, who supplied us, and who will later end up doing recovery time in Bournemouth, turns to me and says, 'You know, you're really *good* at coke.'

I get to the end of my contract at the newspaper, and am let go. During the exit interview, I inform the boss that people are scared of him, and find him unapproachable. Months later, my remaining colleagues tell me how much things have changed since I left, and how much nicer he has become.

tempus fugit

Not long after, freelance aged twenty-five, I discover my first grey hair. It is not really surprising. All I want to do is bang my head against a wall until I die. But somehow I don't. What I also don't do is what all the career manuals and personal trainers tell you to do, which is get back on the horse again as soon as possible. I make half-hearted attempts to get work, but I just feel like crawling into a hole. At a party, I meet Luke who has a house outside London, and decide to leave town and move in with him for a while. A few weeks later, he goes on holiday to Sri Lanka, leaving me behind. He will do this again, to other long-haul places. I should really take this as a Sign, and get myself out of there, but my will has finally collapsed. I just sit in the silent cottage and drink, even when concerned friends suggest, increasingly loudly, that I come home to London forthwith. But I feel as if I have died. I cannot move. When I do manage to drive to London for a visit, the return journey is horribly symbolic, as the Kiss FM signal fades somewhere on the A303, a few miles before the village. The music, quite literally, dies. Stories get back to me, about Kinky Gerlinky and raves and hardcore, but I sit it all out at a silent distance, writing book reviews, and being ill. I manage to find a counsellor-in-training in the village. I play house as a distraction – for fun, I even iron thirty-five of Luke's shirts one day – teach myself to juggle, and learn how to cook, for which I am rewarded with taunts from Luke about my increasing weight.

At twenty-five, I genuinely believe I am washed up for good. I realise that something is missing from my life, apart from the obvious love, sex, and happiness. That something will eventually manifest itself as drugs. There is a dope plant in the house, a feeble twig on the windowsill, but smoking it has a slight effect. That, however, is as far as I get. As I sit and cry over my breakfast tea one day, a friend tells me, breathlessly over the phone, that one of the Portobello crowd is busy being imprisoned in a schizophrenic count's castle somewhere in Austria, having antique guns pointed at her head and getting her friends to smuggle in bottles of methadone. Life is elsewhere.

I wake up most days totally exhausted, without knowing why. One evening, standing in front of me while on the phone, Luke suddenly reaches for the nearest empty wine glass, pulls his penis out and pisses into it. 'Have you ever thought that you might appear to be something better than you really are,' he says

to me one day as we are driving down the motorway. It is never
going to work out with me and his friends, who are bright-eyed,
bushy-tailed, well-heeled, establishment over-achievers, among
whom he has a sort of clown role, although I think they do care
about him, as he has enough money to keep up with them. Two
of them decide to get married abroad, and appoint him their best
man. Although we all hang out together fairly regularly, I am not
invited to the wedding. There is also the matter of the inevitable
threesome involving me, Luke, and the husband-to-be. Sensing a
second-fiddle role, I leave them to it.

I have a repeat of the gynaecological illness that caused me
to take antibiotics in Italy, and I am put back on them. I try to
drink alcohol, but one sip of red wine makes me turn purple
and sweaty. I am told I need an operation to find out what might
be wrong, and what is causing the pain inside me that won't go
away. It is scheduled for two days before Luke is due to leave for
America for the wedding. Those living other lives might wonder
why any boyfriend worth the name would accept an invitation
to something to which I have not been asked, why any boyfriend
worth the name would be happy to leave me alone at home, post-
op, for three weeks, and why any boyfriend worth the name
would ask me to drive him to the airport two days after a general
anaesthetic that, in the event, it takes me several weeks to recover
from. But that is how things are. In the event, apparently, the
bride writes his speech for him, so nervous is she about what he
might say. While he is away, I lie in the garden, and decide to
write a novel.

My first novel is a rambling thing, trying – fatally – to be
comic. Every evening Luke comes home from work and asks
me how many words I have written, with a sly edge to his voice,
and enquires after my latest 'dark night of the soul'. It all sounds
very familiar. I finish the book in four months and send it to an
agent, who rejects it, albeit politely and with some compliments.
'Of course she rejected it,' he says, when I tell him, 'I didn't
think anything would happen. Why don't you just get a job in

publishing?' This, I am to discover, is a fairly common put-down for budding writers.

escape

My grandmother dies, leaving me a thousand pounds, enabling me to go to India for three months. I go round the entire continent clockwise, heavy old camera and lenses with me always, starting in Delhi and ending up in Dharamsala, where I go to recover from terrible flu, and have an affair with an incredibly beautiful Dutchman with an absolutely huge cock. I am coughing too much to have sex, and it is really, really big. Aside from this grounded time of illness, I never stop moving. It's as if I am trying to drink in an entire continent after being trapped in aspic in a sepia-tinted room. I shake hands with the Dalai Lama, and still have the little red string bracelet to prove it. 'You don't look very brown,' says Luke when I get back. Gradually the souvenirs that I bring back mysteriously start to disappear, or are irrevocably damaged without explanation. I finally admit to myself that it's time to get back to London.

Just before leaving Luke for good, I spend ten days at a meditation camp, where I live for nine days without speaking, reading, listening to music or communicating with anyone else. I get up at 4 a.m., sit cross-legged and meditate for several hours a day, I walk round a field, and I eat vegan food, and drink caffeine-free drinks, in silence. Friends worry that I am joining a cult. People who are unused to their own company sometimes have breakdowns during a week like this. One older woman has an angina attack and has to go to hospital. I am so used to myself that I am almost bored by the end of the week. But I don't cheat once. And I do not drink. It is the longest I have gone without a drink since I was a teenager. When I return, my face breaks out in spots for a fortnight. Once I am re-perched in London, I throw the first novel in the bin and start the second. I move in with two people, both of whom have also just come out of relationships, so we are all fresh, angry-eyed and ready to party. But I still do not know how to roll a spliff and, at the age of twenty-six, I have never smoked a cigarette.

So begins a phase of re-setting myself. That is the only way I can describe it. Watching telly with one of the flatmates, a Holland Park boy whose mate Mose nicks Apple PowerBooks to order, and who has been playing me since the day I moved in, he passes me a spliff, and I lie back in a wondrous haze, contemplating what we could possibly be doing together right now, when I suddenly feel a pain in my eye. The vibe spoilt, I go to look in the mirror and it looks as if one of those tiny garden flies has fallen in there and become stuck to my eyeball. All attempts at extraction are futile, and the next morning, a Saturday – these things inevitably happen at the weekend – it is still there, and the pain is worse, so I go to a local GP who advises me to go to hospital.

I stagger up there, and wait an hour or two. I am finally seen by a very nice doctor, who has no idea what it is, but tries to get it out, with no success, especially as my other eye keeps spasming shut, trying to take the affected one with it. The doctor then sticks my head in a kind of metal frame, and tells me that she is going to put yellow dye in my eye to see if there is any damage to my cornea, and then scrape out the offending object with tweezers and a micro-needle. The scene becomes surreal, as she has bleached blonde Marilyn Monroe hair, bright red lipstick and black-rimmed fifties-style glasses. With the liquid yellow filter in my eyes, I feel like I've walked into an MTV video. We discuss what the object could be, and when she tells me it has burned itself onto my eyeball, I finally twig. It is a miniscule lump of hash. I am told to go to another hospital on Sunday morning to be seen by an eye expert. I spend a sleepless night on painkillers, unable to read, or watch television. The next day, a Sunday, I tromp over to the other hospital. The expert is somewhat sniffy about my ability to keep my eyes open, and sends me on my way. I get on the nearest bus, which stops ten minutes' walk from my flat. I have a patch over my eye, and can barely open the other one, so my progress is erratic, and I keep bumping into walls.

People ask me if I am OK, which is nice, but they probably think I am drunk.

loss of street-opiate virginity

I have, at the time, a Best Friend, who has her own best friend among the Portobello crowd, and it is this other woman who supplies us with our first heroin. We debate over where to do it, and decide that my flat is the best place, as it is big, and it will not be too noticeable if we keep disappearing back to my room, as there are usually a lot of people visiting. Portobello woman has made us a starter pack, with the blob ready melted and the tube ready rolled. We slip away to my bedroom. Best Friend has the first smoke, and begins to rant.

I sit on the sofa and breathe my first. I am, to coin a phrase, instantly suffused with golden light. Best Friend's voice fades, and I realise, for the first time, ever, in my whole life, that this is what contentment feels like. This is peace. We go back to join the others in the living room, but I keep slipping back to the stash. 'This is a really crap drug,' says Best Friend, during a moment alone. I don't want to share my revelation with her. 'Someone I know said it was like wearing a nice warm woolly jumper,' I remark. 'Well, that was a really fucking stupid thing to say, wasn't it,' she says. Word gets back to Portobello HQ that I have enjoyed the heroin, but whenever I mention – tentatively, while pretending not to be bothered – doing it again in subsequent weeks, there always seems to be a problem. Finally, Best Friend comes out and tells me that I've been banned from going over to Portobello for one of their smack sessions, in case I get over-excited and 'start making bowls of pasta'.

This is London in the early mid-nineties, where life is about the next party, and specifically about the next batch of drugs. We may all be getting on with our different things, and none of my immediate crowd would call ourselves addicts, but intoxication, or rather the anticipation of it, rules. For me, things will continue this way for the next eight years.

phat head rush

One night at the flat, we all have dinner, dance round the rug, have a smoke and then some of us start having sex with each other. Flatmate sex is really not a good idea. Four of us make it to my bed, where Best Friend cops off with a guy who's just moved in, and I, to my great amusement, with Holland Park boy, who does his best but is totally unable to perform, and slinks away to rant to someone who is crashed out in the living room. To my even greater delight, he creeps into my room a few days later and actually apologises. Time proves that the joke is on me. Not only do I pick up Something Nasty, which they all deny giving me, but I end up with a septic nipple. It is agonisingly painful, and keeps getting stuck to the sheet. Finally it gets so sore that I go, again, to casualty, again on a Saturday morning, for 'proper' painkillers. It is a mark of my then remaining, and totally sincere, naivety that the hospital actually gives me some, as such a request would usually be treated with great suspicion.

This, in fact, is not the first time that Best Friend and I have copped off. There have been scenes with an Iranian playboy, and we once go to a women's bar and pull a 'biracial diva' who runs an art gallery, who we briefly manage to convince that we are in a long-term relationship. She is enticed back to the flat, but the truth defeats us, and she becomes very cross at the sight of our two passively proffered pussies. Actually, I am becoming sick of playing second fiddle to this Best Friend.

tremors

I take temp job after temp job, and after Christmas begin to write my new novel in earnest. For two months, I get up at 5 a.m. every morning and take the tube to the office, where I do two hours' work on the book before everyone else arrives for work, and then another eight hours typing and answering the phone. My curtains never open during the week. The early starts mean that I am nodding off at about ten in the evening, and life is quiet. If I have my red wine when I get home from work, I am fine.

Except I'm not. The drive to write books and get myself a future is all I have. In the meantime, the concept of me even *trying* to write a book is polarising my friends. Most are excited and pleased for me, but a couple of them – disturbingly, the closer ones – do not take it seriously, and one of them becomes very catty. We begin exchanging letters about it – this being pre-email days – and she basically accuses me of posing. I explain that being a writer 'is not about wearing purple hats and storming out of restaurants', and she writes back that I should not give up my day job, even though she hasn't actually read a single page of my book. I cannot work out where all this resentment is coming from. I am working very long hours, and this seems to cause as much objection as the nature of what I am actually doing. It is another echo from my childhood, a little voice telling me that since no one around me takes me seriously, I don't have the right to do so either. I begin to re-evaluate my life. More and more rapidly I am opening door after door, only to find something unexpectedly rotten. When I call my parents, I wonder why I feel nothing but rage for several days afterwards. I still have not learned to keep my mouth shut about anything negative or difficult that might be happening in my life. I still babble away like a child, but most of all about my book and how tiring it is to write and work full time. 'Why don't you just come *home*?' my mother always says, with the familiar sly edge, and the familiar suggestion that whatever I am trying to do, I will never quite manage it, people will be horrible to me, laugh at me, and that I really should give it all up. I begin to feel sick nearly all the time.

When I finish the book, it takes two days to print up on my ancient daisywheel printer. The flat rings with rasping squeaks for hour after hour. It takes ten tries to get myself an agent. The head of my bed is on the other side of the wall from the front door, and the splat of returned manuscript on mat becomes a dreaded alarm call. This is in the days when the post can be relied upon to arrive at 7.30 a.m. One rejection letter tells me that publishers aren't interested in work that is so 'unremittingly dark', another reflects that I am a 'four-letter word writer', and yet another comments that the book is a bit too surreal for her, adding that 'I do prefer my fiction to be based in reality'.

A boyfriend tells me, 'You think too much,' and he is probably right. Of course, I may have misheard him. However, for the first time in my life, I am starting to take my own thinking seriously. I am in fact arriving at what is known as 'the late twenties crisis', when you stop going down the paths that others have made for you, and start finding your own. It strikes me that I have the right not to feel really angry and really upset all the time. Like, duh. I am used to going through life as if the ground is about to split beneath me. Now I can hear the sounds of rocks beginning to move, far below. My father writes to me, enclosing a CD of stuff he's written. Ever since my teenage years, contact with him has made me feel nauseous and slightly panicked, feelings that I have simply learned to live with. Now, something rips inside me. I am fed up with all the secrecy, his toleration of my mother's abuse – of both him and his entire family – and most of all his pretence that everything is fine, and I write a letter expressing this. Years later and sober, I find a draft of the letter, and am struck by the tone, as of a stern adult to a child. His reply, as expected, denies all my feelings, and he tells me that he has destroyed my letter, because if my mother sees it, it will kill her.

frying pan and fire

It takes time to learn that you cannot change people, nor your past. You can wish and wish and squeeze and strain until your eyeballs are about to spit out across the room; you can put on other pasts like clothes, and parade in front of the mirror; you can try on new identities and practise them on people; you can cry yourself rigid until it becomes a fetish; but none of this will change anything. Whatever was going on in my childhood home, whatever went on with two adults who were tied together in some wrecked web of urges and terrors bestowed on them by their own parents, it is not my fault. Neither is it theirs, perhaps, but it is too late for me to do anything about it. I have my own nascent car wreck to attend to. I realise that I cannot take any more of them. I am not in contact with them again for another twelve years. Within days, I have a publisher.

artists in recovery

After learning that writing a book will lose you friends, I now discover that actually having a book deal in the bag gets you a whole lot of new ones. 'The moment we met I just knew we were going to be friends,' says one woman. On examining her more closely, I have grave doubts about this, which in time prove to be correct, but go along with the novelty. I can now consider myself collected by several people. A light comes into their eyes when I mention the book, which they haven't read, and dinner invitations begin to flow. It is around this time that I meet my first Recovery Wonks. Notting Hill types, with trust funds and alcoholic parents, carrying around a lot of very decorative baggage. Steeped in self-examination, they talk about their issues long into the night, sometimes with a smattering of Buddhism thrown in. Some of them are devotees of a Chelsea guru, who addresses his followers in a community hall. The man himself, I am given to understand, is a recovering alcoholic who speaks inspiringly. There is an air of genteel soup kitchen about the meetings, with older ladies with growing-out hennaed hair, and nervous, disturbed-looking artistic men with the look of having crept nervously out of garrets paid for with private funds. I am never entirely sure why some of them are there. I have no experience of self-help meetings of any kind, see them as pointless and something that people with real problems do, not people like me, and feel a bit of a fraud turning up. Others have no such qualms. The problems expressed seem to be mainly social, and it seems almost taboo to mention anything that might actually be distressing to talk about. One evening a young man stands up and says that he was once in a relationship with a girl who was of a different religion to him, and she ended up killing herself as a result. 'After that, I've just never been able to have relationships,' he says. There is a silence, as if someone has come into the room naked, or bearing a dead baby. The guru is speechless for a moment, before saying, 'Well, you must *have* *relationships.*' And that's that.

Someone from this crowd invites me to an Artists In Recovery Meeting. 'But I'm not recovering from anything,' I say. This doesn't matter, apparently, but then I still don't really know what 'recovery' means. Sunday morning, with a steaming hangover, I take the tube to Turnham Green. The sun is already too hot. I get halfway to the address when the reality, or unreality, of what I am doing stops me. I ring a friend from a call box and go off to get drunk.

downers

People keep telling me how excited I must be to be getting published. What I actually feel is a free-flowing anxiety and fear that has always been there, but seems to be increasing every day. I go to a local GP who listens to me ranting and prescribes me Temazepam and beta-blockers. I have never taken a sleeping pill in my life. It is a revelation. At twenty-eight I discover what a good night's sleep feels like.

I am offered a column on a magazine, but manage to screw it up within two issues. I feel exhausted all the time. I go back to the GP and ask for counselling. She tells me there is a therapist attached to the surgery, and I make an appointment. He turns out to be a Jungian analyst. I am still not sure what world we are living in when NHS powers that be, with all the suffering going on that is never truly sorted out, can decide that it is a good idea to have such a specific and rarefied form of help available. The analyst is of a physical type that is shaping up to be one of my nemeses, a softly spoken, prematurely grey-haired man in his thirties. Men like this have always rubbed me up the wrong way. They seem like New Man types, but give off a barely concealed aggression. He sends me off to another analyst in north London, a slightly insipid American woman somewhere near Belsize

Park. I sit there thinking that I could really, really spend a hell of a lot of money chasing this one around. When I go back to the Jungian again, he is disapproving, and says that if I do not become a patient of this woman, there is no other help for me. I realise, for the first time of many, that I have violated an NHS taboo. Take what you're given or piss off, is basically the message. It is one I am to hear many times subsequently.

A couple of weeks later I come in from work, and the pain and anger just won't go away. I am climbing the walls, and I ring a friend who recommends a counsellor in west London, who agrees to see me that night. I trek over to yet another really nice house – go to too many of these places and you start to think that you really are in the wrong job – and spend an hour with her, at the end of which she tells me I should avoid drink and drugs, following which I give her a cheque for seventy pounds, which is quite a lot in 1994. I get home feeling no better than I did before I went there, but the price of such decadent crisis management gives me a brief kick up the bum, and I really should have paid heed to her advice.

stumbling

I go to a party with a couple of Notting Hill girls. The flat has been completely cleared out, aside from a huge bed in the bedroom, and a DJ is installed in the living room. We each gobble down one pill. About an hour later I start to feel odd. I have a sudden urge to walk round and round the party, unable to stop and talk to anyone. I don't know anyone anyway, and the girls have long since disappeared. I begin to see black-and-white diamond wallpaper patterns in front of my eyes, and vertigo begins to engulf me. My mouth goes completely dry, and I run to the kitchen tap, where I fill and refill a pint mug with water, swallowing it in giant gulps. Someone asks me if I am all right – one thing Ecstasy taught people is how to look out for others on the party battlefield – and I promptly throw the whole lot up in a great fountaining arc, some of which ends up on the host.

I feel awful, horrible, as if the air around me is splitting, and my mind is teetering on the edge of a black hole. I find the big bed and get into it, boots and all, and spend the next five hours hallucinating and having my feet rapped by couples who've come in for a snog. As the party empties, the room gets colder, but the beats continue from the other room. One of my friends, tripping her head off, comes in and picks up a tracksuit that has been lying on the floor. She is very petite and it is designed for a large man, and she looks as if she's just lost ten stone, with huge flaps of skin hanging down. The image, burned into my brain, haunts me for days. The other girl cops off with a neighbour, and goes over to his place, I hear later, to have anal sex in his bathtub. Somehow, in the morning I get home. I try to go to work on the Monday, but have a panic attack on the tube and have to rush back home and spend two days in bed. Life goes on. I have meetings about the book, but something just doesn't feel right. The odd wrap of heroin comes my way, and I nip off to bed early to smoke it.

false peak

Another afternoon, another day off work, another version of the sense of the world falling apart. No one is listening, but this is partly because I am not saying anything. I have got really, really good at pretending everything's fine, in daily life anyway. It is lunchtime. Feeling the sun through glass is the worst when I am in this mood. I call my GP, who tells me, quite severely, that I cannot come and see her, and she will definitely not come and see me, because she has miscarriages and heart attacks to deal with. I walk the twenty minutes to the hospital, and am told there is a long wait. I sit for two hours, and then go to the nurse who tells me it is more like four. I go back home to wait there. Two hours later I come back to find I have lost my place in the queue. After another hour I make it into the inside, and am told to sit on another bank of seats, next to a deranged old man who keeps shouting and threatening people. After another hour, I finally see a doctor, who speaks to me for ten minutes. When I ask for medication, she tells me she cannot give me any because she hasn't got my medical records. This is plainly obvious, and I say that they could avoid wasting people's time by putting a sign up in the waiting room about it. By then it is the evening, and I go back to my GP. But what is an NHS doctor going to do with someone like me? I'm not stabbing people in the street. All they can do is hope you'll suddenly decide you're not suffering, and just go home. My experiences are stacking up in favour of the bottle. Bottles of wine don't judge you. Groups of drunk people don't judge you, because they're too busy getting drunk themselves. Somewhere around this time, I start smoking. It might be after a holiday, as duty-free boxes of two hundred are so pretty. Tobacco makes me feel slightly panicked, but this is something I will get over. Around this time, the Alcopop is invented. I am proud to say that, to this day, the number of these that I have consumed can be counted on the fingers of barely two hands.

beauty lighting

The publishing process marches uncomfortably on, and I am sent to have my cover photo taken. This is the first time I have ever been in such a situation. I've gone for years with a phobia of the camera, hiding from lenses at parties, unable to face myself permanently depicted on paper. But there is music to be faced, and at dusk in the late afternoon I go to a flat in north London. I have missed getting a drink on the way from work, and turn up very nervous. The 'flat' turns out to be huge. A small apartment could comfortably fit in each of the rooms. On the walls are large poster-sized blow-ups of the famous men that this photographer has taken previously. Unknown females, any females at all, in fact, do not feature. There has, it seems to me, been an issue about which photographer I am to be sent to, and a sense that I have to be grateful that this much of the budget is going on one person's work.

The woman is perfectly pleasant, with a Sloaney assistant, but I cannot work out why she hasn't noticed how awkward and nervous I am clearly feeling, and why she isn't trying to make me feel at ease. Sweating slightly, I ask for a drink, and whether I can smoke. She gives me a whisky. Somewhere in this domestic cathedral is a tiny baby, which I haven't noticed, which means that my smoking is not totally welcome. But it is tolerated.

My face freezes, but I try. After a few minutes, the assistant comes up to me with a black-and-white polaroid. Expecting some contrasty, husky, rough-but-striking take on me that will catch the reader's imagination, I am horrified. It looks like a school photo of me aged about twelve. I ask why. 'Oh, that's *beauty lighting*,' says the assistant. 'Um,' I say, trying to be humorous, 'I'm twenty-eight, I think I can get away with a bit more contrast. And, ha ha, it might reflect the book a bit more!' The photographer, to whom I am clearly bread and butter and fair enough, but boring, nervy bread and butter at that, ploughs through the session as I crack jokes about my nervousness and ask for more whisky. There is a picture of me smoking, which is actually quite good, but it is not allowed for the cover. I stagger out of there feeling sick, as if I have let a number of people down, most of all myself, and vow that, if I ever become a portrait photographer, I will make a point of putting my subject's comfort first. I rush off to get wine.

middle-class gangs

I am collected by a couple who've got themselves a little social fiefdom in Notting Hill. There is cocaine, champagne, and everyone bitches about each other all the time. It's possible to live a life consisting almost entirely of long, late parties. I'm not even talking about a lot of very rich people who don't need to work, although there is a scattering of them around. Somehow, people keep things ticking over, just, even though they are often up all night. There are rampant infidelities and career near-misses, but we have all seen television programmes, read books, and acted (or not) upon laws drafted by people just like this, people who have cocaine weddings where the guests pile into the honeymoon suite until dawn. If Jane Austen decided to collaborate with

Jackie Collins, this is what might have been produced. However, there is a price to be paid for membership of the group, and if you don't have the money to buy your way in, you are expected to dance a little for your supper.

The word 'gang' is not generally used of people who wear dark suits to work and live in houses with zinc kitchens and blonde wood floors, and who think getting 'tooled up' means making a visit to Homebase. The concept has been hijacked by hoodies toting guns on street corners, but all human beings love a gang. Gangs give people a feeling of safety. One person's business becomes everyone else's, and disapproval is acted out through exclusion rather than physical violence.

To belong to a group is an act of self-preservation, wherever you are, and however cushy your environment. However, although the group protects you, you have to pay a price. You will be expected to defer to the controlling person or couple – often a couple – at the centre of things. This could mean anything from sharing information about your life, to introducing your interesting or useful other friends to them, to making sure you do not offend the other members. There are no hand signs to flash – your signals are internal and social.

The first thing you do with the gang is party. If the crowd is of a like mind, you will be tested on your drinking and drugging abilities, and marked according to your capacity for intake, and for staying the course over a given number of hours or days. At first, I seem to pass all these tests without effort. But I never did groups very well. I never learned to do them, and dealing with the dynamic is like trying to walk downstairs minus my sense of balance, desperately looking for clues all the way.

internal exam

Some time around my twenty-ninth birthday, I am having sex, first thing in the morning before work, with someone I got very drunk with the night before, when I suddenly feel a terrible pain inside. Unlike other moments of pain, it does not pass within seconds. It feels like a red-hot poker being shoved somewhere down there, but which down there I have no idea. Sudden, flaming constipation seems unlikely. 'Hold on a minute,' is all I can gasp, as I disengage from him. Because of the pain, I cannot sit, stand or lie down, but have to crouch. After half an hour or so, the pain hasn't subsided, and it is clear that I need medical help. Barely able to speak, I call the doctor and tell them I am coming. It is too late to ask anyone to come to me, because the surgery is about to open. I ask the man I have been having sex with to call me a taxi, and then to come with me to the doctor's. The fact that I actually have to ask him to do this for me is a warning sign for the future of this association. He isn't happy about it, but goes along with it, as I might even have been begging him by then. As we go through the surgery door, I am leaning on him for support. When my GP, a Polish woman in a brightly coloured suit, comes down the stairs to speak to me, he giggles, 'You can't trust a blonde woman!' actually flirting with her as he passes me over. She thinks I might have an ectopic pregnancy, and sends me to a now defunct hospital in Marylebone Road, where I wait another hour or two, unable to sit, and leaning forward against a wall while people look at me in concern. The nurse holds my hand while the doctor examines me, but can see nothing unusual nor any signs of pregnancy. I am sent home with an enormous bag of pills. The next day I am sent for a scan, where they see something or other that I don't really understand.

A couple of days later, when I can just about stand up, my landlords come round. The directors of the property company are over from the Middle East and want to inspect the flat, as usual with no notice whatsoever. There have been a lot of problems with leaks, broken windows, and mushrooms growing in the boiler cupboard, but the letting agents are determined to do nothing about it. One of them wears reflective sunglasses throughout. They do not appear to notice the raft of pills, and, wearing my dressing gown, I turn my back on them in disgust. After more similar visits by different people, I begin to suspect that the flats in this particular building are not owned by anyone in particular, but are passed around like poker chips. Two nights later, I still have not heard from the man I was having sex with. I call him and suggest he comes over. After a Herculean effort, I get dressed, and light lots of candles round the flat. He finally appears around midnight, and tells me he has a taxi waiting outside because he is on his way to a party. He is gone in twenty minutes.

Back at the doctor's, the nurse says, 'For God's sake take some time off work,' and urges me to get a sick note from the doctor. I have never had one of those in my life. At first I sink into freedom from work, but without the structure of a working day, however irritating, things begin to slide. I wake up exhausted, and am exhausted from morning till night, while still managing to round up the energy to keep up a relatively breezy face to my agent and editor. Still I wait until six before drinking. I research anti-depressants on the internet and go to the GP to ask for some. She gives me Lustral, known as Zoloft in America. Medications researched on the internet, and support groups, tended to refer to things by their American names. I have just broken one of my own taboos, and am determined not to tell anyone about it. That first night, I feel as if I've taken Ecstasy, but without the pleasurable high. I toss and turn, feeling waves of fear and anxiety, sweating, my mouth dry. Still awake at sunrise, I call the surgery at opening time. 'I'm having all these side effects,' I say, panicking. 'You can't be having *all the side effects*,' she snaps. Too fried and terrified to explain the English idiom, I ask her what I should do. 'It's all in your head,' she says, and hangs up.

If there was any justice in the world, my living room would be festooned with Baftas, and every door would have an Oscar keeping it open. I can be sobbing my eyes out, tissues piled up, a glass still bouncing from where I've dashed it across the room. But if the phone rings, I'm fine. Sober or pissed, believe me, absolutely fine. Laughing along, attentive, glad to hear from you, I'm great. Everyone falls for it. I don't think any of my friends ever see me cry.

Gradually the pills level out. Something improves and I don't spend two hours panicking before making a simple phone call. But my rules begin to slip, and there follow vodka Sundays, during one of which a woman I know gets one of her children to phone me. Blitzed on vodka, I have no idea what to say to this sweet eight-year-old girl when I leave a return message, and my attempt at a jolly, friendly message to her is punctuated by long silences on the answerphone at the other end. But, actually, who the hell gets their kids to ring people – people they *know* aren't having a good time right now?

miss beautiful

I am about to be a published author, with only a few months to go. Something's still just not right, but there is no one to tell, as none of my immediate crowd have any experience of being a published author themselves. People are very, very excited when you are about to have a book published, and you don't want to let them down by not being really, really excited too. The time comes for the cover to be unveiled. For months I have asked and asked to see the image they've been planning to use, which they chose ages ago, but this is not, apparently, allowed. The night before, excited, I mock up scenarios in my head, with various versions of the best, and a very definite image of the worst. Chiding myself for my negativity at imagining the worst – the recovery crowd's exhortations have already had an effect – I turn up at the office. A paper is turned over – and there is my worst-case scenario, made flesh, astonishingly almost identical to the awful one I have mocked up in my head. In situations like this, I always think I'll have some New York-meets-Hollywood-style tantrum, with lots of shouting and crying and storming out and threats to call agents. But I just sit there, going redder and redder. 'Um, it's not very *now*, is it?' I manage to say, before going totally silent. After a few more minutes of halting discussion, the others leave the room, leaving me with my editor. Trying to sound bright and positive and resigned, I say, 'Well, it doesn't really matter what I think, does it?' My editor replies, 'No, it doesn't matter what you think.' She has recently been featured in a women's magazine, in which several media people are interviewed about what it's like to be – physically – beautiful.

After relentlessly badgering my eight-months' pregnant agent, and feeling bad about it, I get them to change the colour scheme, but this, apparently, necessitates putting the publication date back an entire month. Odd, for what looks like a Photoshop job of a stock image, even in 1995. I have no idea of the appalling crime I have committed, nor what will happen because of it. I write the publicity material for my book. In my naivety, I read accounts of American women writers, contemporaries of mine, who all seem feisty and fun, and I imagine that similar opinionatedness will be appreciated over here. As I will learn over and over, the American model just doesn't work in this country. You are marked down as mouthy, trying too hard, desperate, or just nuts. The publication date looms. I go by the office to talk to the publicity people, and pop up to my editor's floor to say hello. I am told she is having lunch with another author, one that is not one of hers. She has never suggested lunch with me in our entire professional relationship. I attempt to have a drink with her to celebrate the publication, but it just doesn't seem to be possible. For the launch, there is a party, in a bar called the Flamingo. One friend turns up with what look like blow-ins from a moribund gentleman's club, and insists on standing with them right under the main spotlight near the bar, so they are the first thing that everyone sees when they come in. And then an artist friend insists on pulling out some transparencies of his latest work, which would be fine, except that they consist of white squares on black backgrounds, and therefore do not really come across in a bar. A couple of the directors, one of whom will eventually end up in recovery himself, are wretchedly snide about the paintings, to my face, and then snigger when a friend's much older, quite aristocratic boyfriend hails me along the bar. I do not know where to put myself. None of my newer friends bring any cocaine with them, and none of the members of one particular media clique turn up at all, much to the publishers' disappointment. My agent does turn up, but I do not recognise her. Despite requests, and my proffered CDs, the DJ refuses to play anything but Michael Jackson. It is quite a successful night, all in all.

the new me

I am now a published author, and pour myself into a faster lifestyle. One evening I get some crack from a messed-up, chubby, shouting girl who turns tricks in Soho doorways to put herself through art college. If she was doing that now she would have her own blog, podcast and book deal. Having trailed her and her boyfriend, who I quite fancy, up to the top of some collapsing studios in Charing Cross Road, I finally get a smoke out of them, and a bit of a rock to take home. Afterwards, I tramp across Soho in the rain and decide that crack is not for me because it makes me feel like killing people. Around this time, I buy a book called *Are You Too Nice For Your Own Good?* which I read and then immediately hide.

My novel gets good reviews, and I do a couple of readings, but it all seems to pass in smoke. I go to private clubs in Soho and drink and speak and seem to be joining in for a while, but then other people's faces become hostile. It is like school again. Hostility and desire at the same time, but ultimately rejection. I cannot work out why this is happening. Everywhere I go I seem to put my foot in it. Once, when I am about to watch a talk with a famous columnist who is dying of AIDS, a group of us sitting in the audience remark on how unflattering spotlights are in general, and I say loudly that they are especially awful – timed perfectly with the house lights going down and the audience going quiet – if you've got bad skin. Too late, in a millisecond, I notice the state of the dying man's own ravaged, pitted face. The silence is heavy around me.

I am never clear how much harm I am really doing though, and occasionally wonder if others should not occasionally share the blame for things not always being entirely lovely in the garden. At a big award ceremony, one of the publishers' favoured authors tells me about how his ex-girlfriend was killed in a car crash. I express effusive sympathy, and then later mention it in horror to the publicist. She looks at me with some embarrassment, and thick-as-mince here realises that I've been had. I am doubly surprised because I have always thought he was gay.

The parties crank up. Trouble arrives in the form of someone's old friend, who reappears in town on the crest of a coke wave, and runs rings around the west London crew, selling stories about them to gossip columns, and making passes at all the men. She causes an enormous amount of trouble in a very short time, and I find it odd that none of them really object to her behaviour. Perhaps because they are all coked to fuck as well. One night, not long before Christmas, after the usual variety of party dosages, someone I am sleeping with goes home with her. It is not really a surprise, but I become violently angry and say things that I cannot remember. I confront her on the phone at work, for which I am called 'brave'. I have been called that more times than I can remember. It is only much later that it occurs to me that the crowd are all terrified of her. The invitations start to falter.

I am twenty-nine, and my life feels like a meal thrown against a wall and slowly sliding down it. I have no control over anything. I am, as always, exhausted. Faced with the prospect of spending Christmas on my own for the first time ever, I go to see the Portobello woman, and buy ninety quid's worth of smack. If it wasn't for the heroin, I would have killed myself that Christmas. I spend a week, alternately drinking and chasing in front of the television. On Christmas Day I go to the shop over the road for cigarettes, ignoring my neighbours banging on their windows to get my attention.

It seems a condition of the so-called artistic life to take ill-thought-out journeys in the name of adventure, but, metaphorically and sometimes literally speaking, you still need jabs and a visa, the same as for any holiday. Deep down I always felt that I was nothing, and that the only way I could become something was by being curious and letting things happen to me. Some people's version of this is to climb dangerous crags, photograph bears, or try to be lap dancers. I haven't got that far. My journeys are more internal than that. What is still missing is the capacity to learn. Presumably, if a bear runs at you when you are trying to photograph it, and you survive, you will take more care next time. One of the Portobello lot suddenly finds herself in a mental hospital. Secretly, I am envious of her.

In the new year, I spend a couple of months hearing about parties that I am not invited to. It actually makes me feel stronger, in that if a whole group of people are determined not to talk to me any more because I got annoyed about two other people having sex, they really aren't worth it. I fall off the publisher's invitation list too. I turn up to one huge junket anyway, greeting them with a sunny 'My invite must have got lost in the post!' At one of these dos, I am introduced to a visiting American writer whose book they are publishing over here. We flirt and giggle, and suggest meeting up at the end of the week that he's over here, and he seems delighted. A couple of days later I tell him there will be a dinner. Grandly perhaps, I ask a friend who is a member of a private club if I can give the dinner there, and I start inviting guests. Two days before, I have not heard from him. The dinner morphs from the private club to someone else's house. On the day, I phone his hotel and leave messages. I never hear from him again and feel, not for the first time, a bit of a fool. Despite all the warning signs, I start work on my next novel, telling myself that of course it will be published, because I am a writer now.

go girl

A friend starts taking me to a gay café in Soho which has women's nights during the week. It is an exciting distraction and makes me feel as if I am part of something, but I can't decide whether I am truly sick of men. There is lots of drinking done, and a lot of talk that is far more intimate, first off, than anything I have ever found in a straight bar. 'What do you like?' 'Who do you like?' They are not talking about television programmes. At first I cannot keep up. I have no idea what I like. All I notice is that every woman there, no matter what style she has chosen, basic butch or all done up, is immaculate. Everyone's hair looks as if it has just been cut this morning, and their clothes just out of their bags with the label just cut off. I feel like a ragged, scruffy thing, despite my best efforts. One night, a rich girl from Hampstead, nineteen and just coming out, looks down and points out, with some concern, that one of my footsocks is showing. I am not equal to this.

I have a fling with a newly bi Venezuelan banker, but fall foul of her friends, a long-standing couple whose manipulativeness and control of her matches any straight woman's machinations of men. I consent to being judo-thrown around my bed by a tiny, wiry Australian who I never really fancied in the first place and am not sure why I have allowed her houseroom at all. I finally fake a bout of thrush to put her off me. Later it gets back to me that she has cursed bisexual women to hell. Sex is sex, isn't it? It doesn't really matter. There is beer, there is whisky, there are glances across rooms, some curious, some disapproving – and at least there is company.

One straight friend does stick around, and we continue on our journeys from house to cab to other house and back again, picking up others on the way. One night, back at her place, she goes upstairs and brings down her sweetie bag, the years-old remains of the drugs from when she was nursing a close relative through cancer. There is morphine, Mogadon, and Valium, which we all take turns at, alternating with lines of cocaine, hits of amyl nitrate and Jack Daniel's. The night gets old, the others leave, and another girl is passed out on the sofa. There remain three of us, the third being a man she has been seeing. We go upstairs to her huge bed with its bearskin throw. The sun is coming up. She lies in the middle. Suddenly she thrusts her hand between my legs, and declares, scornfully, that I am 'really dry'. This is not really surprising, and indeed has become the norm, after the chemical cocktail we have consumed. We lie there, cuddling and giggling. Suddenly the doorbell rings. 'Shit! BT are coming to fix my line today.' She goes down to let the man in, and then rushes back upstairs. The phone socket is in the bedroom. I will never forget the sight of a bemused Asian engineer, holding one of those huge yellow toy phone-looking things, having to pass the acres of bed and bearskin to get to the socket, with the three of us in it, sitting up, naked and smiling, with the sun blistering through a chink in the curtains.

Not long after the BT man leaves, things become less pleasant. We somehow swap places in the bed, and her boyfriend gets on top of me and starts to snog me. I really should stop him, but I am stinging from the 'dry' thing, and her rather high-handed behaviour, and so I carry on. She goes downstairs to rant loudly about us to the girl on the sofa. He and I slip out, and decide to go for lunch at a local brasserie, 192. Somewhere on the way there, we run into someone I know, who later tells me she has never seen such pinned eyes in her life. Just as we've ordered the food, I realise I am about to pass out, and we grab the doggie bag and flee. My friend and I don't speak to each other for another six months.

And then I turn thirty.

5. turning thirty

I know I ought to do something for my thirtieth but I actually feel pretty neutral, despite emanating a people-pleasing theatrical fear about it. The celebrations take three forms. The first is a dinner party, at a flat in Holland Park that I have been looking after while its owner is in New York. It is a week night, and I have probably chosen a week night because the guests are the kind of people that will probably have something better to do at the weekend. I cook a vast risotto that takes so long that the guests are there for two hours before it is ready. Then the lights blow. Then one guy pulls out a jiffy bag with one and a half Ecstasy tablets in it. This causes another guest to leave immediately, taking his much younger girlfriend with him. Everyone is home by 2 a.m. The following Saturday I go to a gay bar in Soho with a group of women. We stand and shout and dance and then go home. The third, and I suppose it does count, as I share the same birthday as the host, is a Sunday barbecue that goes on until Monday morning. The always-generous host is a journalist who has surrounded himself with musicians and strippers and hookers and various minor celebrities from Soho. In his large comfortable house, we all fall on whatever lines and pills we can stuff down. One of the guests is a beautiful German girl, from a rich family, who has somehow slipped off the rails and is working in a strip club to support her coke habit. She is pathological, begging people to call their dealers, again and again, raking through her phone looking for old numbers that could release her from her pain. At one point I feel the effects of the Ecstasy, and go off to lie in the bath. As the water creeps up to my nose, I keep jerking awake and observing, with delight, the line of cigarette ash along my chest. At one point the German girl comes in and takes over the bath from me. She gets very cross when she realises I am impervious to her orders to get back in with her. I am too content with my dressing gown and mug of tea. At the deadliest, darkest time of the night, a dealer comes round again, a jabbering woman with orange bleached hair and a small mixed-race boy in tow, who is so exhausted that he starts shouting and crying and punching cushions, and has to be put to bed. Doubtful looks are exchanged among some of us. I end up dancing in my bra and a long black satin skirt, and ranting well into the dawn.

A few months later I am drinking gin in the pub with my father's cousin who is over from New York, and he lets it slip that my father has a daughter from his previous marriage, who I never knew existed.

6. eleven excuses

I've heard all of these. And said a lot of them as well.

1 'I only drink white wine.'
You know you're sophisticated when you've got a bottle of white chilling in the fridge waiting for you when you get home from your high-powered job. You've officially joined the club. You've *arrived*. Never mind that a lot of the cheaper stuff tastes like piss. That's all you drink, so it's OK. But 'www' doesn't just stand for 'world wide web'. Have you ever screeched, thrown food, with or without a plate attached, and cried at people for no reason (and I mean 'at', not because of)? You, my darling, have become a White Wine Witch. It may be a breeding glitch in the Chardonnay grape, or something to do with women's hormones, but if you want to see the effects of white wine in all their gruesome technicolour, go to a publishing party. You may not want to, and it may be totally irrelevant to what you're doing; it may even be offensive to you, but go anyway.

2 'I'm allowed to have a good time, aren't I?'
I often hear this word 'allowed'. 'I'm allowed one vice, aren't I?' But who's doing this allowing? God? The government? Your mum?

3 'I don't want to be boring.'

Boring is in the eye of the beholder. If you're a bore, you'll be one after nine vodkas. Getting pissed may protect you from your own dullness, but no one else.

4 'I'm a smart drunk. People like me.'

A friend of mine once declared herself to be a 'smart drunk', as if it was only a time machine's hop between her and Zelda Fitzgerald. And there were enough Zelda-type stories about her for an entire evening's gossip. Dancing on a table in a club wearing only a sweater. Getting into a food lift in a bar after being up all night, which then got stuck halfway down to the kitchens. Hurling a late-night takeaway at her boyfriend, but only realising she'd done it when she came down in the morning to find chicken bones scattered around the living room. Personally, I'd have left the KFC bit out of the story and replaced it with Thai, or veal cutlets, but the degradation of boozing knows no bounds! It's fun at the time, but what's going to happen when you're sick of being someone else's anecdote? Will the world ever let you be anything else?

5 'I'm creative. Creative people need to drink.'

One of the most important influences over your relationship with booze and drugs, if you're susceptible that way, is all those famous artists who were out of their minds half the time and still churned out incredible poems, novels, pictures and music. If you read about them too much, they start to get into your head. Thing is, they're just the ones you've heard of. For every Keats or Janis Joplin, there are literally a million creative types who fell by the wayside. They may have had limitless potential, but it all went down the sink. A social worker once told me that he had a drawer full of CDs of music made by young bands he'd treated for cocaine and heroin abuse. They got as far as the demo tape, but it all fell apart. Some contemporary artists have flogged their addictions to death in a concerted effort to shift their work, and there's no denying that, post-William Burroughs, a life on the bottle, or the needle, holds a deep fascination. 'My needs are greater than yours' impresses the normies who plod through their salaried lives with only the odd warm beer for company, and exciting bicycle rides. Don't get me wrong. I fell for this one, to some extent, although I'm glad I never got the Burroughs bug at school. I read *Cities of the Red Night* when I was in the sixth form and thought it was utter shite. Remember – the boy genius will be surrounded by enablers, both male and female, who are, whatever the nature of their self-interest, keen to nurture both his talent and his addictions. The girl genius may have this up to a point, but ultimately she is on her own.

6 'I have special needs.'

No doubt you do. We all do. But if you've started telling yourself that your sensitivities are so great that you need some gin just to feel human, you're going to become the worst therapy bore ever. If you choose to stay in that role, you will simply become an object of pity. Later on in your drinking career, however, you may find willing co-dependents all too happy to reinforce your self-image. It's one thing a smoker breaking off to go and have a quick one out the window, revelling in their uniqueness as an addict, but God forbid you one day end up becoming one of those tragic people who has their own special bottle of brandy at the table, like a baby. If things turn out really bad, you may sink into Recovery and never get out. There are those who, even after years of sobriety, still cannot be in the same room as a bottle. If there is a party and they are invited, people have to be warned in advance not to bring alcohol, or even to mention it. It's a shame, as they are not cured of anything, but their needs remain 'special'.

7 'I'm working class. It's normal for us.'

You can set the clock by this one. Before binge-drinking

worked its way into the headlines, there was a belief that middle-class people kept their miserable waster habits to themselves behind closed doors, and it was only the working class who shouted and fought publicly, and happily. The problem is that the demographic has become blurred, and public attitudes more confused. Due to the decline of heavy industry and the rise of the service industry, a lot more people can now be defined as middle class. At the same time, horror at being labelled middle class in turn leads middle-class people to adopt attitudes, accents and habits that they feel will cause them to be called working class, or at least descended from it. (The rise of football is a classic example.) Once upon a time people may have concealed their rich or aristocratic ancestors for fear of being called 'posh'. Now they might conceal parents who are lawyers, doctors or business people, and eagerly assert that at least one great-grandparent was left on the workhouse steps. Having grown up in a council flat is somehow more 'real' than if you swished your way through childhood in a mortgaged semi or, God help us, something larger. Brixton in south London, for example, is a hotbed of demographic concealment. A vast crowd seems to do nothing but move from pub to rave and back to pub again, signing on as needs arise. You will hear Yorkshire, Geordie, cockney, Welsh, Irish and Scottish accents, whose owners expect their grassroots heritages to be taken as read. A quick bit of digging, however, will tell you that the reason some of them don't work is because they don't need to. There's a lot of white money sloshing about down there among the mousy dreads and art happenings. Someone who tells you they are working class may be stretching the definition to breaking point.

8 'I've got Celtic genes.'

Ethnicity trumps class every time, although this one often pairs up with the 'working class' thing. Someone might point to their hair or skin and say 'Irish mum, Scottish dad, pissheads down both sides. It's in my blood.' Of course, no one else is allowed to say that to their face unless they've got the distiller's blood royal as well.

9 'Everyone else I know does it.'

Remember at school, when you begged to get your ears pierced, or to go to a sleepover at that trendy girl's house? 'Everyone else' was allowed to. 'Everyone' is an infinitely expandable population.

10 'X drinks far more than me.'

Sod's law says that there is always someone else who can drink more than you. The tiny little lady who never passes out. The big guy who happily refills his whisky all night and never slurs his words. But is it a competition? Well, yes it is, apparently. I have been admiringly told I have the constitution of a horse, and have dubbed others 'the undead' and 'oxen' when especially impressed by their ability to remain standing after a long night – but if someone compared us to these creatures in any context other than partying, we'd either a) punch them, or b) go home crying and thenceforth spend a fortune on 'age-defying' face creams.

11 'I'm not an alcoholic. I can stop whenever I want.'

Hoo boy, the number of times I've heard this one. Out of my own mouth as well. Even among pissheads, there are stereotypes within stereotypes. Everyone's image of The Alcoholic is the wino with a can of Special – ''Scuse me please darlin', 'scuse me please,' – with smelly hair and an ancient brown coat he sleeps in, tied up with string. I've said it too. An alcoholic is always Somebody Else. So-and-so's father who spends every evening getting slowly soaked in gin, or beer. So-and-so's mother who throws herself at the postman. So-and-so who slaps his girlfriend around and then forgets about it the next morning. So-and-so who ends up writing apology notes every time she can't quite remember what she did the night before. Go on the tube at any time of day, but particularly in the morning, and you'll smell booze. Everyone in the carriage looks pretty normal. No one's slurring or vomiting, or smiling inanely. But don't kid yourself. If you're getting slaughtered every night, even if you're enjoying yourself, and you spend each day fighting physical sickness that you would go to A&E about if you *hadn't* been out the night before, then there's a problem. Isn't there?

7. half a decade of play

People make a huge fuss about turning thirty. There's an orgy of self-examination, and much passing around of round robin emails about 'What Every Woman Should Know', and have done, by the time of this seminal birthday. These might include having had a threesome, or owning matching crockery, depending on the email's originator.

The months that follow feel like a ship turning, nearly capsizing, but somehow managing to go on against the storm. Me and Best Friend finally end things very bloodily during a weekend in Berlin that involves another ill-advised threesome, a staged suicide attempt (not mine) and a very brave emergency doctor turning up in the middle of the night with a briefcase full of injectable narcotics, one of which ends up in someone's bum (not mine). On the way back from this trip, something clicks. I am utterly sick and tired of being subjected to other peoples' theatre. For the whole of my twenties I've been a magnet for manipulative drama queens and people that do not, on painful inspection, seem to want the best for me, despite protestations after the fact. All the pain I've been carrying around seems to go unnoticed among the flashier needs and demands of the others around me. I am tired of feeling like an object of pity, if I am even noticed at all. As always, it is simpler just to drink, but even through this haze, I have finally worked out that something has to be done.

a playpen in a strobe light

I drift from house to house, toilet to toilet, bed to bed. One night, with a management consultant friend, we take a younger girl back to my flat, and I am astounded by her body type, which is solid and earthy and so different from mine. I take home a bloke with extensive psoriasis, who leaves bits of skin behind in my bed, and another time, someone with a small floppy growth that cannot possibly be his penis, but then in my addled comedown state, could be anything, really. All these experiences are wake-me-ups. It seems to, literally, take balls to walk around with such physical imperfections. Most women with even the mildest similar conditions would have hot-footed it to the doctor's years before, either that or remained in self-induced purdah for decades.

I sense another of my own skins shedding. I wonder if you can shed too many. If you don't leave enough time between sheddings you can end up raw. But I feel myself bored and verging on nauseated by the scenes I've been hanging around in – or perhaps sickened by my own capacity to join in with gusto – listening to the same coke-babble of how big the house is that someone has just bought, someone's boyfriend's hundred grand a year crack habit, someone else's weekly spend on handbags, the casual two-faced nastiness, and just how unfaithful everyone is being to everyone else, and the scrabble for the flashiest wedding presents, the less glamorous of which will be swiftly sold. Everyone around me seems buoyed up on a web of lies, told to each other and to themselves. I catch myself staring at cats, and wishing, desperately, that I could be one. Cats know who they are. They eat, sleep, and get kissed and cuddled, and their only obligation is to look cute.

Within a couple of months, I cut my hair short for the first time since the age of twelve, and start doing readings of my first book in pubs. I have not done anything in front of an audience, intentionally anyway, since college. In London in the mid-nineties, the spoken word scene is just taking off. In harmony with the 'chemical generation' going into its next phase, people decide that there is more to words and writing than the mainstream has to offer. Instead of suffering over a manuscript for years, in silence, people get up on a stage, shout, rant, and make people laugh. Strictly, this may have been nothing new, but this is a time when it all comes together. For me, it works. I drink as much as I can, bound onto the stage, shout stuff and then get laughs and applause. I do a monologue at an event in a pub, which is reasonably well received, but am astonished to witness the amount of attention the poetry gets. Ten lines of simple – at times, dare I say it, banal – politics gets shouts of assent and roaring cheers. I am wasting my time still trying to be literary and I want a slice of the attention. After that, I do many, many poetry nights. What these nights have in common is that they are all inextricably bound up with alcohol. I discover that wine is no good, as it dampens you down without killing the nerves. Beer is too heavy, so it has to be vodka, usually preceded by a bottle of something light and fizzy, like Prosecco. A pattern emerges, of starting to drink at four in the afternoon to calm my nerves, and having to take the day off after every gig. I consider this to be normal. Everyone else seems to be the same. It is during one of these nights that I meet Mick, just after he's been on stage, and we swap numbers.

I meet a whole new crowd. God, the relief, to find people who shout at each other, laugh, take the piss, but don't ice each other out after mentioning something that isn't supposed to be mentioned. No one is desperate to keep up appearances, no one tells tales of a vintage bikini they are giving away to the first one to jump up, and has always just gone anyway, and no one suddenly goes into serious mode when dealing with Important People. No one is spectacularly impressed by a seventies BMW, or by stories of house purchases, as most of them live in council flats. These are people who are getting on with art, writing, making films, or music, and who are, for the most part, actually doing what they say they are doing – at least until the crack gets them – and without the word 'million' in sight.

kidulthood

If I need any self-justification for mucking about so much, I am, of course, getting it from the media. The post-rave generation wants to stay young, and live young, for as long as possible. The old idea that you get more sober, more serious, and stay in more, and wear frumpy clothing, is being rejected wholesale by people who don't want their lives to turn slowly sepia, so that all they have left are memories. Actually, after a few years of partying, no one has much memory left. 'You remember *that*?' people say when I remind them of something we did together a few years before. I can usually remember the year, and the season too. I arrange my memories by postcode, which is probably due to the fact that I have moved house so many times. With each attempt at therapy, I do a lot of counting, of looking back over each different year and what distinguishes them, usually in terms of what has traumatised me in some way. I tell a story about something that happened, admit my inappropriate response, and then justify it with 'But I was having a really bad time back then!' This 'bad time' has, effectively, stretched over my entire life.

You can't jump straight from one life to another. There's always an overlap. I take Mick to a west London party, during which he is asked, by a young man far too tall, and too old, to be wearing a camel-coloured duffle coat, with humorous trepidation, whether they are about to have a fight. 'They're not your friends,' Mick announces when we are on our way home. I am always suspicious when men comment on my friends in the negative. Too often it feels like divide-and-rule, as if I am being deliberately isolated, and the ground beneath me, that I thought was safe, is being made to feel uncertain, so that I cling all the closer. But in this case, Mick is right on the money.

my new friend

I sort of know about Mick and heroin, and I am pleased about it. Part of me, a part I have let sit like a soft, forgotten plum at the bottom of the fruit bowl, has, during the moments when my life seems to be at its most pointless, wished ardently, has – in the manner suggested by the Chelsea guru – actually *asked the universe* to send me someone who has access to a regular supply. And lo! It comes to pass.

People love to take ownership of a heroin user, almost more than any other drug user. They monitor, they gossip, and they act concerned, but when something really bad happens, they go all strict and distant. If they've been a user themselves, the strictness is double, with lectures about how much more hardcore it all was when they or their girlfriend were using; the blood that flowed, the regular trips to casualty.

Despite the often gruesome outcomes of out-of-control crack or cocaine use – and, with the rise of skunk, even cannabis – heroin occupies a special space in most peoples' pantheon of Evil Drug Terror. Despite the vast media coverage of rave culture over the last twenty years, descriptions in popular novels, disclosures by everyone from pop stars downwards, and the many debates about dope smoking, say the word 'drugs' to someone who's never done them and they'll instantly think of a hollow-eyed, sallow-cheeked, piss-stained smackhead, his trousers tied with string, living rough in a rat-infested alley full of overflowing dustbins, sticking a needle in his arm, and falling back, his tongue lolling, before going off to mug a granny. If they're slightly more plugged in, they'll think of Leah Betts, who overdosed on water after taking Ecstasy in the mid-nineties.

Weekends are suddenly sorted, and 'sorted'. A gig, a squat rave, and then off home for what I've been looking forward to all along. If I were of a mind to sniff Mick's pockets, I would. Back to my flat or his, music on, telly on, one of us sitting at the table with the tiny paraphernalia all laid out, while the other opens the wine. Together, we make a cosy tableau, almost like a traditional

Victorian Christmas scene, if you squint a bit. The lamp pushed low down over the desk, and a couple of candles flickering. An old black-and-white movie murmuring in the background. Me bent over, concentrating, as if I am sewing a sampler. Him lying back with his works in the soft light.

Even now I get a little hit of reaction at the thought. My favourite drug comes in tiny, knotted, flame-sealed circles of plastic bag, sometimes transparent so that you can see the soft, beige, powdery contents, and sometimes opaque so you can only feel it. I pick at it, carefully, cutting out the blackened knot, and the bag opens in a crumpled, fragile fan, like a just-hatched butterfly. My Swiss army knife, the one with the black handle that got me treated with slight suspicion when travelling in India because everyone else's was red, becomes part of this fetish. Ripping and cutting the tinfoil becomes another fetish point, before trowelling delicately at the powder with the end of the knife. I dig out a small pile of the fluffy powder and put it on the shiny, tinkly silver platter. Then comes the tube, a double layer of foil wrapped round a pen. Holding the foil in one hand, careful not to catch a corner on something and flip its contents onto the carpet, I put the tube in my mouth, and the lighter in the other hand, and gently, gently wave it under the foil where the pile is. Slowly it melts and, as I tip it, it starts to run down in a golden caramel teardrop. As it runs, the smoke comes off it and I suck it down. The idea is to chase the moving blob down and around the foil until it is spent. Later on I will take to picking up the discarded bits of foil out of the bin and carry on waving my lighter under them until I find a magical bit that I missed the first time round. In fact, I am pretty rubbish at all this. I never, even after several years, manage to quite get the technique right, and often char it before it has even run one length of the foil. People say it's best not to use heroin with alcohol, because heroin has a tendency to make the user throw up, and there is a high incidence of overdosing and choking to death on your own vomit. My relatively non-existent puke reflex ensures that this never happens, although I suppose I am lucky.

slow heaven

The body's processes gradually slow down. Going to the loo gradually stops during a session, but I am rewarded with a giant dump when it has worn off. The same goes for sleeping. Heroin actually keeps you awake until the narcotic aspect starts to work. I look in the bathroom mirror and see my pinned vampire eyes, which is a cliché of smack use, as everyone feels the need to do that. There are mild hallucinations, wonderful for a blank blue television screen on a summer afternoon. It is also an excellent jet-lag cure. The only times I give myself cause for concern are when I drink three pints of water in succession, just after the gear kicks in, and am then horrified to find that I can't piss to save my life, and the time when I pass out on my arm and can't grip properly for three weeks. Sex becomes a distant memory.

Mick is way beyond all this. For him, it is the mixing in a spoon, the filter from a cigarette, the getting out of the syringe, the tying off of his arm – on a good day, otherwise it is a finger or a leg – the needle in, the shaft pulled back with blood, and then in again. He is a heavy dope smoker as well, and my sheets and duvet covers, between which we spend many hours cuddling, soon become dramatically holed. Even now, I find blackened spoons in my old boxes, tucked under ancient flyers for poetry gigs, or among old passport photos. I also occasionally find rectangles of foil, burnt black in the middle, pressed smooth, like leaves, between the pages of a book, like material for a collage that I would never make. A few years later, when I am trying, and failing, to get myself admitted to a mental hospital, I tell the admission nurse that I only understand true happiness when I am on heroin.

you can eat when you're dead

Life alternates between dodging beer and puddles of piss at gigs followed by going home to cuddle and flake out in front of the telly with cats crawling over us, and running off to Soho, where I have a new friend who works at a new private club, where we juggle little wraps of paper. That, at least, is my public life. By day I am alone, wrestling with myself to get on with life and drag myself out of myself. I am teetering. But with a drink inside me I am ready for anyone. With my tiny leather skirt, bright blue patent leather knock-off high-heeled loafers, and a jacket, I'm set up for the night. A bottle of wine, some toast, and out I go. Once I am bugged heavily on the way to the tube – always the tube – and I check my bag inside and out. Keys, money, make-up, travelcard, what have I forgotten? As I reach the steps to the underground, I realise what I've left behind – my knickers. Soho in the mid-nineties is an unstoppable blizzard of cocaine. I walk among it in itchy glitter tops from Camden market, and stand in the doorways of private drinking clubs wondering who's going to be the next one to take me to the bogs. Food begins to take second place, aside from huge bowls of pasta scarfed down at home, that recur pretty soon after the first line. Not eating becomes totally normal, and I am only reminded that it is not when having any sort of interaction with mainland Europeans, who look puzzled at my slightly irritated face if they sit down and insist on having an actual meal in a club or bar. Eating wastes both time and money. You can eat when you're dead.

darkest Peru

I begin smoking more, usually B&H, and it is inevitable that, sooner or later, my body is at some point going to put its hand up, and remind me sharply of its needs. I develop a streaming cold, which turns, over a couple of weeks, into a harsh, deep, painful racking cough, on which one course of antibiotics has no effect. I start to feel odd and faint when I cough, and the sound is so hackingly medieval that people look at me in shops and ask me if I am all right. Yet more prescription medicines have no effect. I get a strange pain in my chest. After a few weeks of this, my neck starts to hurt, and my eyes react badly to the least sight of sun. I continue to drink and smoke, and thank the universe for the easily available gear. One Saturday morning – it's always a

Saturday when this happens – I throw up the moment I have eaten my lunch. I begin to worry. My head is banging inside. For once, I begin to feel scared. At about 4 p.m. I call the doctor, who tells me I am showing most of the symptoms of meningitis, and that I should wait a couple of hours and call him again. The fear has already grabbed me too hard, and I decide to go to hospital. Funds being short, I get on the bus. Fear keeps me upright as the crowds get on and off and I totter around the complex of the large west London hospital, a mess of lanes and buildings that seem fairly logical on a sunny day when you're going for a check-up, but facelessly industrial when it's dark and you are delirious. I wind my way up to casualty and wait.

I explain my problem to the triage nurse, but the moment I mention that my GP suspects meningitis, she gives me a cold, suspicious look, and asks me if I have a letter. A letter? 'You're supposed to get a letter from your doctor,' she says. I marvel at the idea of someone who is choking on a bit of steak, or trying to stem a sudden arterial flow, willing their airway not to close any further, or the curtains not to become more splattered, as the doctor taps away at the keyboard – that is assuming they'd managed to get a quick lift to the surgery in the first place. And, if allocated a home visit, I wonder what doctor worth the name would sit there scribbling while the person tried not to asphyxiate. Or perhaps the doctor would expect to borrow the patient's PC. I have an image of the visiting medic tying off a frothing arm with one hand, while asking the haemorrhaging patient if it's OK to save to the desktop. My thoughts cut no ice with the nurse, and with another cold, suspicious look, she dispatches me to the waiting room. It being not only a Saturday night, but an Easter Saturday night, it is rammed. I curl up in a slippy plastic seat, and wait. It has to be said that no one in here looks particularly ill. A family of four children make a lot of noise right by me, and I consider lying down in a corridor. The other nurses, safe behind a glass counter screen, cackle and hoot loudly at private jokes and firmly turn their backs on us all.

I feel as if someone is pushing a hot knife into my face, but I sit, and sit, and sit. At one point, a nurse ushers two old ladies through the waiting room and takes them straight through to the cubicles, stating very loudly, to no one in particular, 'They've got letters. That's why *they're* going through first.' After more time, and a lot more people being sent through to the back, the large, fat man next to me, reeking of booze, begins to slump over and slip off his chair. More nurses appear, and as they are picking him up, one of them hisses in my direction, with theatrical disgust and equally theatrical projection, 'Look at this. It costs four hundred quid to get an ambulance out. It's such a waste of money.' The reception nurses continue to giggle and shriek behind their partition.

I begin to suspect that I am being given special treatment. After four hours, I am finally called, and sit, gowned, in a cubicle, watching a druggie sleep off the wreckage of his day peacefully in a bed over the way. It takes another half hour or so for me to be diagnosed with sinusitis, and be given some painkillers that I have never heard of and which, in the event, do not work at all. Mick has been doing a gig in east London, and claims that he has tried to contact me at the hospital, but no message has been passed on. Actually, I consider dumping him for not immediately blowing out the gig and coming to be with me. However, the methadone tablets he has about his person, when he finally makes it over to my place, more than make up for it. Thank God for junkie boyfriends. I vow to complain to the hospital, in writing, but for the next week I am unable to do more than lie in bed, reading crime novels, gobbling codeines and eating no more than half a banana a day, and by the time the week is over I have lost the impetus. I just want the pain to go away. The positive outcome of this period is that I take up vitamins. I am also interested to note, not long after all this happens, huge public information signs appearing in libraries and on the backs of pub toilet doors very clearly listing the symptoms of meningitis, and urging people, if they have even just some of them, to contact their doctor, or the nearest hospital, immediately.

bad hit

While heroin makes the time pass in waves, the universe, or whatever, likes to give the user – and those intimately involved with them – a bump now and again, to tell them that their lives cannot always move in the predictable fluffy tides of phoning, waiting, consuming and then lying around in a shimmering golden haze until it all starts up again. These karmic tweaks might take the form of a 'bad hit' or a non-fatal overdose, or one of the administrative dramas that a life on drugs inevitably engenders, such as lack of money for a bus journey, or constantly impending homelessness. Then there are the health problems, abscesses and teeth buggered from too much smoking and not enough brushing. With a junkie, what constitutes a medical emergency occupies a parallel universe from that of mainstream society. Actually, a lot of heroin addicts would make very good nurses. Once, when we are all enjoying a stoned Sunday, smoking and injecting among the piles of crisp packets and half-empty tubs of banana yoghurt, one of our number overdoses. I miss the main action as I am upstairs, but I have already noticed that he has turned waxen yellow in the face. However, since he usually looks like that, and is a long-term user, I think little of it. Suddenly there is shouting, and they go into the resuscitation procedure, which consists of walking him around the room shouting his name, and then sticking him in the shower. Sadly, their capacity to take care of each other on the stoned battlefield doesn't extend to themselves. The 'bad hit' is an injection that includes an unwelcome foreign body, such as a morsel of filter. It could also be one that hits the wrong spot, but the former has a timed-release effect, which usually kicks in at the cinema, as the film is about to begin, or as a party is about to start. There is hissed swearing, excessive sweating, and an atmosphere of complaint and general bad temper. I am reasonably content as long as I've smoked my own little bit before going out. It never occurs to me that the situation isn't normal. I would never say that this was a bad time, or a difficult time, or even an annoying time. As long as there is heroin at the end of the tunnel, and preferably at the beginning of it as well, I can put up with a hell of a lot.

We occasionally fantasise about robbing a chemist's, or taking a doctor hostage, but frankly I am far too lazy, and Boots in Queensway is so hyped up on Drug Terror that every time I go in to buy a bottle of Benylin Original the assistant simultaneously rings a bell and flashes a light. At times of murderous skintness, when all we have between us is fag and wine money – aside from the sacred twenty or fifty pounds necessary for a bag – Mick suggests kidnapping one of my richer friends, and sending her mother a toe.

One day the band is playing at a gig out of town. Mick has forgotten to get his supplies in, or woke up too late and has to get in the van before sorting himself out. Either way, I am entrusted with a precious task, which involves turning up at his mate's flat and watching him cook up a syringe-ful for Mick, which he wraps up and places inside a spectacle case. 'Do you know what this is?' he asks. Mick's line to the waiting band – which by then no one could possibly have been fooled by – is that it is 'cortisone' for his 'bad foot'.

I never get myself a full-on smack habit. The possibility is there, there is just about time to fit it all in, and there is very little stopping me, beyond Mick's protests that I've already done too much of it that week. But, I am just too lazy. And my writing keeps me going through everything. If there isn't a space left for that, forget it. And alcohol is still my number one. It is easily available, and I don't have to order it in advance by phone, while making reference to 'little fellers' or 'glasses of water'. Luckily, also, I have become friendly with the guys in my local corner shop, who give me credit when I'm skint. Am I depressed? Probably. When you're hung over every day, you are perpetually depressed. The only thing that keeps me going is the thought of the next session. It's warm and safe, cuddling up after a smoke. With hindsight, I must thank the Powers That Be (misc.) that I had, at this point, no credit anywhere, for I would now be bankrupt, for sure.

I have always avoided married men like the plague. I always feel that the married person of the two will have the upper hand, and that if you are married, you should only sleep with other married people, which is really what they are there for. What never occurs to me during all this time, is that a person doesn't have to be betrothed to another human being to be married. A person can be married to their work, and a person can be married to a substance. It might help if someone had pointed out to me that to get into a relationship with an addict is a sign of gravely low self-esteem, but my guardian angel is, by now, on perpetual dialysis.

1997, Dr Junk

A month or so after my lengthy flu attack finally dies down, it looks like this summer is going to be a good one. There are more gigs, deep drug benders and festivals. We come back from Glastonbury in a Winnebago, having partied for three days. After a weekend like that, it's always straight back to the gear to come down with, and a giant sofa, and two tabby cats patting our faces and staring into our eyes, just in case we don't wake up.

One sunny lunchtime, I am just waking up, with an ashtray stuck on my chest, when the phone rings. One of the crowd that runs around with the band has hanged himself. There are tears and a benefit gig and a funeral, and off the back of it all, someone decides that Mick should clean up. I forget whose idea it is, but this someone has also decided that he should do a new kind of detox. Naltrexone is a drug that works by blocking opiate receptors. Basically, with your system full of it, heroin has no effect. One of the early adopters of this treatment is a private psychiatrist who is well known in the music industry. The plan, unbeknown to Mick's manager, who is kept in the dark about it, for reasons I cannot remember, is for Mick to go into hospital, be knocked out for six hours while his system is pumped full of this stuff, and then woken up, the idea being that his system will then be free of heroin, and as long as he takes the Naltrexone in pill form every day, he will not be able to go back on heroin, and all will be fine. The five-figure fee is being paid by the band's record company. I ought to be pleased, but I have very mixed feelings about this, for reasons both altruistic and not.

We go to see Dr Junk for a preliminary chat. He is an olivy, slippery man, slick with private funds, with a famous band's gold disc on the wall behind him, and a little jar of downers on his desk, like sweets. At the time Mick is crashing at various peoples' flats, but it is decided that he will convalesce at another junkie friend's house, a pad knee-deep in discarded syringes, and which is currently inhabited by a young artistic boy. It also seems to have been decided that I am going to be chief nurse, which I do not fully comprehend. The idea of forking out a couple more grand for Mick to spend a couple of weeks in a nursing home, to recover from a major operation, does not seem to have occurred to anybody else, either.

I take Mick to the hospital. It is a hot summer day. Something doesn't feel right. But then nothing really ever does feel right in the mornings. Actually, part of me doesn't want him to clean up either. A very nervous, very young, northern boy sits with his friend on the scratchy armchairs in the waiting room. They are going to detox two at once. Mick is very nervous. Despite the fact that he has self-medicated to the point of coma on literally thousands of occasions in his life, the idea of having someone else do it for him is understandably a frightening one. The next day when I go to get him, he looks small and drained in his hospital bed. Already I am wondering what on earth is going to happen. Dr Junk gives me a list of the drugs that Mick should be taking, which are mainly downers of different kinds.

We take a cab back to the flat, which has been partially cleared of syringes. It is hot in Bermondsey. Mick sits in a chair, and another and then another. We are all sweating. He asks for hip hop. The bass stops the fizzing feeling as the drug he has been taking for twenty years has suddenly been unceremoniously removed from his system. He can barely walk. The day goes on.

Early in the evening there is a loud bang in the hallway. On the way back from the loo, Mick has fallen to the ground like a stone, as his blood pressure has dropped so much. The artistic boy swears quietly because *The Simpsons* is on and it is his favourite programme, but he pulls himself away from the television and helps Mick up. I walk back to the hospital through the late afternoon heat for diarrhoea tablets. The young doctor I explain the situation to gives me a look that tells me everything I need to know. Sweating, I also bring back some red wine, and we manage to knock up some spaghetti between the three of us. I have no idea what I am doing. Everything is melting. Even the knives in the deadly little kitchen bend as soon as I try to cut anything. Mick can't get up without falling down. The next day he is the same. I have Dr Junk's pager number, but he is not replying. For some reason I switch on the television – and there he is participating in a television debate about the treatment of heroin addiction. At least we know where he is. We go to see him again, during which meeting he waves his little sweetie jar at us as if we are children. He seems to accept without much question Mick's testimony that he is such a hardcore druggie that Valium will not touch the sides, and hand-writes a prescription for Tuinal. I have no idea what Tuinal is, except that it is known as 'traffic lights' in certain circles, due to its colourful capsule, and is way, way more powerful than Valium.

I start to get the message when, the following evening, I go off across town, clutching Dr Junk's prescription, to get some of this Tuinal from Bliss Chemists in Marble Arch. I am put in mind of the wording on the inside front page of my passport, that Her Britannic Majesty's Secretary of Gear Requests and Requires in the Name of Her Majesty all those whom it may concern to allow the bearer to get a supply of barbiturates, freely without let or hindrance, and to afford the bearer such assistance and protection as may be necessary. Oh ha ha. Dr Junk's handwritten prescription, albeit on posh paper, is getting pretty sweaty and dog-eared from being in my pocket for a couple of days. I have no idea how frayed

I am myself, from lack of sleep, from the mixture of red wine and Valium that I've been living on, and from listening to Mick hallucinate, first of all that I am his ex-girlfriend, then that I am one of the cats, and then shouting 'Satan!' repeatedly. Then he tells me that he might not love me any more. I am now fried to the point of collapse, and would really like some fucking smack. My attempt at getting the script filled at Marble Arch ends with me snarling loudly that someone or other is 'dicking me around', and security is called. Next, I go to a phone box and try Bliss Chemists in Streatham. A nice man answers but is very cagey on the issue of whether he might be able to give me any Tuinal, and asks me to read what is on the page. I am aware that sometimes doctors use secret marks to indicate a genuine prescription for something pleasantly mood-altering. After this chat, which enlightens neither of us, I hang up and go back to the flat. The next day Mick asks me to go out and get him some needles. I finally walk out of the flat and go all the way home without phoning. Later, I get a torrent of abuse from him, during which he tells me that he has been out, but when he went to a garage and tried to pay for a box of matches with a twenty-pound note, the man behind the counter threatened him with a baseball bat.

I see Mick a day or two later. He has injected himself in the leg, and an abscess is forming. The hard dark purple rotten patch on his calf is hot and getting hotter. I offer to take him to the hospital. He refuses. I tell him to go to the hospital. He refuses. I go home. On the phone he tells me it is the size of a fist. I tell him to go to the hospital, and that is that. When I try to find him the next day, his ex-girlfriend tells me that he has now actually gone to hospital, and very pointedly does not provide an explanation as to why she did not tell me before. First thing in the morning, I phone his social worker, and explain my concerns that Mick has gone off to hospital, and is staying with his ex, who he used to use drugs with, back in the day. His reply is to ask me what she does for a living. Puzzled, I reply that she works in radio. 'Well, you're a writer, aren't you, so I don't think there'd be any competition between you.' Floored, I go off to the Notting Hill Carnival on my own. I drink half a bottle of vodka before going, and the other half while I am there, and end up being rescued somewhere around the Sancho Panza sound system by a very nice social worker from Ealing, called Clarence, who saves me from my initial inability to walk, looks away politely when I squat to wee under various lorries, and squires me very pleasantly around various parties in the area, including a Cameroonian do in an upstairs flat, during which a man makes a pass at me while I am on the toilet.

The following day, Mick's manager finally has to be told, as the abscess on Mick's leg is even worse. He freaks, understandably. We go to the hospital, but Mick refuses to see me. After sitting for two hours in the waiting room, shaking, I am taken to the pub, where various friends of his joke about their junkie pasts, and the fights and all the blood, and I am a bit speechless at their lack of concern, and feel at a disadvantage. It doesn't feel right to be so jocular when Mick is ill in hospital with possible early-day blood poisoning and botched chemical-induced heroin withdrawal. They are acting as if it is a bit naive of me to be upset, which I find, frankly, shallow. The trouble with crowds of people that are held together by drugs is that life becomes very cheap, and trauma a very casual currency.

The following day I go back to the hospital to try and see Mick. When I am finally allowed up to the ward, I am greeted with a scornful glare by the nurse who, Mick is quick to tell me, grew up in the same rough district as he did. I am done for. He snarls abuse at me for abandoning him, and the nurse appears to agree. There isn't a lot I can do here, and I go away. I feel as if I am being hit in the stomach, but slowly. The person I've spent the whole of the previous year with now barely recognises me, except to shout abuse. I email the boy from the record company with a long list of my concerns about the medical treatment Mick has received. We have by then been pretty much abandoned by Dr Junk, at least in any meaningful sense.

I begin to feel that I have been made responsible for something. The final straw comes when Mick's manager tells me first that Mick doesn't love me any more. When I see Mick again, with his leg in a bandage, he tells me that he and the record company boy have been sitting in a restaurant, sniggering over my apparently hysterical email. This is the final straw. I wake up the next day almost unable to breathe, and get out the Yellow Pages. I find an Al-Anon meeting, for the friends and relatives of addicts, and ring the contact, a posh-sounding older woman who listens to me ramble and suggests I come to a meeting the next morning.

I find my way to a little room in a community centre. It is my first ever 12-step meeting. I sit down. There are laminated cards on the table. I am in a terrible state, and the last thing I need to do is listen to other people, but I just about manage it. One lady, also new to meetings, who is having a problem with her daughter, keeps trying to speak while the others share, but is shushed each time. Everyone around the little circle tells their story, a litany of their abandoning, abusive nearest and dearest, who have scammed money and love off them in equal measure. When it comes to my turn, I cannot speak. I try but all I want to do is cry. Worse, though, is my rising horror that I have anything in common with the people in this room. I am ashamed to think this way, but when I look at my companions' strange, outdated clothes, their funny eighties shoes, faded jackets and tired frizzed-up hair, it's like walking into a time warp. Does being involved with an addict regress your own life that much? Clearly it does. I feel such horror at ending up like any of these people, even for one minute, that I flee the meeting as soon as politely possible. I feel bad that snobbery is the driver, but it kind of works.

this unusual woman

The next day a friend rings me, early in the morning, and tells me to put the telly on because there's been a car crash in Paris involving Princess Diana. I am barely awake but I dive in like one lost in the desert, into the pool of wondering, the endless shift of newsreaders inviting each other to speculate, over and over again, about what has happened and what is going to happen. Hand in my mouth, I barely move from the television all day.

Days pass, and I lean into the public mourning as if into a soft grassy mountainside. I am so tired. I go to see the flowers. Piled up and glinting in the sun, the metallic pinks and blues and yellows make this corner of London look like a street scene in India. A friend tells me that his coke man stopped taking calls for twenty-four hours, 'out of respect for Diana,' – his voicemail intoned, pausing for the comma – 'Princess of Wales'.

A few weeks later, Mick's manager and I go to see Dr Junk, as Mick has rapidly returned to heroin. His manager tries to shush me while I tell Dr Junk about all the things that happened, my voice rising, and how stressful it was, and the effect it had on me. Dr Junk looks at me from in front of the shiny gold disc and tells me that I have been 'too stoical'.

Hindsight tells me that in seeking out men with substance problems, I have been looking for some cover, so that I can quietly get on with my own intoxication. Who would ever take me for a drug addict, or an alcoholic? If you surround yourself with people with worse habits than you, and who are notorious for them, you will always seem like the Normal One. I am with Mick for another two years.

playpen

After Mick and I split up, I find a new, much cheaper place to live. My life seems to be split down the middle, between my outward and inward life. Outwardly I am merging with all the other people around London who are just keeping their heads above water, filling their bodies with chemicals, yet barely hanging on inside. Naively, with the new place I plan to make a new start.

First, I go to New York for a wedding. With hindsight this is a foolish decision, given how much the trip costs, and how much I will desperately, desperately need that money, which is all the spare money I have, in the forthcoming months. During the wedding dinner, the many speeches get shorter and more explicit as time goes on, and the sex and drug references become less and less veiled, to the twitching of older relatives. Later, we all end up in the couple's suite at the Four Seasons. Finally, there are four of us left. We decide to let the newlyweds go to bed, and go to look for a taxi. I have arrived in town, my first ever visit to the Big Apple, expecting a three-day binge, against which the last days of Caligula were as nothing, of which tonight is presumably just Part One. I start to ask these three denizens of the town where we could go next, but the woman gets out, saying she is staying with her sister and cannot wake her up. One guy says he is staying on a friend's floor, so ditto the noise issue. The other is not forthcoming with invitations back to his hotel, even though I know full well he is still 'holding'. I am shocked that the evening is ending so soon. I am so wired I manage to run up the twelve flights of stairs back to the warehouse flat where I am staying. Normally I have to rest on each landing. I stand in the huge space, my head singing and ringing. It is only 4 a.m. The next morning I have lunch with a friend of a friend, who is a Famous Cultural Commentator, who I blow it with, first by shaking and actually appearing to need, rather than just want, a beer before lunch, secondly by farting in his flat, and thirdly by appearing genuinely shocked when he tells me that he once went and bought some heroin for an article he was writing about the availability of it in New York, but flushed it down the toilet without trying it. Months later, after the millennium, I am strangely hurt when someone tells me the newlyweds all came over to England to celebrate. I never hear from any of them again.

kaleidoscope

Sitting on the floor in the late morning after a long night, a friend says, 'Look, I can come really easily,' and she sits back, shuts her eyes and begins to strain, the tip of her tongue showing. Nothing happens. Someone yanks a framed photo off the wall, which happens to have a long white line down the middle of the image, like something from *The Omen*, and we joyously snort cocaine along it. Her husband takes his trousers down and insists we look at his balls, barely able to speak. A huge bowl of loose change thrown again and again round the room until the walls ring out. A television hit with a chain and little chunks of glass everywhere. 'Guess what! I'm going to do DMT and MAOIs!' A huge rock of cocaine, left hidden behind someone's television, goes missing, and a vast search is put on to find it. A day later, it is accepted that it must have been removed by the presumably ecstatic television engineer who'd come round to fix the socket. Going to put a tampon in and finding one there already, and trying to remember when you put that one in, and wondering whether there is yet another one behind it. Very occasionally, there is. Hotly debating whether it is possible to make a citizen's arrest of a yoghurt. 'They didn't even have the decency to put a numbing agent in it!' Going out into the garden first thing on a summer morning, scattering cats, and waving a large pink mosque-shaped alarm clock around, which emits a thin and scratchy but loud call to prayer, over and over again, over the neighbour's fences in the sun. Someone wanking over someone else's dress and then smashing a brandy bottle over someone's head. Fight clubs. Back to someone's first thing and doing coke round the baby's cradle. The motto 'They don't know', when at work after being up all night. Bored of the party, but too scared to exit the capsule into the real world air. Too scared, even, of a taxi. Public transport unthinkable, due to potential terror. Mick tucking into some new prescription sleeping tablets, Zopiclone, washing them down with Jack Daniel's, and becoming so aggressive that I run out to a phone box in terror at seven in the morning to call the Samaritans. Going in and out of cubicles. Blood tests. Sitting on banquettes in a pub at nine o'clock in the morning, shouting, 'Cunt cunt cunt cunty cunt!' while attempting yet another rendition by the Tourette's Choir. Tourette's renditions are always PC, as racial epithets are never used. Squealing with laughter at puke stories, such as when a friend, arriving at work after being up all night, cannot get to the loo in time and sends a fluffy pink substance, formed of Ribena and a hastily scarfed-down banana, all over a wall. Mixing cocaine and Ecstasy and red wine and Seroxat and seeing flashing lights. Taking speed alone at home and customising a pair of Camden market dungarees. Tossing and turning all morning during a heatwave after an all-nighter in someone's spare bedroom and finally going home, wired to hell, clutching a Tesco bag containing a pizza and a jar of rollmops. The train stops between all the stations and I am convinced every man in the train is staring at my breasts. I am so hungry I could kill. At home I stuff in a rollmop and they have already gone off in the heat. After thirty minutes I get the pizza out of the oven and instantly drop it on the floor, face down. I eat it anyway. Becoming mesmerised by a muscle above my top lip that only twitches when I'm putting a tampon in. After hearing the news of Paula Yates's death, sitting at home alone taking cocaine and writing a long letter to her.

If pushed, a lot of people say they prefer drugs to sex. Actually, a lot of people prefer drugs to a lot of things. After New York, bad things happen. Someone decides that I owe them a lot of money, and gradually I slide downhill into a domestic situation I could never have imagined, involving fleas, slugs, rats, rotting food, deadbeat stoners who never pay bills, and psychological warfare for which I am totally unprepared. I end up sleeping on friends' sofas half the time, and am prescribed Librium by my GP. The knock-on effects of it are painful and embarrassing and have a profound effect on my life. I am still a slave to my own desire for things to be nice. I never thought it was possible to feel this stressed and helpless, but it is too embarrassing to admit it to anyone. I go and see psychiatric nurses and say that I cannot stand my life any more, and they ask me what I would like to happen, and I say that I want to be an in-patient. A few days later I get a letter saying I am being referred. I am over the moon and for once want to cry with relief. A month later, I go to see the hospital, which is a kind of special living community, but they refuse to take me, because I tell them I am taking drugs. The admissions person, a Germanic Nurse Ratched type, clearly considers me a potentially disruptive influence. A nice older lady shows me round and one of the patients, a pretty girl of about twenty, appears in a doorway, all smiley, playing with a toddler. She looks at me very nicely and says hello and asks me if I am a journalist. The nice older lady says no, and explains that I am a potential in-patient. Instantly the girl's face turns savage.

8. women – when drink is the only solution

moral panic

You can't open a newspaper, watch television, or check out a news site, without seeing yet another story about pissed-up women taking themselves to hell, and the world with them. You'd think that getting drunk was a brand new disease that we'd only recently invented. There are echoes with the rise of HIV/AIDS. Back in the eighties, the chief constable of Manchester police, James Anderton, said that gay men were 'swirling about in a human cesspool of their own making', and much the same is said today about women out on a bender.

In the UK, fierce, highly paid columnist-led resistance to whatever human behaviour is under this week's spotlight is known as a 'moral panic'. Moral panics occur whenever the poor, the foreign, the very young, ethnic minorities, and, of course, women, do something that goes against a set of unspoken rules that may have been prevalent among the parents of those currently in their fifties. Gay sex, immigration when not coming from a war zone specifically endorsed by the Foreign Office, those on low incomes attempting to boost them, intoxication with substances currently deemed illegal, dancing together in groups to a background of repetitive beats having ingested said substances, children using mobile technology, the availability of fizzy drinks in schools, and pretty much any female behaviour that could not be undertaken by a paraplegic nun, have all been excoriated savagely in clouds of fear, with dark warnings that the end is even more nigh than it was in the writer's previous column.

Those promulgating this week's panic may not lead spotless lives themselves. Secret – or overt – affairs, abandonment of children, tax evasion, bigotry, and a drink or drug problem that may cause misery to those around them, or at least ridicule, are as prevalent in the houses of the commentators as anywhere else. Hypocrisy aside, the trouble is that once you have harangued your readers or listeners at such a continuously high level, you are not going to have much energy left for the issues that might actually merit such heavy-handed sermonising, such as the fact that if I am interpreting hundreds of news reports correctly, children are in far more danger from other children, and their own parents, than they are from any escaped nonce, that those who do not own property are left to fend for themselves in a society that has pretty much written them off, and that of the estimated 15 per cent of rape cases that are reported, between only 5 and 6 per cent of those result in a conviction.[8] It is not that the latter issues aren't mentioned, but that they are juxtaposed, with equal seriousness, with fulminations about subjects such as school food, traffic wardens, or an erect penis appearing in a television programme, all of which compete for space with increasing numbers of celebrity stories and spin-offs from reality TV. So it's not really surprising that people are paid to trump up moral hysteria, because otherwise no one would know what to get outraged about next.

The quickest way to prod the public into a reaction is to remind them, yet again, that women are increasingly out of control, even more out of control than they were last time, and that Something Must Be Done. Alcohol is a great lead-in for any story like this, because the use of it can, fairly accurately and without much effort, be attributed to women having more sex. More sex leads to the spread of disease, and unplanned pregnancy. However, the disease bit is just the icing on the cake, because the very notion of women voluntarily having more sex, alcohol-induced or not, is enough to set pulpits shaking from Swindon to Inverness.

the curse of the hen night

The most potent symbol of the scurrilous state of British womanhood today is the celebration of a woman's impending marriage. The pre-wedding single-sex knees-up is a time-honoured tradition, like circumcision, or the blooding of a pubescent child after a fox hunt. Once upon a time, however, it was the men who got the prenuptial spotlight. The stag do was a staple of situation comedy – blokes get their mate wrecked, hire a stripper and watch the UHT fly. More complex pranks might involve someone being comatose enough to be placed on some form of transport, to wake up the next morning tied to a lamp-post, naked, in a small Hebridean village. It is a staple of movies and, on a domestic scale, anecdotes that may surpass anything that any of the participants subsequently achieve – even if, in actuality, none of them felt very comfortable with the stripper, and did not enjoy their first attempt at mixing MDMA and cocaine.

As our expectations of the night expanded, it stopped being possible to have the gender party on the once-traditional night before the wedding itself, as the groom might have to, for example, get himself home again and sober up, as he might not have been to bed at all, or simply get himself tested for sexually transmitted diseases. Likewise, as the expectations of the night became more than getting a few beers down you in the back room of the local pub, participants started to find themselves expected to go all the way to Tallinn, or further. It has all become a much bigger deal, and women have raced to catch up.

A group of women very specifically out on the piss, and very specifically out to make use of a waiter's tackle, can be a spectacular, if unedifying sight. You can spot them on station platforms on their way into battle, wearing matching cowboy hats or feather boas. Either that or you'll see them in rented stretch limos, screeching out of the windows. Hearts sink as they enter their chosen venue. The old-school placing of knickers on one's head seems like harmless social play compared to the battery of dildos, vibrators and suggestive cakes that must now adorn the table. After the requisite number of vodka shots, screaming and being sick are pretty much obligatory, or at least you'd think so from the hum that comes from any restaurant that's hosting a hen do. Entire areas of cities have been written off, after one chain bar accepts them, and the rest topple and follow suit, one by one.

It is all too easy to be snobbish about this, but there is really very little difference between their behaviour and that of their posher sisters, who may have access to someone's huge house, or a hotel, to do all this in and are therefore not on public display. The difference is that the more well-off will have better alcohol, possibly higher quality drugs, and fewer chocolate penises. Their particular use of a stretch limo will be distinguished from everyone else's by its obvious irony.

It is interesting to note the number of hen nights that seem to go on every day of the week. This must be heartening to family values campaigners, as it means there are an equal number of weddings about to occur. The fact that the event may produce a number of children not biologically related to the groom is neither here nor there.

An observer from Mars might say that these nights are a symbol of female maturity about to be gained, a rite of passage as the bride passes from one stage, that of freedom and exploration, to the next, that of contributing to the stability of society. However, this would not be strictly correct. Nowadays, by the time a woman comes to getting married, she has probably enacted a similar night on at least a hundred occasions, and will probably do so many times afterwards, stopping only – hopefully – when she is pregnant. There is no such thing as a ritual any more.

screaming orgasm up against the wall, madam?

In 1998 or thereabouts I went to Paris to visit a friend. The French version of Berlin's Love Parade, a big rave with floats and club nights, was happening that weekend, so we decided to go along. On the way, we dropped in on some of her gay friends who lived in a beautiful top floor apartment near the parade route. There were about six of us there but, to my utter horror, only one bottle of champagne. I offered to go to the shop for more, but my friend looked nonplussed and said it wasn't necessary. I remembered the words of another French man to me, many years before: 'The English cannot have a good time without drinking', and I did not want to make myself stand out. So I butched it out, sweating. After an hour or so of chat, I felt the familiar panic rising, and, while fielding questions about myself, finally said, 'I'll answer that if you give me another drink.' Finally, after what seemed like years, we went down to the street to join the walking crowds, heading for Bastille. The first thing I noticed was that all the cafés were open, with not a boarded-up shop front in sight. The old ladies with their small dogs, and the couples with children, were there as they always would have been on a Saturday afternoon, and I didn't spot a single beer can in the crowd of techno-heads as we ambled along. I was amazed, and getting antsy in the hot sun. We hooked up with some other people, including a couple of suntanned and very cute straight men. I perked up a bit, but after an hour of wandering, I finally asked that we stop so that I could grab something to eat. When I was in the shop, I bought three tiny bottles of Heineken. When I got back to the waiting group, I waved the bag and offered one to one of the cute guys. Utterly bemused, all he said was, 'You're having a *beer*?' I felt the full weight of my nationhood for a moment – before realising that there was all the more for me, then.

Take a hen night, multiply by ten, and factor in hot sun, the like of which the visitor may have never encountered more than once a year, and an endless supply of drink at prices only dreamed of back home, and you have the UK's chief cultural embassy to the rest of the world. Men paved the way with football but, as always, women are not to be outdone. The main goal of these trips is to have sex and drink a lot. This is not a new phenomenon. It has simply, like everything else, become grander.

The Bacchae of ancient Greek myth were wild women who went out, got wrecked and then literally tore men to pieces. Their legacy lives on in the eyes of any pissed girl out on the town with her mates, where the noise seems to have a life of its own, tearing up the walls like a flame. So it seems somehow fitting that British drinkers have adopted places like Faliraki, on the Bacchae's original home turf, with such gusto. One thing I've learned in all my travels – package, rucksack, or five star – is that the Brits in general are seen as the world's biggest drunks; and British women in particular, of all their Western sisters, as the world's biggest whores. You can tire of the self-inflicted pressures of cultural relativism, and in many cultures, a woman might be called a whore just for wanting to get an education or drive a car, but even so. Who can forget the pictures of yet another girl, showing us acres of lobster-striped pasty flab, legs behind ears, skirt around her neck, lying in the road outside a taverna with a squaddie or three on top of her? Luckily most images aren't high res enough to reveal the botched tattoos, nor the weeping scar from the spontaneous belly-button piercing she can't remember getting after yesterday's tenth tequila slammer.

It's important to note that while there is always a vociferous group of island locals ready to comment on the iniquities of the British package tourist, there are just as many whose bars and clubs are greatly benefiting from the revenue, and who are happy to give holiday reps plenty of money to encourage the 'invaders'. Resorts like Faliraki have enjoyed some of the highest-profile horror stories in recent years. In 2003 there were several deaths, involving someone falling under a dustcart, someone else expiring simply from overdoing it, and an actual murder by glassing. In a twist worthy of a *Carry On* film, a girl was arrested minutes after winning 'Best Bottom 2003', which got almost as much publicity as the deaths.

fire down below

There's a darker side to all the fun of screeching, flashing your tits and throwing up in public. There's a lot of extra sex happening, and not all of it planned, or even wanted.

In early 2006, the Home Office started a campaign to warn men that they should ensure consent for sex.[9] There are relatively few convictions for rape and this is partly because alcohol is often involved, and the woman can't remember what happened, only that something did. This is not enough for the courts, and judges have sometimes thrown cases out because of it. Around the same time, a study by the Metropolitan Police revealed that over a third of women who reported a rape had consumed alcohol immediately before the attack.[10]

A lot has been written about 'date rape', i.e. non-consensual sex between two people who already know each other, even if for a very short time. A lot has also been written in the last few years about the concept of drug rape, i.e. where a predatory male has covertly spiked a woman's drink with the intention of making it easy to have sex with her. In 2003, Essex police performed tests on two hundred empty glasses in a club in Chelmsford, and found that seven of them had traces of benzodiazepines (i.e. Valium) on them, and another had traces of Ketamine. The figure of 4 per cent was said to be a surprise, and they said that they had been expecting no more than 1 per cent.[11] This, and other news programme follow-ups where reporters did their own research, led health spokespeople to assert that a vast amount of drink-spiking was going on, and thus most reporting in recent years has assumed that drugs are to blame for all incidents of acquaintance rape.

The trouble is that women – those that do them – really, really love drugs. Years ago, I remember a close friend saying 'I would fuck a man for drugs. You would too, wouldn't you?' I celebrated my thirty-fourth birthday in a bar in Shoreditch. As the lock-in hour approached, out came the Green Fairy, the imported Absinthe that had hit London a couple of years before, and then the disappearing to the toilets began. 'Oooh, give me some of that,' I said to the man I was seeing at the time, shoving him downstairs to the bogs and ordering him to chop a line out. 'The thing is, it's not really coke,' he mumbled. I must have started up some kind of 'Go on go on go on' thing, because he relented and gave me a tiny, greyish-pinkish-coloured spider's leg, and we went back upstairs. Within fifteen minutes I was slumped on a banquette, my head in his lap, demanding soggily to be taken home. I woke up the next morning barely able to walk. It felt like I was tramping through a field of glue. I never worked out what it was; Ketamine, MDA, who knows. Back at the bar, a friend, who'd had the same stuff, was also waking up, trousers down, having apparently been penetrated, not entirely at her own choosing, by the bar's resident nutter.

Despite the occasional new story about the vast number of banknotes impregnated with cocaine and other street drugs, the outside world has only recently woken up to the fact that poly-drug use is pretty normal now, and during an ordinary evening out drinking, someone might well also have consumed a chemical buffet of cannabis, cocaine, speed, Ecstasy and prescription downers. A few years ago, a news programme did some random tests for cocaine in pubs and bars and found, to their surprise, but perhaps no one else's, that traces of it could be found in any establishment where you can get a drink, on everything from glasses to door handles and even on a baby-changing table.

an inconvenient truth

Although women are a lot more savvy these days about what it feels like to be under the influence of many different drugs – and hopefully when they've taken something they didn't mean to – unfortunately, none of this really matters, because it simply isn't necessary for a woman to be spiked with something extra to end up having sex that she didn't want – enough tequila, vodka or JD and Coke and you're pretty much anyone's.

This situation hits at the heart of gender relations in twenty-first century society. There is always going to be tension between the idea that a woman has the right to dress as she likes, and behave as she likes, up to and including fully intending to go out and get shagged in a bar toilet, even if she has no idea who with, nor whether she'll be able to remember doing it; and the fact that a drunk woman with her legs open out the back by the wheelie bins may well appear to be up for it to the nearest geezer who's totally wankered himself, and had only nipped out for a piss. At the core of this superficially well-suited pair is the idea that the woman should at least be able to choose who she does it with, and whether she does it at all.

But take a look at the animal kingdom. What creature, in the whole of nature, allows itself to become so intoxicated that it cannot protect itself from predators, or even accidents? It seems an aspect of human privilege, that sets us above animals, that we allow ourselves to do this. And then, to play devil's advocate for a moment, isn't this what getting really, really drunk is all about – letting the spirit of Dionysus slip in and take you wherever it wants to go?

sex – the new sixties

In fact, Dionysus must be having a right laugh at the moment. Magazines exhort us to liberate our inner geisha, screeching *10 Ways To Please Him* at us from the shelves. And after we've exhausted those ten ways – actually, make that forty – how many more? How far can a girl go, constantly upping the ante on herself? After the ice cubes and the placing of doughnuts or carved fruit on her boyfriend's penis, what is she going to do when he gets bored? First of all, she'll spend money on ever more pricey underwear. Then she'll do the ironing wearing it. Then she'll find herself doing things she may well not be comfortable with – anal sex; him watching her with another girl; threesomes. And after that, what will she do then? Dogs? A horse? Through the internet, sex practices that were once seen as minority pursuits, such as bondage and sadomasochism, have now become totally accessible and are regularly written about as just yet another life choice to be ticked off on a list. In many ways this is a positive thing. But it also means that what were once seen as ordinary sexual relations have now morphed into the dreaded 'vanilla' – or 'lightweight' – and activities that you might have seen in a porn film at someone's house one night, that once seemed like circus acts, are now treated as an expected part of any ordinary woman's sexual repertoire, no matter how gymnastic, or – depending on personal preferences – how degrading.

And the targets are getting younger and younger. Not content with women of legal age, marketers are targeting girls who not long ago would have been thought of as children. When I was growing up, childhood ended at about eleven. Now it's more like eight, and descending. The female ideal now looks like a teenage boy with pith helmets stuck on his chest. What was once seen in the late nineties as an ironic porn clone look, when everyone was sick of the post-grunge paleness that had been in for years – the caramel face, blonded straightened hair and frosted lipstick – has become the norm. Many female pop stars have embraced it wholeheartedly: white women colour their faces beige and bleach their hair, and paler-skinned black women put blonde extensions in, so there's a kind of racial smoothing of boundaries which ought to be a positive thing. (Incidentally, I've heard it suggested that white people are descended from aliens, because aliens are described by those who claim to have seen them as tall, white-skinned and pale-haired. As, traditionally, angels are also fair-skinned and golden-haired, it's interesting that the pornoisation of our culture has brought on this increase in the presence of angels.) But the Californian-Aryan sun-kissed look doesn't go well with British light and pale skins. If you're a pale Caucasian, it's just not very attractive to go around looking like you've spent the weekend sitting in a bath full of chicken korma.

I swallow!

There's a lot in the media right now about how free and cool teenage girls are, that they live their emotional lives very close to the surface, and do what they want when they feel like it. I hope everyone under eighteen is having a good time, I really do, but a batch of fashion shoots do not indicate a mass increase in inner self-confidence, and neither do positions of the month, bellies hanging over waistbands and more freely available morning-after pills, however important the latter. And boozing definitely doesn't.

Actually, though, if you'd come to Britain on a package holiday from Neptune, you might, dare I say it, wonder what the fuss is about. While she may not have 'asked for it' out loud, a girl's T-shirt may already have done the talking for her. In one of the listings in the *TVGoHome* annual of 2001, for a programme called *Cunt* which eventually produced the television character Nathan Barley, a girl is described as wearing a T-shirt bearing the legend 'Dicktoy Slut'. At the time, it might have been a mild exaggeration, but nowadays having 'My Nipples Get Harder Than Most Guys' Dicks' emblazoned down your baps seems positively coy.

We live in a world where women who are famous for having huge plastic tits and not much else are held up as desirable icons for our female children. Double points if they get called a 'survivor'. For these girls, the few who make it seem to have everything anyone could possibly want – clothes, jewellery, a house or two, lots of foreign travel, loads of freebies, and their physical form celebrated from every angle. The fact that these women have had to get their bits out to succeed, no more, no less, and have had their lives examined in the most brutal detail, at times viciously, seems to pass their fans by. Among intellectual, chattering-class women, it's fashionable to go on about how it's fine and even cool to do that, even though not a single one of them would ever take this route herself, preferring to pass exams, go to university, and claw her way up the media ladder.

And I cannot see any of today's female commentators miming a post-orgasm face for money either. Whatever her own family of origin, a media commentator will say that it's OK for a working-class girl to get her kit off for money, as this is, apparently, one of the few options open to her.

Now that you can buy thongs for seven-year-olds without risking arrest, it's become increasingly unfashionable to sound a note of concern about a girl selling herself for money, whether through actual sex, i.e. prostitution, or the never-fulfilled promise of it, i.e. dancing or being photographed. There's a whiff, fanned by certain elements in the media, that you must be a real prude if you're not comfortable with this. This is true at the time of writing, and I suspect will remain true for a while to come. From the media, you could be forgiven for thinking that every other female student is a part-time escort, and anyone who isn't having sex for money to support their studies just hasn't really got with the program, and is doomed to a life of eating beans and taking buses, rather than seared sea bass and limos. Mind you, when one of the contestants on a reality TV show is famous only for deep-throating a football coach, and allegedly charges quite a lot to do so, you could be forgiven for asking yourself the simple question – after taking all those exams, reading all those books, and re-writing your CV maybe a hundred times over the years – 'Why the hell did I bother?'

watching the clapometer

Sadly, sex doesn't have to be random and drunken to bring disease and unwanted pregnancy, but there's no doubt that boozing and 'accidents' go together like fish and chips. Being perpetually hung over can mask the symptoms of something nasty, and an infected person might unknowingly, or uncaringly, be spreading gonorrhoea, herpes, and other nasties, like chlamydia, which existed but was barely heard of even ten years ago in the mainstream media. What we're seeing more of is conditions that have no symptoms, but can still be infectious. This must account for the fact that people are continuing to have sex when infected, as these diseases are not fun when they finally make themselves known. Alas, the female reproductive system is a perfect target for these bugs, and if an infection is not caught in time, infertility can result. Someone, somewhere, will have cynically suggested that at least that would spare someone the effort of obtaining, and asserting their right to use, contraception. What's more, those who are catching these conditions, and spreading them, are getting younger and younger. There's a frightening contrast between the early years of extreme HIV/AIDS awareness, and the situation we're in now, but these potentially fatal conditions are seen as an old person's thing. This is ironic because some of the older generation, who thought they were too old to worry about this kind of thing, have now taken up swinging and are catching everything in the book.[12]

As for teenage pregnancy, our rates are the highest in Europe,[13] but few seem willing to actually do anything about it, or admit the powerful connection with alcohol. It's too much of a political football, because any solution might have to take into account that sex actually happens. It's a shame for all sorts of reasons, not least because it seems logical to assume that, boozing aside, the younger the mother, the healthier the baby. I may have missed a biology class one time, but if a woman is born with all her eggs, surely they are exposed to whatever she puts into her body during her lifetime? Surely the egg of a sixteen-year-old is in a better state than one that's been battered by thirty-plus years of smoking, drinking, drugs, junk food, medication, pollution and stress?

Unfortunately, we can't assume a minimum level of education for every girl that gets pregnant. For many people, their first drinking and their first sex go together like a cornet and a 99. I wonder how many of these babies of teenage mums have already had their first taste of alcohol before they were even born. And I wonder how much the rise in ADHD (Attention Deficit Hyperactivity Disorder) can be linked to it. It's time someone did some proper research on this. On the television, it was heartbreaking to see a teenage girl, eight months gone, off on the piss because she didn't know any better, and another one doing the same because she didn't want to be left out when her mates were having a good time. It's very, very odd that society comes over all gooey when someone is pregnant, no matter what a mess their life is in, nor what harm may come to the future child. You'd think that people would heed the call, after being scared witless by the concept of global warming – the biggest licence to print money since the Y2K bug – to scale down their own reproduction, and recycle, by adopting all the poor, abandoned children who haven't got parents.

The problem isn't confined to poorly educated teenagers, though. I once knew a woman who, on discovering she was expecting, bragged endlessly about the amount of drugs she'd done during the first three months when she hadn't realised, and how she was going to write a book about how it was fine for women to carry on partying while pregnant. Six months into her pregnancy, I started wondering why her bump hadn't got any bigger. She hadn't been going for scans because she'd decided they might, er, harm the child. Finally she was persuaded to go for one, and, sadly, the baby had died. If still in doubt, a read of Michael Dorris's *The Broken Cord*, about Foetal Alcohol Syndrome, should be enough to keep anyone on the wagon when they're going to have a baby.

body battlefield

Women have 10 per cent more fat than men, on average, so we have less water in our bodies to dilute alcohol. This makes us more vulnerable to alcohol-related diseases. From a standing start, we burn fewer calories than men, because we have less muscle. Cruelly, therefore, we put on weight quicker than men do. Our bladders are smaller, and we need to go to the loo more often, which is a shame because there are only the same number of loos for women as there are for men in most drinking establishments. Our hormones flood our bodies every month, and due to processes still not fully understood by medical science, we react differently to certain chemicals depending on what week it is in our menstrual cycle.

rant – some things that are not fair

My book – my rules. Here is a list of things that are not fair, that you are welcome to skip if you wish. My point is, they might drive anyone to drink. Only recently, a judge decided to tighten up the law on 'crimes of passion' and declared that 'provocation' over a long period was not enough to give a murdering husband leniency. Too many husbands were getting away with short sentences for manslaughter, while it was only recently that women were allowed to take years of abuse into account when in the dock for having finally been driven to kill a violent partner. There are still debates about shortening working hours in the UK parliament, and there is still a relentless push-pull about how to make working hours more flexible for women who have families – whose children are, after all, the next generation. Then there is – *still!* – the matter of equal pay, and of how staying at home to look after children is seen as an inferior choice. Younger and younger children are getting anorexia, as what is reported as 'average' in the media is further away from human norms than it has ever been. Globally, rows about what women should wear cause as much chatter as wars, and these rows, when exported, cause a lot of heart-searching in Western countries, but only half-hearted suggestions for change, cultural relativism always being cited as the preventer of more robust law-making. The fear of being called racist now overrides all other considerations. Thus we have absorbed 'honour killings' and genital mutilation with as much uncomfortable but bland tolerance as labiaplasty.

In the UK, sexual crimes against women are actually legally designated 'hate crimes', but you don't hear much about it. The awareness of globally curtailed freedoms has a butterfly effect on Western women. We get angry, then berate ourselves for getting

angry, because 'it's their culture', and then quickly dash off
yet another 'gratitude list' for everything we've got. Grotesque
though the idea might be of covering yourself from head to foot
when leaving the house, you are at least making a deal with
society that says, 'OK, I've covered up now, I've obeyed the rules,
now leave me the fuck alone.' Some non-Western cultures would
rather enforce this on women than attempt to change their male
way of thinking, which is why any Western female tourist, even
dressed fairly discreetly, causes such intrusive sexual hysteria. A
flash of white skin, even just the back of the hands, is enough.
Girls who have not yet fully developed are getting plastic surgery
for their birthdays. Anti-abortionists consider a woman to be no
more than a field to plough, and a child to be no more than a
philosophical entity. Women still do not have rights over their
own fertility, and laws worldwide still vary, and waver over
whether we are forced to have something growing in our bodies
that we don't want to be there. Such is the urge to control women
that everything must be subjugated to it, even the welfare of the
unwanted child in question. Women's problems are medicalised
when they may simply be a response to an inadequate and hostile
environment, and natural body hair is only seen in the freaks'
corner of porn websites.

And we act it all out on ourselves – cutting, anorexia, overeating,
exercise obsession, self-starvation – without any encouragement
from others. We are more likely to win prizes for our looks,
even though the criteria for the prizes may have nothing to do
with physical beauty. Even women's magazines are occasionally
exposed for making youth and looks the chief criteria for awards
supposedly set up to promote women's achievements. With each
new generation, a whole new raft of rights, entitlements and
expectations appears, and every mother has to grit her teeth and
rise above it all as she watches her daughter take so much more
for granted. Our reward for allowing these situations to continue
is that the English language has grudgingly accepted various
enlightened phrases, such as the wretched 'me time', 'mummy

time' and 'empowerment', which reek of desperation, but are, apparently, the best that the world will tolerate.

if you can't beat 'em...

Perhaps as a result of the above, it's very important among women not to be seen as a victim. The word has taken on the worst possible connotations, even though, if something bad happened to you, that's exactly what you were, even if just for a few minutes. Women are increasingly phobic of being seen to feel anything other than all-powerful. Some women already know all this, and cultivate hobbies traditionally seen as male whilst playing the girly card when necessary. For the rest of us, this is very confusing. When you've applied your girly dispensation and refused to either get on a motorbike, become an expert on beer, or learn the offside rule, it's dismaying to discover that the really cool girls have been into those things all along. Some of them have even imported cocaine. What to do? You are bored to death by football, are scared to go on a two-wheeler, and avoid beer like the plague because it makes you fat, and you've never dealt drugs because there seemed to be so many other people doing it that what was the point? Oddly, though, few women take up philosophy, which is arguably the most masculine pastime of all. But whichever way a woman chooses to live, it is only under torture that she would ever admit to having ever, in her entire life, been a victim. In fact, the demands of self-PR being what they are nowadays, she would probably have to be tied to a board and be dunked repeatedly in a cold bath by five mocking insurgents, for at least twenty-four hours, alternating with being sexually molested with electrified probes, before she would admit that anything had ever been done to her that was beyond her power to stop. Alcohol increases testosterone in the female body – no wonder we get feisty when we drink.

mine's a double

A 2005 Amnesty International survey revealed that the majority of people think a woman who gets raped while drunk is asking for it.[14] However, logic says that if you're going to drink yourself into such a trance-like state that you really have no idea of what is happening to you, it's best to stay in the vicinity of your own home, or at least surround yourself with about fifty friends. As soon as you enter the public arena, you become public property if you allow yourself to be so. It's a jungle out there. Until every single mugger, murderer, rapist or just out-and-out bad lot is behind bars or dead, and no more are born, everyone in society, men too, is at risk from someone else if they are really, really unlucky. And the problem is that while 'No' may well mean 'No', 'I'll have another double JD and Coke, please' also means just that.

As a consequence of all the boozing, women are spending more and more time – and money – in a state of *detox*; a word, ironically, that was once used solely to describe coming off drugs, and now inevitably involves *pampering*, a horrific marketing concept used to sell ceramic tealight holders and thrush-inducing bubble baths. We all ought to know by now that neither an economy-sized crate of scented candles, nor chucking it all in for an aromatherapy course, is going to sort anyone's life out. We might all do well to remember the Wiccan rule: 'An't do no harm, do what thou wilt.' And this extends to the harm we're doing to ourselves.

9. the final countdown

oh God
oh God
oh God

After forty-eight hour fun in Brighton over the weekend, went to a gig in Brixton Monday night. Just got in Tuesday 10 p.m. after twenty-four hours of the usual, except this time also involving oral sex in public with two men in a bar in Clapham High Street.

don't even ask
don't even ask
will tell all v soon

After a heroin Christmas, during which I spend four days on a sofa with Mick although we are no longer a couple, I decide to stop drinking for five days a week. I manage this for nearly three months and am incredibly proud of myself. I also give up wheat because I am being slowly driven mad by stomach problems. My life changes dramatically, albeit in chunks. I am trying to restart my life by going to evening classes and staying in all the time. I also lose weight. But I spoil it a little by caning it so hard at the weekends that I don't feel like going out the rest of the time anyway. My suicidal emails to friends are a wince-making testimony to this. The trouble with the part-time wagon is that you are still dominated by the calendar. It is one of the traditional signs of an addict to start marking off days and awarding yourself points for managing to stay clean for forty-eight hours, thus entitling yourself to a bender afterwards.

It is during this particular mini-wagon that I go out for drinks with a group of writers. As we sit among the pints, me with various soft drinks, someone asks me if I am OK. 'Yes,' I reply, 'I'm just sober.' A few days later I am told that someone who was there thinks I am a bit weird and aloof.

how to be a token bohemian

My writing is praised, but this praise does not turn into money. This means that I just can't chuck another twenty quid in the pot for late-night supplies and, in the main, restaurants are totally off limits to me. Living that life, I learn to eat before I go out, and then turn up late pretending to have been held up. My clothes are all one-offs from charity shops or designer sale outlets. So far, so normal, but I am also aware that I am becoming a bit of a pet artist. A Token Bohemian, in fact.

'Oh sweetie, it's just so great that you're a writer. Don't stop, will you? I wish I was as brave as you!' I have heard this many times. On the surface, this is a nice, encouraging thing to say, and is probably well meant. But look again. It's very easy for a person on £100K+ in the law, media or finance to say that, when you're wondering how not to lose your internet connection, and are spending hours looking for drinkable wine at under three pounds a bottle.

Being twice published is a ticket to being interesting, and collectable. There are always advantages to be gained from an artistic identity, but there are rules. It's fun being collected, up to a point, but there's always a rumble of give and take below the surface, which generally translates into singing for my supper, and this usually takes the form of using my 'wild' private life as a bargaining chip, because I don't have a credit card to wave around. And then arrives the pumpkin hour, and the others go back to their paid-for houses, while I slink off to get the night bus back to my rented perch. Of course, none of this matters if you have inner self-confidence. For me, it is yet more fuel for pain and yet more excuse to drink myself out of it.

Despite the apparent cosiness of the gang, it doesn't take much to elicit punishment. One night, just after midnight, when the coke has just run out, one of our crowd suddenly remembers that a friend, who's already gone home, still has a gramme on her. As all our faces begin to light up and we start to salivate, she begins ordering us to get into a cab with her and go round to the other girl's flat to get it. At the last minute, I back out and refuse to go with the two of them, eliciting comments of 'Chicken!' When they return, triumphant, they tell me that when they got to her house, these two diminutive women, suit-wearing, law-upholding, and relatively sober by day, began kicking her door in, waking her husband, who had to get up early for work. Apparently, she handed it over without a word.

What I need is a kind of social decompression chamber. I don't find it the night I cop off with a lawyer, after having taken him upstairs to talk him out of hitting someone. At about 7 a.m., twelve hours after we started out, I take him back to my flat where we play records for about another ten hours, after which we pass out on the bed. Sex is out of the question, due to incapacity. We wake up at about 10 p.m., starving. The first thing that comes into my head is fish fingers, and I suggest he goes to the corner shop to get some. He looks at me with utter disgust and says 'Ergh, how can you eat those, they're really bad for you.' It is simply beyond my mental ability to point out that, during the previous twenty-four hours, he has consumed probably at least two grammes of cocaine, four or five Ecstasy tablets, a bottle of vodka, at least ten pints, smoked about sixty Marlborough Lights, possibly alternating with ten or so B&H, and five or six spliffs.

South of the river, the sessions continue in parallel. No one cares whether I have bought a property or not, but I get dark looks from a girlfriend when she comes back from making a post-up-all-night pot of tea to find me having lines of charlie snorted off my breasts by her boyfriend and one of the participants in the Belgo's Bierodrome Oral Sex Spectacular. I have an affair with a man who is registered blind. He is a 'real' alcoholic and needs two bottles of cider to get going in the morning. I feel very normal.

A group of us take a villa in Majorca. This, with hindsight, is the last gasp for this particular combination of people, which is probably why it is so much fun, a bit like sex at the end of a relationship. Our combined annual salary is probably approaching a million pounds, although mine at the time is negligible. I am about to embark on my journey to the final frontier, although I do not know it at the time. In fact, people have been very kind and offered to pay for me, which is nice, if damaging to my already half-gone sense of pride. This group is held together by cocaine and dominant women, who would be ladies who lunched if they were not too busy working in important jobs, jobs which were more important, in society's eyes anyway, than mine and that of another of our number, which is why she and I are requisitioned as the Special Transport Crew.

On the evening of departure, we meet at someone's house to tank up. My friend and I each set about inserting the small clingwrapped packets, she with the Ecstasy, I with the cocaine. I later discover that you should never trust a muling package that has been made by someone else. A group of other people turn up just for the craic, one of whom, David, will turn out to be my guide to the aforementioned final frontier. I have just started taking Seroxat, and am still in the honeymoon phase of feeling very pleasant but more susceptible to alcohol than usual.

people like us

There follows a cheap night flight, accompanied by singing, but there are no fights or glassings. Having arrived four hours before we can get access to the villa, we decide to spend the morning in a bar. After the wake-up beers and brandies, it is suggested that we broach the mule-wraps, to tide us over till we can get the keys, so my friend and I adjourn to the loos to unload. Each squatting in a cubicle, we dig around and chat loudly until I hear my friend's door bang and she goes merrily back to the party. Just after she leaves, the thread holding my package all together breaks off in my fingers, and I am left with the slippery packet stuck inside me. I can see the morning sun under the cubicle door, and hear the voices and music from the bar. Shouting 'help' is pointless. I ruminate. If *I* was going to make an intra-vaginal drug transportation unit, the string, and it would be string and not cotton sewing thread, unless it was doubled or tripled, would be integral to the whole thing, and wrapped around all the way up and down. I attempt botched yoga position after yoga position as panic sets in, wondering how I can ask the bar staff for a crochet hook without arousing suspicion. Well aware of the time-stretching capacity of intoxication, it would be at least an hour of real time before anyone realised I was gone. Pulsing every muscle in there that I can, I finally extract the thing with the tips of my fingers and get the hell out of there.

The contents of the packets are never destined to last long, but they cover the first twenty-four hours of the trip very nicely. By mid-evening, everyone has removed a lot of clothing, and I am walking around with a bunch of grapes in my knickers. We smoke the rest of the Ecstasy for breakfast. I haven't felt so good in ages. One thing they don't tell you about Seroxat is that it masks hangovers, or at least it does with me, and I am sleeping better than I have in years. Wherever I am, I'm normally the first to get up, boiling the kettle in silence among the snores, and doing the washing-up, but this time it is me who scrapes up the end of breakfast while everyone else gets their beach bags ready. At this particular breakfast, my fruit salad, lovingly created from the grapes, each cut in half or more, remains uneaten. I suspect a thrush rumour, but say nothing.

I don't remember a huge amount about the rest of the trip,

except that we laugh a lot. My fellow mule, however, is having a funny turn that week, and one night wakes her husband up at five in the morning to offer him half a sleeping pill. Somewhere, there is a shot of all the women, topless in the pool. I still have my booze weight then, and I apparently win 'best in show' when the picture is shown to others later. The flight back segues us back into English ways, engaging other passengers in subterfuges to get more wine when the flight steward suggests that some of us have had enough.

I return to my flat, a basement studio with junkie blood spatter on the ceiling and a currently unoccupied crack-hole under the front steps, with an arrangement of stained mattresses in it, where the gas meters are – card meters, naturally, which I inevitably end up feeding in the early hours of the morning when trying not to hallucinate. One thing about drinking, and drugs too, is that for a few hours you can buy your way into any life, and believe yourself part of it.

one-way ticket

My final journey starts one night, as things often do. We have all been out somewhere, God knows where, and a group of us end up back at someone's flat, as you do. This someone is sleeping with David. The fourth person is a Danish woman who is, apparently, David's best friend.

He produces more cocaine and we sit around the kitchen table, trading sex stories round the circle until the other two women have dropped out of the game and gone quiet and there is only me and him left. 'Come to bed now, I'm going to shag you senseless!' says his girlfriend, at about seven in the morning. Crashed on the sofa, I listen to them humping for a while before passing out.

David and I trade numbers, and we end up having lunch during which he gives me a pair of Gucci sunglasses that have been given to him as a present by one of his employees. It is fitting that they break in my bag a couple of weeks later. He has a powerboat (customised) and has on several occasions been bumped up to Concorde for work, is familiar with hotels in Monaco, and is still, technically, married to somebody else. He never, ever, runs out of cocaine. Cocaine makes the clock run and run. You can have an entire relationship in a night, and then keep repeating it over and over again.

We have been up all night when I finally take him back to my flat. Even in my addled state I am aware that I am revealing more than perhaps is safe in the status stakes. I have had to move here at the last minute, there being nowhere else to go at the time. Before my hasty decorating session, the walls were dark turquoise, the colour of pine bubble bath, and the floor was brown lino squares, curling up. There was a discarded rice cooker in the kitchen which had probably never been used to produce food. The flat was boarded up, and I have been assured that it had been so for many months. The desperate knocking and flapping of the letterbox in the early hours – 'Junior? Junior!' 'Likrish! Likrish! You there?' – that begins as soon as I move in, and my subsequent researches, tell me that it is more like six weeks. Later, I find out from a neighbour upstairs that there was a near-murder in there just before the inhabitants were evicted, and the whole house was under siege by crack dealers vying for attention on the lawn. I have already had cause to wonder about the place. At the Notting Hill Carnival a couple of weeks before I moved in, a friend and I were standing in the road outside, swaying along with the crowd, and I pointed down to the flat while telling a friend about it. A man standing next to me suddenly became animated. He didn't hide it either, looking between me and the flat and back again rapidly. At the time I thought he was just checking me out.

It is a novelty for David to come anywhere near such a place. His career trajectory has only gone one way, and that is up. We lie around, we do more lines, and then he suggests we go away the following weekend. He goes on the internet, and suggests the south of France. The night before we leave, David says, 'You will turn up, won't you? It's rude when people don't turn up.' I am amazed. The idea of not turning up to any trip, let alone one that is a gift from someone else, is alien and odd. A few weeks later he says 'You talk a flaky game, but you're so solid.' He is, as many rich or famous men are, surrounded by a committee of protectors and self-interested parties, eager to place their stake in his affections, and run around for him. Otherwise, they are a self-centred lot. The women are all a bit corporate, a bit successful, and, as far as I can see, thoroughly shallow. He has never met anyone like me before. The women, all of whom have happily listened to him going on about his marriage for several years, are enraged that a usurper has appeared to shove them down the hierarchy, as it is clear that several of them have been waiting patiently in the wings for their moment to pounce.

As I am leaving my flat to meet him at Liverpool Street, it occurs to me that even before the bus fare there and the one home at the other end of the weekend, I only have four pounds in the whole world.

I don't tell anyone I am going. It is more fun that way. On the way back, we get to Victoria and then go our separate ways. He waits in line at the taxi rank, and I go to wait for the bus. We watch each other standing there, and for a moment our differing modes of transport really ought to strike me as significant.

Our usual evening's ritual consists of vodka-juice, cocaine, and red wine, and back again, with cocaine throughout. Twenty-four hours, thirty-six hours, watching the sky go dark behind the blinds, watching it lighten up again, watching it go dark again. Talking, talking, sex, talking, and more sex, more lines and another bottle of wine. One night we get back late and his corkscrew has gone missing. We open the bottle with a power drill, sending red splatters all over the kitchen wall.

I've been out with someone much richer than me before, and vowed never to let it happen again, but by that stage I have lost all sense of self. I have become a leaf on the wind, waiting to experience things because anything has to be better than the daily reality of my life – no stable home, suicidal hangovers, attempts to get therapy, and antidepressants. All this prevents me from seeing even the most basic warning signs, like the time when he says, 'So let's say this goes on for about, say, six months, right?' One evening, David is very keen to watch a documentary about Jeffrey Archer, which puts forward the hypothesis that he is, medically speaking, a psychopath. Ologists are wheeled on, and someone boils the definition down to seventeen features of a person that indicate that this is more likely than not. He applies them to himself, and counts fifteen. His career has been a scramble from one shafting of someone to another, eventually culminating in getting his best friend, who works for him, made redundant in order to save his own job. One time he comes round with bloody knuckles, but refuses to say why. Throughout this, he still manages to get me to feel sorry for him, and I supply him with sex on demand and listen to him talking about his soon-to-be ex-wife, long into the night.

I bring a sex toy on one of our trips, but it doesn't get used. Then one morning he suddenly gets up and leaves me draped over the sofa and comes back into the room with his electric razor, which he puts inside me and switches on. It hurts a bit, I suppose, but I am numb.

And so the summer passes, and we spend nights with vodka and red wine, and line after line chopped out. After a while he gets one of those little glass bottles with a valve on it, so it is easier to snort it in public, while pretending to blow our noses. I keep the affair secret, telling only two friends. I am so sick of people knowing things about me, and all those things being sad, pitiful ones. His Danish friend lives in New York, and he suggests we go over there to visit. I should perhaps have thought a little more about the potential repercussions of this trip. The night before we go, we've already been up all night, and I end up sleeping on the floor when his nightmares become too violent.

The Danish woman is living with her boyfriend in a Lower East Side apartment. There is bar hopping, Chinese food, and a small party. I have previously wondered about this woman's proprietorial behaviour and what is really going on with her and David – if anything, as some people are expert at destabilising situations even when nothing's going on at all. He tells affectionate, frequent anecdotes about her – 'mad as a box of frogs' – and her vast capacity for cocaine – 'Dyson' – and her flashing her tits in public. Over the bed, the one she shares with her fiancé, there are framed photographs on the walls, of her and David. This causes me to cock my head, mentally at least. After all, I am seeing a married man. Although who he is actually married to, in any meaningful sense of the word, is unclear. His only true life partner so far is white and vaguely petroleous-smelling.

We are up all night. By 6 a.m. I find myself crying in bed. In early September in New York, it is still hot, hot enough for us to spend the rest of the day on the terrace in bikinis. Preparing for the evening, David and I have a shower together, which we manage to break while having sex. My period has just started, and my blood is all over the shower curtain, the towels and the sheets. When we are tidying up the room before leaving, I notice that a big patch of my blood had seeped its way through to the mattress.

One evening she asks me, and her boyfriend, to leave the bar we're all sitting in, so that she can have some time alone with David. Enough is starting to be enough. I thank her for her concern, but assure her that I'm fine where I am. When I later ask why she behaves the way she does, David replies, with theatrical exasperation, that he does not know. A pattern emerges. Every time I mention something like this, he makes a great show of how open he is being about it. 'Look, I'm not hiding anything, I'm being completely open for the first time in my life.'

fallout

Our night flight home is delayed due to violent storms, and we don't leave until midnight. Luckily we are in business class, and the staff open the bar, especially for me, it seems, before we have taken off. My entreaties to the steward get me a lot of sympathetic attention. I finally get back to the flat in the early afternoon the next day. The first email I see is from a close friend, asking me if it is true where I have just been and who with. The second is from another close friend, the only person who knew about the trip, telling me to put the TV on because something has happened to one of the Twin Towers. Oh yes, I write back, there were terrible storms in New York last night. That's probably got something to do with it. I don't think it's storms, she replies. The rest of the day is history. I leave messages for David, but receive none from him all day. I send our hostess a sympathetic email but never hear back. Later, she tells David that she has found a used condom behind her printer, and is derogatory about the amount of semen in it. She never mentions the bloodstained mattress.

out of the bag

Locally, as globally, the next few weeks are a blizzard of accusations, text wars, and demands that I make amends for what I have done. Locally, as globally, it becomes apparent that a lot of people feel a great sense of ownership over the situation, and over my life in particular. It's clear that I have previously earned myself a label, the victim devoid of volition, who sings for her supper to earn herself a place on the ride. The wronged girlfriend has neglected to tell the gang that 'the love of her life' is in fact married, but still manages to earn herself a Bafta for her theatrical wailing, and is rewarded with lunches and long supportive talks into the night about my general badness. I butch out a party with them all not long after, and she sits there with artfully smudged mascara.

And then I have to move house again, during which time David decides that we will take another holiday, this time to California. I dare to question his choice of dates, and he later apologises for his snarled response. We decide that we will not take any cocaine with us, as LA is a bit far for that. I drink so much on the ten-hour flight that the hangover kicks in before we land, and by the time we arrive I am ready to lie down. Only the profoundest effort of will prevents me sitting on the floor whilst in the queue for immigration. Ahead of us, the officers are asking everyone if they are carrying meat or vegetables, and I begin a muttering rant about whether cocaine is a vegetable, and David shushes me with a quick flash of rage.

cunning stunts

We arrive at the hotel, and our host, an old colleague of his, is dispatched to get supplies. He turns up much later with a couple of grammes, some porn movies, and a huge pink butt plug, for some unaccountable reason. His much younger wife has stayed at home because she doesn't like cocaine. Time passes, and it is decided to phone a couple of girls. When they arrive at our beachfront hotel room, they are a sorry pair. One of them keeps banging on about her ADHD diagnosis. We lie around on the bed and chat, and then David and I invite them into the bath with us. It is a huge corner bath that can sit four easily. I have just got my dressing gown off and slipped into the bath, when the two of them start having some kind of standoff – which is doubtless staged – and then leave very rapidly. I am cross and disappointed, as I have not been with a woman in several years and am feeling extremely up for it. The cocaine is turning sticky in the damp West Coast air. It is getting light outside. Two more girls are ordered, and our host disappears with one of them down to the beach for over an hour, while we chat to the other. There is something charming about being presented with a credit card swiper before all sitting politely on the bed while the business is done. The bill racks up and up, to nearly two thousand dollars, and the cocaine is now liquefying sticky lumps. This time, the door to our hotel room remains ajar, with the girls' minder's foot in it, and he spirits them away quickly. David is cross that the last two were duds and we try again. The lady on the phone tells us that the only one she has free at this time of the morning is really not that pretty and, in fact, is black, and do we mind? We assure her that we do not, and she arrives later on, announcing breezily in the morning sun, 'I don't do girls,' as soon as she sees me lying there.

Back then, it never seems to dawn on me that cocaine is an anaesthetic. Despite being aware of its medical uses, I have never applied them to myself. By then I feel mummified, and lie immovable on the bed. 'You're a bit shy, aren't you?' she says, and when David is in the loo, asks me if I would like her to blow him. I forget what I say at this point, but I don't think anything actually happens, and we all just have a nice chat.

We ride out the comedown with Apple Martinis in Palm Springs, and then head for Vegas, where we have a row, partly because, for some mysterious reason, his dealer is also holidaying in LA and is suggesting that David drives all day to meet him, and then bring him back to Vegas. Filled with horror at the prospect of a car journey with someone who will probably have slept a total of one night in the previous five, I manage to squash this one, but I have to pay for it. As with parents, when dealing with a rich person, you need to use gentle reasoning and debate. They cannot actually be told anything directly, and will simply remind you that they are paying for whatever it is. Now I think about it, this must be how stay-at-home wives of wealthy husbands live, twenty-four hours a day, if they haven't managed to get in the saddle on day one.

The theme continues back in London. We're out drinking when he gets a call which is clearly a bit urgent and embarrassing. We go back to his house, where he explains to me that he recently got a hooker for a friend of his, but the friend didn't pay her, so she is coming round to collect. How odd it is, to be sitting there as the woman comes in, shakes my hand and presents the now familiar credit card swiper. And so on and so on. We go to Venice for a weekend, and don't leave our hotel the whole time we are there. For Christmas he decides we should go to Thailand, and who am I to argue? I have to move house again and I am totally adrift.

A week or so before leaving, I go to his flat to collect him before going to dinner with some friends nearby. We were going all the previous night, and I have gone gratefully to my bed. No one is answering the doorbell, so I manage to blag my way into the building. When I get to his flat, the chain is on. I sneak my skinny wrist round the door and open it easily. I find him passed out in his bed. Something feels distinctly whiffy. I go into the living room and see a lot of glasses on the table, one of which is marked with lipstick. I then pick up his camera, a large, and at the time very expensive, digital one, and idly flick through the images. It's odd how quickly you learn when you're in a total rage. I remember a friend managing to do the Rubik's cube in minutes while being bollocked for copping off with someone at a teenage party. And there they all are. He finally gets out of bed, and a row ensues, during which he tells me that he got the girl for his godson's eighteenth birthday, that he didn't do anything with her, after which he smashes his phone against the wall and says that I can go on holiday on my own, and dares me to end it. Somehow, we still manage to go out to dinner, and on holiday.

splice the mainbrace

I have never been on a yacht before, and now I am helping someone sail one around Thailand. As is not unknown among wives and girlfriends of trained yachtsmen, I learn quickly to let the captain's snarling wash over me. It is, as you might expect, unbelievably beautiful, chugging from one tiny idyllic island to another, with very little sailing to be done as the weather is so calm. Our days take a pattern, early rising, sailing all day, dropping anchor at about 4 p.m. and then getting going on the cocktails. We eat and then pass out. Sex is all but forgotten. There is, of course, no cocaine around.

Then, one morning, David says that we have to go to a small port town because he has to pick up something for the boat. It is a bit of a diversion from what we have planned, but there is nothing more to be said. As we approach the harbour, he says, 'I really need someone to jump over the side and tie us up. I suppose you're not capable of doing that, are you.' We find a restaurant for lunch and sit on the terrace. Suddenly, as we are tucking into our giant prawns and the first beer of the day, there's an 'Awright mate!' I turn and look up. On a remote island in Thailand, we have been found by his dealer and his mate. For some reason, I am not surprised at all, and do not react beyond an 'Oh, hi,' which throws them all a little. And then David and I have a hissed row while walking up and down a road at the top of the hill. We don't have sex for the rest of the holiday. Valentine's Day comes and goes. He does not bring me anything, apart from the usual cocaine. Much later, probably about 7 a.m., he says 'I don't want to be patronising, but I don't want to marry you.'

One day in March, I have a premonition that I have still not hit rock bottom. Despite years spent contemplating suicide, I have somehow stayed afloat. Just. Even before that time, I have been telling people that the water is 'just up to my nose'. I feel terrible fear, but show nothing.

Eight in the morning at his flat, he becomes very emotional and asks me to read a letter he once wrote to his wife before they were married. I cannot remember how it has come to this, but he insists that he is revealing all to me and wants to have no secrets. I have heard this quite a few times by now. It is as if he needs a confessor of some sort. Alarm bells ring when I see the word 'tolerant' in the letter to his wife. My ears sing in the morning sun, which I think I have learned to love. One morning he comes over at 10 a.m., having been up all night in a casino in the Edgware Road. I curse, as I have been about to call an agent about a book proposal, but have always felt such terror at making phone calls like that that it takes me hours, sometimes days or weeks, of psyching up to do it. After chatting, and he is after all off his face, I tell him to come back later, whereupon he says that he can finally tell where he actually stands, and that I am putting work before him, and leaves. And then I have to move house again.

freefall

It would be convenient if we all spotted the exact moment when we have lost control and gravity takes over and our lives start to slide downhill, so that we could catch them in time, yank them back into touch, make an inventory of everything we've been doing wrong and make some real changes, the way the books and magazines exhort us to do. Only hindsight can tell us about these moments. Just when you think life can't become any more exhausting and uncertain, there's more exhausting uncertainty. That's what life taught me, that there's always more. It is much easier to open another bottle of wine.

Available flats consist of a tiny seventies concept bedsit, a warped rhomboid that would need a network of pulleys on the ceiling to get around it once my possessions are in there, and whose kitchen does not contain enough room for a fridge, a flat previously occupied by a crack-addicted prostitute, most of whose possessions are still in there, and who has started operating, child in tow, out of a flat on the floor below, and an unheated basement in Fulham which is so damp that you can almost cut chunks out of the air. In the latter case, the previous occupant, who is being evicted for non-payment of rent, has not been happy about the damp, and has left huge scrawls of graffiti attesting to the fact. 'ASTHMA', it says on one wall in foot-high stylish letters, clearly the product of an artistic training, and every wall has a story of what it is like to live there, in black marker pen.

It is like living two lives. Actually, it *is* living two lives. One night I am chopping and chatting on a glass table in someone's expensive ultra-clean minimalist flat, and the next I am acknowledging that I am bordering on homeless. David offers me ten grand so that I can rent a place for six months and write. It is a very generous offer, but something inside tells me not to take it.

virgin island

During all this time, a close relative of his has become very ill. He has mixed feelings about her and becomes very depressed. I am far too bound up with my own problems to deal with it, and the only things I look forward to are our caning sessions. We go sailing in the Virgin Islands. I am the only woman on board. A terrible mistake, as seasoned sailors subsequently tell me. One of the others is a young man who, on his thirtieth birthday, is apparently going to inherit a sizeable chunk of England, and who appears to have a thing for his own sister, another is a friend of David's coke man, and the third is, alas, David's soon-to-be ex-brother-in-law. It is not the merriest combination. One evening, David starts talking about the Danish woman, apropos of nothing, and, yet again, her amazing capacity for cocaine. I have had enough and storm down the jetty to the barbecue.

The British Virgin Islands is not the happiest of places. The locals are not very friendly, but when you see how the irritable, peevish posh yachties behave towards them, you can't be surprised. Having no idea what to expect, I assume that everyone who sails will be letting their hair down and wearing gold dresses once they have docked. I step up on land wearing a very short satin leopard-print slip, which barely covers my bum. The reception I get is extraordinary, as if Madonna has arrived amid the sea of chinos and jeans. There is muttering among my male companions, and David does nothing to stop it. He seems almost embarrassed by my presence. The rich boy gives me a lecture about not getting a round in. I am not sure who would be the most embarrassed by the fact that we have a thousand dollars of David's money, in cash, stashed away in my bag. Rich boy calls his girlfriend every morning from the boat, at vast cost, but still cops off with a crew-girl from another yacht. David and I don't have any sex during the trip, aside from something short and masturbatory, as he is always so drunk. One night he falls asleep on the toilet. Another time he snores so loudly that I wake in fear, thinking a giant powerboat is trying to dock with us.

I run around with the various cameras we have brought, but not one of my companions picks one up and takes a picture of me. To make a point, I end up taking one of myself, camera at arm's length, before realising how odd it will look on the negatives. One morning I have to almost force David to do the same with the pair of us. When we land, he discovers that his relative is dying.

I get stopped in Customs, and they all vanish to another part of the airport, as they are so loaded up with cigarettes. As we all get off the train at Victoria, no one says goodbye to me, and I have to shout and wave very pointedly to remind them all of my existence. I wander back home, my tan and short dress getting me more attention than I want.

Why I don't face facts and leg it right now remains a mystery. I continue to see David, as if I am on a mission that I must see through to the end. We have sometimes said to each other, flying high, 'Don't abandon me!' but now I have become a pit of need, while desperately trying to keep up appearances. I lie in bed while he goes off to the funeral. When I get up, I find love letters that he has left for me outside the bedroom door. This is unusual to say the least, and I should be suspicious, but I am still too buzzed and coshed from a two-day session and my final Valium the night before. Absentmindedly, I turn over and look over the piece of paper that one of the notes has been written on. It is a demand for service charges from his landlord. So far so normal, except that when we first met, David told me in great detail about how he discovered the building when it was first being renovated, and how he got a look at the plans and got the architect to alter them so that the living room was bigger, and how they were cool with that because he paid cash. The last bit is true, at least. I remember joking with him about how we are the only two people we know who don't have mortgages.

denouement

I walk round and round the flat, trying to walk myself awake as the sun beats outside. In one room I see a piece of paper on the floor, with train times to a town in the north. The name is familiar. It's a woman he's mentioned before, who runs a vintage clothing shop. The dates refer to the previous weekend, when he said he was seeing his dying relative. Through the haze of chemicals, I begin to feel something. That something is a culmination of everything I have let pass in the previous nine months, like the Danish woman theatrically grabbing one of his sweaters and saying 'Oh I love this jumper, it smells of him,' and phoning him at 3 a.m. on a Friday night; and other calls from women in America at similar times; him telling an ex-shag of his at a party, in front of me, that he'd had dinner with his wife the night before, and saying he hated dancing and never did, but then going off and dancing with her just after saying this, albeit appallingly. It is incoming rage. But this rage is not going to stop at the next station.

I make my way back to the living room and begin to go through all the receipts that are spread out on the table. And, within seconds, as you do, I find what I am looking for – a credit card receipt for a strip club, dated the Saturday that I thought he was away seeing his dying relative. Something makes me get down on the ground, and there is part of a condom wrapper. We have hardly used them in our entire relationship, and certainly not recently. I grab a beer from the fridge, and then another, and again I walk around and around and around the flat, smoking, trying to calm down but only getting more and more angry. Suddenly I pick up a pot plant and hurl it against the wall. It leaves a dent in the plaster and a spray of earth that clings to the white paint in a huge fan. Up to this point, I have choices. Sober, or at least only slightly hung over, I might have weighed up the fact that he was at a funeral – whether the loved one had been abusive, or not – quietly left, cried, ranted to my friends, and planned a spectacular dumping with some revenge thrown in, holding back a little for bereavement's sake. I could, in other words, keep some cards back and play the game.

But the trouble with holding everything in through fear of losing *everything*, the kind of everything that means you think you will have no life left, is that you end up tolerating situations that few others would, or at least not for long. And to have the deal you have made with yourself, and tacitly with others, ripped up in front of your face, is too much. Just as cocaine does not give you energy, but takes the energy you already have and concentrates it into something else, repressed rage and fear takes whatever you have inside you and crushes it into a black hole that can do nothing but suck away at you until you let it out. If you continue to accept lies from someone, even after you know they're lies, you may as well live in a prison cell. I am already in one. I weigh up again and again that there has been a decent trade-off here – I got nice holidays and all the booze and coke I could shove into myself, in return for sex on demand and all the therapeutic listening anyone could ever need. But it is too late. The feeling of betrayal goes far deeper. It feels like my whole life being repeated. I call him and leave a message, during which I say things I will not be able to take back, drink another can of beer, and walk out of the flat, ripping a book I have given him to shreds on the way out. It takes me about three miles of walking before I finally run out of energy and collapse at a bus stop.

Days later, we meet in a pub, where he subjects me to a torture session during which I, to my everlasting disgust and shame, actually beg to go back with him. In the sweep of the past nine months, I have almost forgotten that I have a life of my own that needs care and attention. Of course, nothing is ever the same again. After a relationship ends badly, you go back in your mind over all the times when you had a ripe opportunity to dump someone, and really should have; wince-making moments of anything from mild disrespect to outrageous cheek, that you can't believe you let pass. There is something familiar here, from long ago, about people paying for things, and this absolving them from all criticism.

Amazingly, things continue, on the surface, but I feel as if I am nearing the edge of a precipice in a very high wind. I know it is there, but I battle on in a haze. One Friday night we arrange to meet, but he doesn't call. Instead of sitting down rationally and telling myself that what I really need to do is end this and move on, I have another vodka and start calling his friends. His dealer sounds suitably vague about where he is, but concedes that he has seen him moving from one bar to another. I ring a friend in fury and go off to get drunk. Later I am treated to reams of abuse, and self-pitying rages about his job, which he has resigned from. I can never understand someone as rich as that getting worked up about a mere job. An hour or so of him hanging up on me ensues. I have, apparently, violated a taboo. Going out with someone in a band, you get used to phoning around everyone, before starting on the hospitals, to find out where your man is. It's pretty normal really. But not this time. After that, I cry all day, most days.

signs

Two days before my birthday I wake up, and just after that quarter-second of delicious peace, before I remember why I have to cry, I hear a loud bang in the bathroom. I lie there, thinking perhaps someone has thrown a stone at my window. But I am high up on the third floor. Thirty seconds later there is another one. The blinding morning sun blasting me through my tears, I get up and go to see what is happening. The mirror, the old mirror that was there when I moved in, has spontaneously cracked all the way across. It is a sign. I ring a hospital and a nice lady tells me to go to casualty. I get on the bus. In the waiting room I sit, trying to drown out the ranting and shouting, and finally slump down over my knees. Instantly a security guard runs over and barks at me. He thinks I have OD'd. Eventually, and I will not use that word again, although it applies to every leg of my journey through the hospital, I see the triage nurse, and after more waiting I am sent to a cubicle and given a blanket. My curtain is not closed and I am sitting in full view of a man with a broken ankle and his girlfriend, who are sitting in their own cubicle, nattering, and staring at me from time to time. I sit numbly. Finally, as I am about to invite them to tell me what they are looking at, they close their curtain, which muffles their voices.

After an hour or so, I am finally sent through to see a psychiatric nurse, who takes me to sit in a larger private room. He begins by asking me whether I had a difficult birth. I am baffled, and struggle to reply. We talk for two hours, during which he suggests that I stop drinking and taking drugs, because I clearly can't handle it, and tells me that they aren't going to give me an emergency bed. When I mention medication, he suddenly looks at me sharply and says 'Why don't you go to your doctor?' I have already mentioned my lifestyle so I am screwed. He rounds off the session with the suggestion that I go home and have a nice hot bath, and offers me a sandwich. I go on to make three suicide attempts in the next ten days.

What now? I get home, and look around me. There is nothing left to do but drink. The night before my birthday, zombie-like, I invite some friends to a bar to celebrate. David texts me earlier in the day to say, in strangely formal language, that he isn't coming. I am so hung over that I cannot see anything beyond the fact that he isn't coming and, in a now familiar pattern, beg him to come. Somehow I get through the evening, getting drunker and drunker and watching everyone laughing. One friend gives me a laminated photo of himself, blind drunk, upside down with his head on the floor and his feet against a bar, with the words 'Not dead yet!' at the top. I still have it.

The next morning, my birthday, I wake up knowing that I want to die. I drink all day in my flat, crying and crying. David does not call. At midnight I get out my collection of Valium and Temazepam and begin to swallow them. I text David informing him of what I have done, and the phone begins beeping with texts and rings. I drink more vodka and lie back.

I wake up the following evening thinking it is the morning. I am woken by the phone. It's a friend inviting me over for supper. I ask her why she is calling me so early in the morning. Amazingly, I actually get up, have some more vodka and get on the tube. I am having trouble walking. Later, ranting incoherently, I have to be put to bed in her spare room. The next couple of days I retreat to Mick's house, where he is now happily living with his girlfriend. There is to be punishment for this. David and I scream at each other on the phone. I manage to go through all this without really telling anyone. No armies of friends come over to look after me.

My capacity for shame is boundless. It is just too much to tell anyone, as if I will be shunned, even by my own friends, to whom I am tolerant, friendly, and predictable. So I feel.

A couple of days later I get some heroin, drink more vodka and try to cut my wrists in the bath, but I just cannot get it right. Every day begins and ends the same way, waking with that blissful moment of normality before my feelings come back and the tears come. Coffee, vodka, cigarettes, crying and crying, lying on the floor. Writing out a suicide email to about ten people, but not sending it. More vodka, more heroin. The sun is vicious through the windows of my flat. There is no sign of David.

I plan yet again. I will get it right this time. I spend another day semi-passed out on the wooden floor next to the ashtray. This gives me a certain relationship with the neighbours across the way, who, I only realise weeks later, have been watching me with great interest. Perhaps I should not be surprised. I walk around the flat naked, going to the kitchen for a refill every twenty minutes or so. I am also screaming like a dog in a trap.

Another day spent drinking and crying. Another hour, another unsent text. Marlboro Lights. Vodka with a bit of mango juice to take the edge off. Charred tinfoil. My thumb stinging from the lighter wheel. A hot bath. My ears ringing, my eyes starting to roll. Goodbye everybody.

Four hours later. A cold bath. My neck hurts from where I've passed out with my head on the side. It's light outside. Shit. Hello world!

10. day zero

I wake up, and I'm not dead, which is a start, but it doesn't seem like a fresh start. There are no immediate, miraculous changes. In the coming weeks, statues will not weep when I pass them; aura-readers will not stop me in the street and beg to take my picture. And to say that I suddenly know what is right, and this is it, would be an exaggeration. I still drink vodka and cry for a while. But something has changed. It is like a switch in my head. It is like waking up one morning and realising you're not in love any more, or that you've got over a breakup, or have finally let go of a lifetime's cherished ambition that was never going to work out.

The sun shines with the same violence, and the floor is still hard when I lie on it, but something inside me knows that twenty-three years of blotting myself out is about to come to an end. About five years previously, I wrote a poem about suicide. It tells the reader to basically lay off that idea, as they have no idea what's on the other side. The first time I performed it in public, people came up and thanked me for it, and continued to do so every time I read it out.

The pain doesn't evaporate overnight, and nor has my urge to obliteration, and I continue to sniff around heroin-using friends. Before finding a source in Kilburn, I beg Mick for a contact number. He responds with irritable concern, and gives me, as it turns out, a fake one. On my first visit to the Kilburn flat, I go out at 4 p.m., so drunk I can't walk straight. Someone later tells me they met me on the stairs of my building that day and had a chat with me, but I have no memory of it. Going down the road, I have to grip hard onto the railings in order to remain upright, but I put one foot in front of the other and somehow get to the tube, and somehow get to the dealer's flat. The dealer and his friend fuss over me, listen to me rant about my now-dead relationship, and make me eat a meat-and-two-veg dinner, and give me a lecture about the checklist of daily necessities, and how food and basic self-care come first. The dealer listens to me ramble while injecting himself, and gives me a stern talking-to about not accepting abuse in relationships. Along with my fifty-quid bag I get myself a great bargain and I am very appreciative.

While heroin remains a temptation, I realise that cocaine has not taught me very much. A couple of weeks later, in a spirit of truce, David and I meet in Soho. A matter of minutes after we meet, he asks me, with faux casualness, if I've seen a friend of mine who has very large breasts, and who once threw herself at him when I was out of the room.

We sit down in a restaurant but, true to form, he disappears to the loo, then becomes agitated, tells me I am despicable, and then rushes off, refusing to take my calls, and leaves me pissed and starving on a crowded and noisy Saturday night. It is symbolic that I get on the wrong bus and it takes me over an hour to get home when I could have walked it in twenty minutes. Over the next few days, I write long and embarrassing emails to him. He is determined not to see me and becomes extremely vicious. I finally tell him it is over one night on the phone, and he ardently agrees with me. I decide that I will never touch cocaine again.

I go to a clinic to try and get therapy. The assessor looks at me with concern. Since my first overdose I've got into the habit of slumping when I sit down anywhere, especially on the loo. I clutch onto banisters, and shuffle slightly when I walk. He asks me if I have gone for any check-ups after my various attempts to end it all. A week or so later I get a letter saying that they will not treat me while I am still drinking, and that I should come back in six months when I am sober. This, on the surface, is a responsible thing to do, and it is the prospect of getting help that finally persuades me that I should give up drinking. However, I have already discovered that if you turn up somewhere expressing suicidal depression, and are 'self-medicating' with drink and drugs, it can be used as an excuse not to see you. Philosophically this may be valid, but the reality is that those who need help *right now* don't get it. At best, you have a nation of walking wounded who are just about functioning. At worst, you have homeless drinkers abandoned on the scrapheap. Sadly, we have a health service that places mental health somewhere at the level of a verruca as a priority.

I persist, and manage to get myself referred to an NHS alcohol clinic, and I start seeing a counsellor in Soho. He seems to speak very slowly. When you've been used to coke-fuelled rapid-fire ravings right in your face all night, normal speech comes out like molasses. He gets me to fill out a drinking diary, with where I am when I have a drink, what mood I am in at the time, and how much I have consumed. I am regularly topping one hundred units per week, and he is horrified, as is the nurse who examines me. I try to explain that sixty units is just the baseline – a bottle of wine a night, in other words – but that's just home drinking. Parties and socialising is extra. Most of the women I know are no different, and some would be much worse.

Although I am still drinking, I start taking Seroxat, a drug for which I am – still – eternally grateful. It calms me and takes the edge off. And so begins a journey. Living from day to day may be a cliché, but it applies here. Somehow I still keep up a face to my friends, even managing to go out at times. I am very wobbly, but I manage it. But I spend most of the time at home, sitting in a chair, reading the paper, on the internet, or sleeping. I haven't properly unpacked from moving in a month previously, and the first day that I manage to tidy up is a huge breakthrough. Nobody knows about the heroin overdose – I am like the schoolgirl who has secretly given birth on the gym toilets. Over the next two months, I gradually cut down my drinking. I feel like a scientist, a pioneer, with my careful observation of my intake, my little rules, my numbers of glasses.

Then there is the issue of money. I have none. I wonder what to do next. In the middle of this fugged madness I try, unbelievably, to get yet another agent interested in yet another book idea, and, unbelievably, I try to get an editor interested in yet another feature idea, all to no avail, and probably just as well, as I most likely come over as ranting and bonkers, or coshed and vague. In my addled state, I go to see a friend who's worked as a dominatrix to see if I could do that. I turn up at her lovely house, babbling, my left wrist covered in a plaster to hide the crusting cuts. We drink some white wine and take some Ecstasy and lie on the floor, and she – fatefully – sends David a text on my behalf, and as soon as he sees that a woman is contacting him, he replies with the kind of hopeful, friendly message that I haven't received from him in months.

I am learning the meaning of living from day to day, which is actually a great luxury. The house-movers managed to split the hose to my gas cooker, but I cannot face anyone coming to the house to fix it. Someone explains how to put tape round it and look for bubbles, but in the state I am in, I cannot face doing this, which must mean that at least I have some sanity left. A friend lends me a small meths burner, the kind normally used for camping, on which I will cook all my meals for the next eight months.

I have a final all-day blast, on the weekend of the Queen Mother's birthday, with a gig and an all-nighter. I drink vodka all morning before turning up. Later, I fall over while dancing, unwisely dressed in a long, tight skirt and high boots, and bang my back so hard that it hurts to walk for two weeks. I leave the party with three friends and we go back to someone's flat, where we dance, roll around on the bed and pass out – me before the others, as the Seroxat is still kicking in blissfully. The next day we watch the Red Arrows fly past the window over the Thames and I feel something like hope. In the pub later on, I finally tell them about what has been going on, and one of them says 'The thing is, Tania, the truth is that life is pointless, the world is a pointless place. You just have to make the best of it.' He is, in a sense, right. You can sniff all the flowers you like, kiss all the babies and tithe your earnings to charity, but what is it all worth if you cannot live?

I am begining to see more clearly, but it is a slow and bloody rebirth. My body starts fighting back when it realises that the familiar chemical drip is finally deserting it forever. After weeks of living on a diet of all-day vodka, fruit juice and slices of salami, my blood tests start showing that my liver is affected. For the next six months, on and off, until long after I stop drinking, I have night sweats, and my skin breaks out. One minute it is almost flaking, the next you could use it to fry up a perfectly respectable full English. I search high and low, cheap and expensive, for a moisturiser that works, grinding through a range of beauty products that would impress the most dogged marketeer. A tiny thread vein on the side of my nose, that has been there for years, suddenly grows, seemingly overnight, until it looks like a lipstick mark, and will take electrified needles and lasers to remove. I get a lump in my right breast and am sent to the Royal Marsden. They have a handout for women suggesting that Evening Primrose oil might help. Confusingly, one consultant I see there sniffs at the idea, but it works.

Over that summer, through the blackness, light begins to come through. My lack of money is strangely liberating. I walk for miles and miles, but the only shops I go into are charity shops. Without choice, I am free. A successful journalist friend is asked to write a sex column in a magazine, but has to go abroad for six months to research a book. At her goodbye party, where I am still wobbly from heroin and eager to get back home for more, she suggests I try for it. I do, and succeed. It seems like a miracle.

I rejoin an internet support group, one that I joined a year before and then left when the coking and flying around the world took over my head. That group teaches me a lot. It is a bipolar and depression support email list. Most of the contributors are Americans, and the range of people is enormous. There are people with good jobs who are struggling with medication, and people whose lives are utterly horrific, living between the edge of barely funded care and nothing, dealing with past abuse and present medication, abusive spouses and parents. Some are physically disabled as well. I am utterly shocked that poorer Americans have to beg their doctor for free samples of antidepressants when their insurance has run out. What I learn from that group is that it does not matter how different my circumstances are from another person's, I can still try to make a difference by responding, even if all I can offer is a cyber-hug. Another thing I learned is that once you have been through a certain number of things, you become both more tolerant and less so. I learn about why people behave the way they do, and not to take it personally, and you learn where to draw the line with someone who refuses to be helped. I feel that I am on a crash course in personal development. I keep this a secret from my friends.

Since the age of fifteen, I have had a horror of the summer. Summer Seasonal Affective Disorder, you could call it. As soon as the clocks went forward I would start to feel dread, and a depression would fall around me which would only lift after the August bank holiday, and I'd wake up on someone's sofa after the Notting Hill carnival and feel the nip of autumn in the air and feel total relief. For me, summer represented loss, being left behind, people disappearing to enjoy themselves, burning sunlight behind glass windows, exposure. Winter was my time, with dark corners and places to hide, leaves turning, candles in dim rooms, wrapping up. One day I mention this to the group. One man suggests I do a ceremony, go out into the dawn light and thank the sun for my life. It has given me life, he says, and I should thank it, not avoid it. It sounds desperately hokey but that one email changed everything. I do not, in the end, go out – it is still cold, and bomb scares and the impending war in Iraq mean that my area is full of police. But I look out of the window and think it, and it works. This could be called sentimentality but for me is a simple appreciation of life.

In recovery, the theme of sentimentality comes up again and again. I learn to stand still in my home and appreciate the small things, the view out of the window, the clouds, a flower, a cat. Other people I've met in recovery say the same, and I have to ask myself what happens to our consciousness in the adult world, when you lose sight of your environment to the extent that you have to apologise for noticing it. It is as if I am finding my own skin again.

I see a very attractive psychiatrist briefly, who listens to me babbling about fancying people, and spots the drug head I still have on me when I ask about taking Ritalin on top of the Seroxat, to stop me falling asleep. He warns me off relationships and points out my vulnerability. Everything seems to be pointing in the same direction.

I go to a festival in south London, the wonderful Lambeth Country Show, and sit on the grass with a cup of cider, relieved to rest. Everyone else is always so drunk that no one will notice how shaky I still am. I tell a party friend that I haven't done cocaine for three weeks. '*Three weeks*?' he says, incredulous at my momentous achievement. I manage one gig, at an East End literary festival. A woman makes a snide remark about me as we all file in, not realising I am standing behind her. When I respond she flees to the loo. I have a vast vodka, and trip as I get on the stage. It is very hot. A local photographer keeps trying to take my picture, but the sun is just too bright and my eyes just will not open. The writer who is on after me, and who is topping the bill, starts shuffling papers long before I finish. Perhaps I ought to care more about the bad atmosphere, but I am already flying far above it. One friend comes to support me, and later we go to a party on a rooftop in Clerkenwell, full of trendy celebs. People ask me how I am, knowing nothing of the past few weeks, and

I manage to find a story to tell them. For a few tiny moments I feel as if I belong, that if I stand on the merry deck listening to the coke chatter, and hearing all the stories of screenplays and launches and exhibitions for long enough, I can somehow weave my way into a real life. I have finally learned that Dutch courage doesn't work. Downstairs in the darkness of the house I see a girl, stoned out of her mind, with a huge green lizard on the table in front of her. 'Wow,' I say, 'amazing.' She can barely wrestle up the energy to reply.

It takes me several weeks to stop drinking altogether. I almost stop going out, which cuts my intake in half. Spurred on by the dodgy consequences of drinking on top of medication, I tackle drinking at home before dealing with it socially. I gradually reduce from a bottle of wine, to half a bottle, to two glasses, to one, and then a bottle of beer instead. And then nothing. To be at home alone in the evening without a drink suddenly turns into no big deal.

I take my last drink on the 11th September 2002, exactly a year after so many things kicked off, and the following evening, I do something that I have barely ever done in my life since I was a child. I go out to a bar, and return home sober.

11. day one

On my first night of public sobriety, I go to a small party in a bar in Brixton. It just feels odd, not terrifying. I know a few people there, and it dawns on me that you can sit somewhere and just be normal, and I don't have a panic attack or bite my nails or cry or abuse people or suddenly have to go home. I notice a lot of things that are completely new to me. There are too many lights coming from too many different places. There is too much noise, and too many different faces to take in. My booze sonar, the one that lets you ignore what you don't want to hear or see, is not operating.

Two months later a friend invites me to her hen party. To my acute embarrassment, I have to ask her in advance if it is OK to just pay for the dinner, and that this isn't just because I have given up drinking, but in fact because I am so broke. I arrive at an apartment full of women, most of whom I don't know, and bottles and bottles of alcohol. I sit quietly as the corks pop. It is the smell of champagne that nearly tips me back. The warm, sharp, strawlike aroma of summer days and falling back onto grass laughing. I think about it, and think about it, and think that perhaps it might be OK to have just one or two, because it is a party after all, and women together have such a laugh. Someone tells me how much she enjoyed reading a piece I wrote for *Penthouse* a few years before, but another woman is being oddly hostile, and keeps taking my tobacco without asking. And then the hostess suddenly stands up, asks for silence, and announces to the fifteen or so women in the room that I am only going to pay for the meal, and not the alcohol. I am floored. This gets me a snort from the tobacco-grabbing woman and I feel, as they say, a right twat. At my first proper party since becoming sober, it is the first time I've sensed being in the spotlight, that I've chosen a path that is very different from most. It is my first proper punch through the mirror from drinker to sober person, and yet another reminder of how money defines us, more than ever.

Money and sex are very similar. If you're in a relationship and the sex is good, you barely think about it and it constitutes about 15 per cent of the relationship. When it's going badly, it's about 90 per cent. With money, if you've got enough, or more than enough, you barely notice it. If you haven't, and are counting the bus fare in your wallet, and spending an entire morning phoning all the utilities to tell them you can't pay them, and they are saying 'But it's only fifteen pounds, madam', it's everything. It's like a hammer bashing away at the inside of your head. This is why the phrase 'It's only money' – so apt when you've just tossed away twenty-five quid on a black cab home because you just couldn't be bothered to wait for a bus, or when you've hit the designer sales and bought twice as much as you intended – rings so hollow.

When you've been swathed in a liquid blanket your whole life, getting sober is a chilly, bloody rebirth. When you sober up, you find a lot of what you thought or felt before is just not true any more. People or situations that you happily tolerated, in your numbness, will become intolerable. And others may, in turn, find you intolerable, simply for your transgressive stance in declining alcohol. In the early days, I encounter one or two sour faces when I ask for 'Just a Coke', and overhear whispers that I have become 'boring'. For 'boring' translate 'not falling in with whatever is going on'. This is nothing compared to what some people go through, having to deal with their closest friends teasing them, trying to goad them into drinking again, and even starting to ignore them. I've heard too many stories like this. Actually, I am lucky. As with the 'when are you going to have kids?' intrusion (sorry, 'question'), very few people, bar staff aside, give me a hard time over getting sober. I must have underestimated my friends. Thank you, friends. I've heard again and again how difficult sobriety is for anyone who's enmeshed in one group of people. The group will always worry when one of their number stops behaving in the accepted, even demanded, way. There's safety in numbers, but there are rules too. Perhaps all too aware of my fragile boundaries, I tend to put them up at the least sign of being taken for granted.

The first thing that giving up alcohol does is turn up the volume. I am still astounded by noise. If you've had people in the house all night, try turning on the music or the television when you've all woken up later on and see how loud it is. Noise is the first thing I begin to find hard on a regular basis, and still do. Sometimes, all I can hear is a wall of technicolour noise and people shouting. It's very disorientating, like a kind of vertigo, and all I can do is go quiet. It's instructive, if quite boring after a while, to soberly witness the progression of a night out. People talk louder and louder, interrupt with increasing vehemence, and begin to repeat themselves, becoming more and more emotional and insistent. This was, of course, me, once upon a time.

Someone persuades me to do a gig. I am desperate for cash, and I return to the typical scene of a crowded bar and shouting oblivion in Brick Lane. I've never done a gig sober. I stay safe and do oldies. Later the promoter says it is the best one I've ever done.

As the weather gets colder, I get warmer jackets out, and marvel at the number of old paper hankies in the pockets. I had forgotten how wiping my nose had become a way of life.

Since my midsummer overdose, the weight has been dropping off me like a silken veil. All those years of booze bloat fall away and by Christmas, when I am three months sober, I will be down to 8 stone 12. For a 5′ 10″ person that is not a lot. My xylophone ribcage reflects the light along its ridges, and I catch sight of myself in shop windows and am appalled by the thin girl, and pitying of her, until I realise it's me. But at least I'm alive.

12. getting help

I don't regret one minute's partying, although I regret the sadness behind it. But I feel that its cultural significance as a bonding ritual has given way, both nationally and globally, to a helpless urge that barely resembles the 'good time' everyone likes to say they're having. It's worth remembering, though, that if you decide to stop drinking, you're taking on a nation as well as your friends.

The first nosy query, only the first of many nosy queries that the newly sober person gets to deal with, is 'Are you doing AA?' This may be followed by a question about rehab, often from a person who doesn't really know what rehab is. I'm aware that I didn't take the conventional route, and after six months my counsellor told me that I have had an 'unusual recovery pattern'.

Giving up anything is a grieving process, when the relationship is as long-standing as this. Anger, denial, bargaining, depression and acceptance are all there, jostling for your attention. In my case, however, surviving three attempts on my own life is enough to send me running towards the horizon like a wind-up toy. At the start there is just me and a life force that was half buried for most of my existence. There is no time to sit in judgement on myself. I've been told more than once that I have a will of iron. This may be true, but willpower doesn't work. Willpower may get you across the water when it's getting dark, or help you win a cycle race, or help you lift a car off your granny, but it won't keep your addictions at bay, physical or emotional. In my case, from the start, what saves me is a switch in my head. But I know I'll need support from somewhere.

the internet

My first stop is the internet. As the booze leaves my system, the medication kicks in, and my concentration levels go up, I begin to take an interest in my surroundings. My primary world is my computer. I spend at least an hour and a half a day on the support group, but I decide that I need to find something closer to home. Problems may be universal but sometimes the UK and the US are just too divergent. I have to be careful with some jokes, and when I tell them about my 'broken cooker' they think I am running some sort of speed factory. I discover a UK-based alcohol recovery site and dive into the forum. As with most help forums, there are lots of good and helpful people, and a small handful of tossers, trolls, and self-styled gurus. True to form, I argue with the guru, become dismayed with the sheep-like behaviour of the other members, and then eventually leave. Superstition is rife among the people on there, and their lives seem drenched in fear, and I wonder if there is something wrong with me that I do not feel the same way. I joke about going into a pub in order to test my sobriety, and get a terrified response from a woman, saying that I shouldn't put myself through such a thing. *But I nearly died this summer!* I want to reply. *Who cares if I go to a bloody bar?*

pills

I often wonder how many people I know have an unblemished medical record, in the sense that the only conditions they have sought help about are physical. One man I know tells me that he once exercised his right under a new law to see his medical records, and found one page – *one!* – among hundreds, on which he'd been reported as asking his GP where he could find a counsellor, several years previously. 'I tore it out and chucked it away,' he says, almost crossing himself. 'No sense having that in my file.' Christ.

I have a coffee with a news reporter in the pub opposite the ITN building in Gray's Inn Road. The reporter turns to look upwards at the building and says 'Half the people in there are on Prozac.' I smile. Seroxat, sister drug to Prozac probably saved my life. Yes, at first I drank while taking it, but to get any of the more specific alcohol recovery drugs – the pleasure-blocker Naltrexone (oh, the irony!), or the old-school Antabuse that makes you sick if you drink on it, or the craving suppressant Campral, or the benzodiazepine Librium – I would have had to fulfil a fairly major condition: I would have had to already be sober. Perhaps one day there'll be a patch like the nicotine one for smokers.

Perhaps one day there'll be a ban on public drinking, like there is already for smoking.

the NHS – a quick rant

I've been treated by many helpful and sympathetic doctors and nurses in my life, but it's the bad ones that stand out, simply because one is too many. In the months after I picked myself off the floor, I was lucky to find a helpful counsellor, a spot-on psychiatrist, and, once, a psychologist who describes my childhood as 'chronically invalidating', which made me feel validated like nothing else had. This was in striking contrast to my previous experience of being turned away from hospital in a crisis. The thinking behind it seems to be that when you go home from your failed attempt to get help you will be suddenly jolted out of your malaise by shock at the fact that there is no help for you, because your problems don't really exist anyway, and they hope – to say 'assume' would be harsh – that their official, rubber-stamped rejection of your feelings will somehow jog you into a higher state of awareness, and that you will go merrily on your way, like a fresh convert. It doesn't happen that way, although I suppose that if you don't actually commit suicide, technically their ruse will have succeeded. Funding being what it is, the fact that you remain alive, however miserable your life, will therefore not negatively affect their monthly statistics.

Beds are limited, unless you're rich. They can only treat you as an emergency if you appear to be an immediate danger to yourself or others. Being good little English people, we spend our whole time making everything easy for others. 'I must have made a mistake', 'It's just a flesh wound', etc. I don't want to recommend trashing the place to make a point, but if you were to get yourself sectioned under the Mental Health Act, you would at least get a bed and possibly the treatment you need. I do sometimes wonder about the levels of prejudice against mental illness, even within the health service itself. If they can persuade you you're fine, they will, despite all evidence to the contrary. Unless they can see blood, you've got a lot of explaining to do. And there's a catch-22 in all this – if you turn up on your own, and you're lucid enough to make yourself understood and explain what you think is wrong with you, then you're not ill enough to merit treatment. So by trying to be a 'good patient', you're actually doing yourself a disservice. It's all part of the fear of mental illness that causes so much bureaucratic brushing under the carpet. If you break your leg, you get patched up in hospital. If your mind breaks, that option's rarely there, even though the consequences for your well-being may be far worse. And yet no one would think of tying your leg together with a bit of string and sending you home there and then, as they do with so many minds – you would be crippled for life.

If you are unlucky, you will get whiffs of a double stigma – that of mental illness itself, and the issue of how, if you are white, middle-class and educated, you can possibly have problems. And if you do have problems, you are doubly pathetic in their eyes, to have had all these chances in life and still be in a mess. It can be summed up in what is known as 'that look'. You don't get it from everybody, and it can be benign; it is not necessarily hostile. Sometimes, I have turned up somewhere, and they have thought I am an inspector, or a new manager who's got lost on the way in.

alternative therapies

On the positive side, complementary medicine can make you feel better, because it is sympathetic to the whole person. On the negative side, it fosters a permanent state of unwellness, as people constantly take their own emotional temperature, and declare themselves 'out of balance' for the day. Luckily, I've rarely had the spare funds to throw at any of the really silly stuff.

alcoholics anonymous

Long before I give up drinking, I had a suspicion of Alcoholics Anonymous. While acknowledging and respecting the fact that many, many thousands have passed that way and got tremendous support out of it, a lot of those from the programme that I meet personally do not seem to have benefited from it as people. It seems to turn them into automatons, full of pat little phrases and sayings – 'just for today', 'take what you want and leave the rest,' – sending each other birthday cards for every year they've stayed off the sauce. It seems to me to be replacing one addiction with another. One day, when someone tells me that they've just been to a meeting where one of the regulars turned up and told the group that her son had died two days before, I am baffled. Your son's just copped it and you're babbling away in a goddamn *AA meeting*? Of course, she simply may have been trying to avoid drinking at such a terrible time, but this did not occur to me.

Now that I have more experience with the public health system, I can see why people go to AA, for purely practical reasons, apart from anything else. A friend says it is 'group therapy for the price of a cup of coffee' and when you've tried and tried and mostly failed to get help on the NHS, or realised that you cannot afford private therapy once a week, let alone more than that, group meetings of people in a similar situation, who have chosen to be there, start to make sense.

Two months into sobriety, I decide to try it. I choose a big meeting, where I can hide. There are about a hundred people in the room, perhaps more. I slip in, get myself a tea, and sit at the back. Not long after I sit down, I become aware of a tanned man who looks as if he might be famous, trundling round and round the room going up to people, seemingly unable to sit down, and giggling maniacally. I immediately feel on edge, but try to zone him out. If it even needed saying, going to your first meeting on your own is a big deal. A couple of minutes later he comes right up close to me and asks me, in a loud, complicit, stage whisper, if I want a vodka. I am completely thrown, wondering if this is an initiation. I am sure that this is against the rules, but have no idea what to do about it. I look at some of the people and think, there but for the grace of God, and then feel obliged to reprimand my own judgementalism. But I don't like the sense of superstition that dogs the world of self-help. Naturally, *mea culpa*, despite feeling uncomfortable, I still cast my own eyes over the crowd for a possible date – a sober guy, fantastic! – but sense trouble wherever I look. I manage a few of these sessions, but feel somehow drained by trying to avoid the annoying man and wonder why no one takes him aside and calms him down, and eventually stop going.

I find another meeting, much closer to where I live. I am overjoyed, as it is only five minutes' walk away. When I get there, I am one of only two women in a room full of men, either funny old geezers, kind of *Last of the Summer Wine* meets somewhere near Waterloo bridge, and young guys who can't stop jumping up and down and taking calls on their mobiles, as if the raves they used to operate at are still going on in their heads. There is a reek of stale wine coming from far too near me. I stay till the end, but do not return.

I try several others, and my impression remains the same. My view is that a mixed-sex AA meeting is no place to go if you are a vulnerable woman trying out life sober for the first time ever. There is too much troubled male sexual energy there for me to get much help from it, despite diligently listening to the chairing, some of which is very inspiring. I share this thought on the internet and am told off for being judgemental. I argue that gender is a factor in recovery, and that men and women have different needs in the early days, but the online recovery guru is having none of it. A couple of years later, I go to some women-only meetings, and wish that I had found them before.

talking cures

In an ideal world, as we talked and shared our problems, we would shed each layer of experience in regulated waves. But the past doesn't burn off so straightforwardly. Bad memories are enemies of promise as much as prams in hallways are said to be. You have to do something about all the people who are living rent-free in your head – a phrase I wish I could claim as my own. Throughout my life, to therapist after therapist, I have apologised for myself. Look at me, look at the things I've achieved that have all come to nothing. I wasn't starved as a child, not passed from care home to care home, not forced to work from the age of twelve. I have a good education. Sorry I'm here. Sorry I'm alive and wasting your time like this. After I've been sober for a few months, I conclude that therapy, this solipsistic game of sofa tennis, is the last thing I want or need.

Besides, I've got it all worked out. Constantly being examined in a harsh spotlight is what led to me drinking. After a while, the low hum of continuous criticism became maddeningly loud. There was something wrong with everything about me – the shape of my body; the colour of my hair; my personality, my level of intelligence. So, thanks to the proximity of alcohol and drugs, I got out of my head because I couldn't stand being me. Having been brought up told what an uncaring and incompetent person I was, I then fell into that role. I sabotaged everything as hard as I could, and then fell into black depressions as a result. The predictions became true. I was branded irresponsible, and a disruptive influence, and even, at times, a bully. But I felt bullied the moment I got through the door at home. I always felt like a victim – how could I possibly bully others? I had been trained to see myself as unlovable, and I was. I drank because it was an instant, relatively low-cost membership of a club, of sorts. Others began to accept me.

I spent half a lifetime slipping and sliding, one step forward, two steps back, drowning out my feelings and my own needs. Those who know me might not realise that; to many people, it might seem as if I've always lived for myself. But in the end I couldn't work out where I ended and the pain began. I went through an illness stage, a 'blaming everyone else' stage, and an 'I'm fundamentally flawed' stage, and finally got sick of all three. When you start boring *yourself*, then you know there's a way out. But it was a long, long journey to get there. I lost my dignity many times over. Sometimes, when I'm walking down the street, a memory of something I said or did, whether five years ago or fifteen, will suddenly pop uninvited into my head. I still wince, physically, if I'm not paying attention.

The number of people whose parents divorced when they were under fifteen, who then go on to become addicts, is enormous. I, however, grew up a rare animal – with both parents. My parents weren't alcoholics, or junkies. But as I discover more about them, I see greater and greater parallels between alcoholic parents and my own. At one extreme, my mother would decide, always at the last minute, that she couldn't handle a long-prearranged trip, and take to her bed for several days. At the other, she would enter a screaming fugue state, hitting, smashing things and threatening. I was never allowed to forget her self-imposed martyrdom, of which my father was the enabler. Of course I fought back, in my own way, but it didn't feel like it at the time. When it dawned on me, in my thirties, that just because someone said something to me didn't mean it was true, I flipped over and became everyone's therapist. In my final pre-sobriety relationship, my contribution consisted almost entirely of listening to David's problems, with sex on demand thrown in. I even knew what I was doing. One night, in a drugged-up haze, I declared, with the intense sentimentality that only cocaine can induce, that I was officially compensating for my selfish behaviour as a child, and was trying to give something back. Give something back! After that relationship, if I'd been charging by the hour I wouldn't have needed to work, ever again.

It's now scientifically proven that continued exposure to stress can cause permanent chemical change in the body of a young, growing person. It can permanently affect your brain chemistry forever. Anyone who abuses a child is laying the groundwork for a miserable adult. And it's not all about physical violence. If someone can control their child with a look or verbal threat, it lets the parent off the hook. You only have to go to a smart supermarket like Waitrose in the King's Road to see the effect of the middle-class version of toxic parenting. A father lecturing his small son from a great height, the boy's mannerisms already taking the form of fearful people-pleaser; a snappish camel-coated couple driving past in their huge airless Mercedes, a small silent child in the back, bricked up behind tinted windows.

My theory: an unhappy person who is unhappily married will see their own negative traits, and/or those of their partner, coming out in their child. But they won't blame themselves, or the universe. They'll blame the child.

analysis versus astrology – the debate continues

Psychoanalysis and astrology are two paths to relief of suffering that are championed in equal measure by their supporters. But which is the most valid? My forays into psychoanalysis were not edifying, and I can't believe it was even suggested to me. Oddly enough, though, no one ever suggested astrology. When, early in sobriety, I found a vast, and free, Swiss horoscope website, I dived in with joy and felt better very quickly. What was really spooky was that when I read the predictions of events that had already occurred, for example, the time of my suicide attempts, and a major fallout with a group of people, the site was accurate almost to the day.

I don't want to crap on a whole school of thought that has provided many insights, and given birth to many other, perhaps more considered, schools of thought, but if you are in any kind of crisis, I would advise you to scream and run at the very idea of psychoanalysis. Lying on your back counting your analyst's antiques is not going to cure you of anything, unless it jolts you back into some kind of reality at the absurdity of what you are doing and how much it is costing you. Psychoanalysis is a very interesting literary game, but not for anyone who's stressed, depressed or in any mental trouble. Being expected to wait a week after being smugly told some nasty 'truth' about yourself such as how selfish you really are, is no fun, and can be actively detrimental. Of course, if you are rich, you might only have to wait a couple of days. But it is still of dubious value to the sick, unless you are willing to devote your entire life to it.

If you're in a state where you have to approach any kind of oracle for an answer, you already know you're in trouble. Lots more people read horoscopes than will ever admit it. And why do so many people read them, particularly women? Because a lot of people, particularly women, feel helpless every day and need some kind of endorsing support structure – and preferably one that doesn't reply by asking what you think about in bed. There are those who say astrology is judgemental, because it labels people ('I won't employ a Gemini,' etc.), but psychoanalysis is all about labelling, or tearing off your labels to reveal the next set beneath. There also those who say astrology is total bollocks, because how can the position of a planet at your birth possibly dictate either your personality or your future, and that it is no more valid than referring to the four humours. The traditional response to that is 'The sun rises every morning, doesn't it?'

Daily horoscopes in newspapers give astrology a bad press. They are not a good way to approach it, because they are so generalised. Detractors ask, how can one-twelfth of the world's population have the same thing going on with them at any one time? The answer is that they don't. The astrological chart is far more complex than that. What excites people about doing their chart is that it can endorse parts of you that you like, and help you confront the parts you don't like, because people need to define themselves. It's a form of self-identity in an all-defining world where we are often afraid of what we are. Everyone's birth chart is unique to them. Psychoanalysis will also pick away at the layers to find the 'real', unique you. But it can take a long time, if not forever. I've met miserable, fucked-up people, in their eighth year of analysis, who say 'But there are so many more things to find out,' before shuffling off, pale-faced and broke, to their next timed meeting.

Astrology doesn't moralise – in the wrong hands, psychoanalysis most definitely does.

positive thinking

You know the score with positive thinkers. You can be sitting there, feeling abandoned by all, newly unemployed, with an embarrassing medical problem that won't go away, and going to the shop to get milk is about all you can manage. You call a friend for support, but whenever you try and mention the apocalyptic gloom that is pervading every corner of your mind, they keep interrupting you and saying 'You've got to think positive!' and won't let you go on talking about how you feel. In case there are any positive thinkers reading this, just for your information, this is a really crap way to be a friend.

Positive thinking means many different things to different people. Frankly, I have never heard more bollocks spoken on just about any other subject. In life you have a choice as to how you see what's happening to you, good and bad. It is pointless, fatalistic and passive to continually imagine the worst in any situation, but you're really dumb if you don't take a good look down there now and again. A therapist would say you have to 'reframe' your past bad experiences (in other words, choose to see them in a less damaging context) if they are continuing to hurt you. If you have a potentially fatal illness, you are sometimes advised to visualise the forces of good erasing the disease inside you, and this works well for some people. But there's a very fine line between positive thinking and denial. A lot of people who have joined the recovery movement appear to have programmed a mantra into their heads that involves never saying anything negative about anything, 'just in case'. Ditto a disturbing number of westerners who have decided to become Buddhists. In fact, some of the most mind-blowingly self-centred people I've ever met were newly self-declared western Buddhists. There is, of course, an equally fine line between all this and superstition. I once knew a woman who'd had rotten parents, and had spent a lot of her adult life desperately trying not to be like them with her own children. She was doing pretty well, but she had bought the PT line to the degree where I could not say anything negative in front of her, even something faintly derogatory about a convicted mass-murderer, without her going, in a finger-wagging tone '... or he could just be a kind, loving human being!' Likewise, I knew a talented singer, and Nu-buddhist, who had got pregnant just as her career appeared to be taking off. Late on in her pregnancy she was not able to work so much, and was obviously frustrated about it. I asked if perhaps this might make her resent the baby on some level. She shivered and said 'Resent? *Resent?* Don't even say that word!', practically crossing herself.

Once, when I am freaking out with a morning panic attack, one such friend happens to call me. I am dying to talk, but he cuts me off with: 'Can you feel your feet?' Silence. 'Can you feel your feet?' Silence. In desperation I follow his bullying demands that I express awareness of my body parts, right up to the top of my head. As you might imagine, this was no help at all, to put it mildly. I came off the phone feeling really abused, even though he may have meant well.

I wish some of these people would just chuck a rabbit's foot over their shoulders when they speak their minds, rather than censor themselves. I'm sure the Great Adjudicator In The Sky wouldn't give a toss either way; she/he/it's got far more important things to worry about.

Oh yes – I forgot! Positive thinking means never having to say you're sorry.

trading one substance for another

If you get depression, you can't do drugs, or drink. I'm sorry. I really am. But I'm speaking from over twenty years' experience. Alcohol may not seem like it, but it's a depressant. Like a sexy but shallow new lover, it takes you up, then it drops you like a stone. Depression gets worse over the years if you drink. You stop knowing where you end and the misery begins. You take medication, as I've done, but you don't stop drinking at first because, sssh, some of those pills actually make hangovers less bad. Your horror, at your own life and the state of the world, will become real. It isn't real; it's the chemicals talking. But since you're made of chemicals as well, they're all in there getting it on with each other, because you're letting them. Buy a couple and wait, as they say.

Cocaine makes things ten times worse. No, make that a hundred. Coke comedowns, two days later, are a loving kiss with your own death. Emails I've sent to friends on those days are foetid puffs of air from the dark side. Red wine and Valium take the edge off, but they don't erase the horror in your head. Don't go there. I was hung over every day of my life. Coming down too, some of the time. Not necessarily the worst of the worst every single time, but that aching dullness in my brain, piqued with hyper-awareness of my position in the world, and the consequent pain.

'Drugs and all that,' I said to a therapist one day, 'they're just masks.' She looked baffled.

hungry, angry, lonely, tired

To borrow, for once, from the AA movement, hunger, anger, loneliness, and tiredness are four things to watch out for in the early days. These are the things that can catch you unawares and drive you back to the bottle. One day, a year or so into sobriety, I ring a friend and say that I can't work out why I'm not feeling either really excited about something, or really traumatised. 'I think it's called an even keel,' she says. Then I begin to worry that I'm not worried enough.

13. birthdays

My thirty-seventh birthday is a long affair. Beforehand, I wonder how I'm going to stick it out, sober, all day in a bar, but I manage it. Ten hours of it, in fact. Drinks last me much longer than they used to. Soft fruity ones set my teeth on edge and become a bore, so I alternate them with Coke or Red Bull, but Red Bull makes me feel murderous after two cans, so I decide to drop it. Coke is always there as a sweet hit, but the racing heart and dehydration are ugly after two or three. The closest I get to a decent 'sophisticated' soft drink is a half-and-half mix of cranberry juice and ginger ale. If you squint, it could almost have alcohol in it. Friends come and go all day. I make a sort of a speech about how happy I am to be alive, when we have taken over the room upstairs, and staff members keep nervously peering through the little window in the door. We, everyone except me being plastered, are making a lot of noise for only about eight people. But they know no one is getting glassed, so they leave us to it. On his way back home in Brixton, one of my friends is buying a kebab when someone grabs the tenner out of his hand and runs for it. My friend sets off in pursuit. Luckily for him, in fact, he is wearing brogues, and slips and falls before he can catch the boy thief. Even though he dislocates his shoulder and has to go to hospital, he is still lucky. If he had caught the boy he might have been stabbed or shot. He is very proud of the fact that he ends up in hospital dosed up on pure morphine, when his assailant will have to make do with a crappy bag of whatever, cut with the ubiquitous baby laxative.

I think about nature documentaries, of sticky little foals and calves just born, getting up off the ground. This is how I have felt for a year now, when I get to my first sober birthday. Sometimes I feel disturbed, but this has nothing to do with wanting alcohol. Sometimes the only music I can listen to is jungle or dark, moody drum & bass. It is the music of madness. No wonder it goes so well with crack, but I have no desire for drugs either, even though the wall of fast beats is the only thing holding me up. Three years later, when I am giving up smoking, a friend tells me to notice whenever I get to something that I am doing for the first time since giving it up, and gradually I will rack up the smoke-free experiences and soon it will only be rare occasions when I notice that I am not smoking. With drinking, I don't really find this. When I go out, all I notice is the fact that I'm noticing something.

For now, though, all I have left is smoking. Smoking becomes my pet, my friend, my Linus blanket, my drink substitute, and, actually, my companion. I am writing columns for a problem page. A column every two weeks is all I can manage at first I am still so mentally drained. Unbelievably, out of the dust on my living room floor, the wisping ashtrays, the crying, the too-much-coffee, I have become a sex journalist. The flood of memories comes out as if I have opened an old wardrobe. The daily actuality is that I don't want anyone to come near me. I am happy to raid my memory banks, and am proud of not actually lying about it in any of my columns. For the first time in my life I am not, however secretly, looking for a boyfriend, or sex. As they say, it's time for Me now. After the last one, a relationship would be as lethal to me as a dose of TB or Legionnaires.

I have nothing, but for the first time I don't feel like nothing. There isn't time to feel like nothing when you're on a mission. It is a strange kind of freedom. Sometimes, several years later, when things are hard in other ways, I remember this time like a fetish. Having no choice gives you a twisted kind of liberation. The only pressure on me is to stay alive.

hobbies

And so it remains. I wake up earlier and earlier. My body demands tobacco and coffee. I get up at 5 a.m. and start a blog that is also a problem page. I answer questions that I have posed myself, anything from domestic – 'How Do I Get Peanut Butter Out Of My Hair?' – to gender-political – 'Bitchez On Testosterone' – to relationship-related, such as 'Should I Date A Married Man?' Gradually I build a small fan base and people start to write to me. I make business cards for it, and write it every day. Of course, I write about alcohol and drugs, and mental illness. Of course, I write under a pseudonym. A quick Google shows me that its traces live on, but the domain has been hijacked. A further Google shows a very cross comment I left somewhere, about a week before my last-ever drink, about not winning the *Guardian* weblog award. Despite the disappointment, this blog counts as My First Recovery Project. Somehow, though, it is fitting that the moribund-looking geranium that I inherit with the flat, little more than a bunch of dried twigs, slowly comes back to life and flourishes into a glorious red flowery bush within a few months. The geranium, like me, is unkillable.

No, I really don't want therapy at all. I've spent so much time slathering about me, me, me, to so many people, in person and online. I've officially been there. I'm alive. I just want to get on with my stuff. Paradoxically, as the months turn slowly into years, I feel the wind of a time tunnel taking me back and back, as if I am reclaiming something from the past. In other words, I start to get in touch with my inner nerd. Fiddling with the blog gets me interested in my computer, and I seek out people on the internet who can help me, some of whom become real-time friends. I am well old enough to remember what life was like without the internet, but I have no idea how I survived.

the real world

Slowly, slowly, I come back to work. I go to fetish fairs, write about clubs and chat about brands of rubber underwear. I interview a man who runs a shop that sells a machine you can fuck yourself, or someone else, with. I receive a metal butt plug in the post, sent by one of a burgeoning number of online sex shops keen to promote themselves. All this between bouts of simultaneous exhaustion and euphoria. Keeping up a normal, sane face to people is a challenge that others perhaps take for granted. No wonder I used to drink. Naturally, new acquaintances ask about my sex life. I take the stance that I don't believe in one-night stands any more, and that I've 'moved on from all that'. To say I have taken a vow of celibacy would get me a bit of publicity as a sex columnist, but despite the fact that my name is starting to appear in various publications, I don't want anyone scrutinising me. I am still raw. Maybe I always will be.

I actually shed very few friends, however, apart from those who just don't seem so nice when I don't have a bottle or two inside me. I become painfully aware that a lot of my old friends still think their time is more important than mine, and expect me to be available for house-sitting and other unpaid duties. I cannot, for I am on a mission.

smileys

It takes me eighteen months to emerge into the world and try to sell myself, and I get lucky quickly. Old friends from over a decade back appear and offer to help out. It all feels like serendipity and glory and all the things I feel I have deserved for a long time coming home to roost in the soft dawn light of my new life. The going soon gets tough. I take my first commercial writing job in a very long time, and after half killing myself working, with bronchitis, my employer tries to do a runner and not pay me the two grand he owes. Everything from 'cheque's in the post' to telling me I have to recover the money from the client. I am skint. I am in a terrible panic as I really need this money. I do not buckle. I do not fall off the wagon. I fight and fight, and threaten legal action, and finally have a chat with a friend who knows large shady blokes who will come and make suggestions to the guy as to why he should hand it over PDQ. Finally, without the help of the blokes, I get it. I have fought and won. Likewise someone else who doesn't want to pay me. Likewise a small host of others who do not know that I have looked death in the face and am every day still holding on as if on horseback or a small ship in a storm, and although I am kind of fine I am kind of not – but of course they don't see any of this, and I win my fights.

I become frustrated at peoples' lack of consideration for others. Was I like this too, when I was hung over every day? I think of the adage that everyone should work in retail for six months, to teach them what it's like behind the counter. I also wonder if everyone should do bondage-and-discipline training for six months, to teach them about transfer of power, and control over themselves, before they even think about assuming control over other people.

the bell curve

As I fall back into work, my emails fall somewhere on a bell curve. If I am writing to a close friend, or someone I only know on the internet, the message might well be festooned with smileys and exclamation marks. Moving up the curve, as the relationship becomes more formal and distant, these decorations fall away. As I reach the top of the curve and go back down it my mood changes. If I am writing to a work contact who I perceive to be messing me about or just being a flake, the smileys and exclamation marks increase – 'Hello! :-) Just checking in!' – and I realise it is me hiding my rage all over again. That the tiniest implication that I am not getting exactly what I want has instantly driven me to the edge of sanity and my world is about to crash, but I must hide it at all costs lest I am revealed to be who I really am, a person with needs, which would be the worst thing in the world – so the smileys continue. My return to the working world is bloody.

Sometimes all I am armed with, in truth, is a smile. I want the world to share my happiness and be nice and not try to rip me off. I cannot buckle and fall because now there really is nowhere to fall. And then I am reminded, as I start to come down from my cloud of survival euphoria, that personal PR is what I am going to need more than ever, as I swing towards forty.

sex 2.0

The response to my column is good, but I wait for a while to be headhunted. All the therapy books say that you shouldn't wait for things to happen, so I don't, and then a nice bloke appears, and asks me to present a radio show with him, all about sex. We are fully uncensored. We are groundbreaking. We are proud of what we are doing. I am still dizzy with medication. I am lighting up first thing in the morning, and drinking strong coffee half the day. I have become preoccupied with feeling all right, and I feel as if I have a hangover all the time. Then I become involved with a charity that raises money to help isolated disabled people find friends and sex partners. Their annual ball is the Glastonbury of sex, where people do all sorts of wonderful things to each other in front of others. After a while I realise that I am inhabiting a bubble. When I tell people what I do, sometimes there are twee little sniggers. Being involved in sex media seems totally natural to me. But then so did taking heroin, at one time. There is a lot of sex in my life, but I'm not actually having any of it. But it doesn't seem to matter. I am alive.

I am often asked 'But what do you do when you want to get off your head?' At thirty-eight I have not yet fully worked this out.

a note on noise

Increasingly, even after six years of sobriety, I can't stand loud drunk people. I mean I'm really allergic. I also dread loud places because I have to lip-read. As the years pass and I stay sober, I realise I am gradually losing some people. This may also be because, sober, I cannot tolerate what I put up with when I was drunk. I start to realise that I'm losing one problem-drinking friend when I take part in a public discussion about erotica, as part of a festival. The following morning I get a desperate call from the organisers, asking me to chair the main debate that evening, because the original person has had to drop out, and they really liked my contribution to the discussion. Not long after, this friend rings me and I tell my exciting news. Barely missing a beat, she goes into a rant about how it took her two hours to get there and then it was sold out, and no offence but she didn't think that any event that I was taking part in could possibly be that popular. When she can't make my birthday party, I feel so relieved I feel guilty.

14. eight people-friendly excuses for not drinking

Newly sober, you need to get yourself some defences, and quickly. As soon as you go out the door and interact with others, you're going to be pushed to the limits of your personal PR. It's not about lying, or making others feel better – although it might, loosely, involve both – but it is about gently guiding them away from your weak points, as you might give a stray cow a shove to prevent it knocking you down. As with most jobs, life is 30 per cent what you're doing, and 70 per cent the person or persons you've got to do it with.

People who've had cosmetic surgery – which seems, on the surface, to be a far more serious decision than merely abjuring alcohol – sometimes tell everyone they've been in a car crash, to explain away the bandages and the disappearing act. Nowadays, though, if the far higher proportion of television programmes about cosmetic surgery than those about giving up alcohol is anything to go by, to pay someone else to cut you open is far less radical, apparently. Although all those very personal and medically explicit programmes seem at first to be freak shows, they are really advertisements, spreading the word more effectively than your most gossipy friend. Here are some pacifiers that might, if you're lucky, get some of your interrogators off your back.

1 'It's just for now.'
In other words, 'get off my back,' but nicely.

2 'I'm doing a detox, actually.'
Ah yes, the famous 'detox'. Once upon a time this word applied to hardcore addicts or full-on alcoholics who needed to go into hospital just to get everything out of their system. Nowadays, in popular terms, to 'detox' means buying infusions of acrid or tasteless herbs, sacks of odd and expensive pills, and clutching a vast amphora of very expensive labelled water and swigging it wherever you go. Vast tracts of money are being made on the back of detox culture, and although you might feel a twat saying it, you could always hop on this particular bandwagon to get people off the scent. Throw the gym, running, and yoga into the mix and everyone will be cheering you on. 'I'm trying to lose weight' is a variant of this.

3 'I just got tired of it.'
This is a nice, simple way of getting people to back off, because it makes it sound as if you made a calm, adult choice in the midst of far more important things going on. You could also throw in something about an increased workload, or a Very Important Deadline at some unspecified point in the middle future.

4 'I'm/we're trying for a baby.'
Unassailable and unarguable, this one. It helps if it is true, though, because otherwise, in a few months' time, people will be asking far nosier and more offensive questions, this time about the state of your uterus rather than your liver.

5 'The hangovers were becoming a nightmare.'
Throw them a bone. Admit there was a problem, but only to do with the aftermath, which everyone understands because they themselves talk about it all the time. You might want

to throw in a vague muttering about an 'allergy to alcohol'. Allergy talk is, again, safe. Everyone's got one!

6 'Something scary happened to a friend/relative and it got me thinking.'

This might be true. If not, you might get caught in your own web of lies, once you've invented the friend, their lifestyle and the story of what happened. But it's always good – or, at least, easier – to pass the responsibility for your choice on to someone else.

7 'The doctor said I should.'

A bit more cast iron, this one, and can be linked with allergies, or worse. You could say you were getting a liver or kidney problem that runs in the family. Again, this puts the rationale onto someone else, but with the added lofty back-up of the medical profession.

8 'I've been getting blackouts.'

Another bone. It's personal without admitting any inherent mental or emotional faults on your part. Said in a mysterious tone, you can draw them in by implying some secrecy to this disclosure. A story about repeatedly losing keys or phones, or falling asleep on trains, even being attacked while semi-comatose on a bus, or by a cab driver, could give it substance. An embellished story, involving violence or great personal danger, gives more *grand guignol*, but, again, watch the lying.

Of course, you can just tell everyone to sod off, and to take it or leave it.

15. welcome to my world

hullo birds, hullo trees

We live in a society where the greatest taboo is contentment. I only went and broke it. Make no mistake – other people are the problem. And there are a lot of them around.

the first rule of giving up drinking is:
you don't talk about giving up drinking

Well, you can talk about it to a therapist or support group, and hopefully your close friends, but telling it to the rest of the world is a minefield. Tell people that you're 'going on the wagon' and they'll pat you on the back and say, 'Wow, I wish I could do that. I really admire you. What a great idea!' There's something convivial about the idea of 'the wagon'. It throws up an affectionate, pastoral image of old-time prohibition posters and ladies in bonnets and bustles shouting 'Cast out the demon rum!' outside factory pubs. There's something comfortingly temporary about doing a wagon. You'll get on it, and rumble for a while over the bumpy road, straw in mouth, waving to your friends as you go, and then you'll climb down off it in the next town and meet them all in the nearest hostelry.

Tell them you've 'given up drinking', however, and their faces will tell a different story. A mixture of concern and slight confusion will darken their countenance – unless of course

you're a known hardcore boozer who's been pissing everyone off
for ages, in which case their faces will express barely concealed
relief. But if you're not known for ringing around more than five
people to apologise the morning after every bender, and your
friends' mantelpieces aren't festooned with apology cards from
you, you'll be in for a grilling. Let me ram the point home again.
'Oh? Was there a problem?' is a *really stupid question*. If you reply
'No', you may be gently castigated for going on a 'health kick'. If
you answer 'Yes', it will double their confusion – 'But you always
seemed fine to me.' This implies that a) perhaps you don't know
your own mind, and b) that you are a bit of a lightweight. In fact,
when I told my two then closest friends – both of whom had
issues with drinking – they both said, 'But you were never that
big a drinker, were you?' as if I must have had a medical reason
for doing it – because if I had stopped, my intake being less than
theirs, then they really ought to stop too.

'no offence, but...' – social survival

You go out to meet someone. You're sitting there, clean from the
shower, clean clothes, smiling or trying to smile, and you have
said you'll have a lime and soda or whatever, and then at some
point in some way you will drop into the conversation that you
don't drink alcohol. And the interrogation begins, even if you
were gossiping about the telly, or your friends, or discussing the
NASDAQ. It's a rude intrusion, a breaking of the conversational
hymen. What, I ask, am I supposed to say? *Yes, of course there
was a problem, I drank till I puked every single day*, which is the
lurid stuff they want to hear, or *Well, in a way, but it was just that
I thought that it was time to* – and you waffle on and hope for
a nearby handbag to explode, as a distraction, because actually
whose goddamn business is it that you were lying on the floor
half dead for several weeks with your head in an ashtray when
you should have been in hospital? And then they say that they
had a friend or relative who was an alcoholic and, no offence,
but you don't seem like that at all. There you are, pinned and

wriggling and waffling, your ears seeking out a distraction, any distraction from the inevitable pool of heavy silence you can feel gathering around you, and suddenly your past flashes before you, the crying, the suicidal fantasies, the rejection, the – and hold on, this was supposed to be a date!

When people ask if you went to meetings and rehab and detox, although they may not know what those words actually mean – you are actually expected to help them with their terminology as they look vague, and talk about 'one of those places, you know, like the Priory,' – you actually start telling them all about the twelve steps and halfway houses, things that they might have heard a little bit about. Of course, people are often only being well-meaning, but intention means nothing. 'But you don't seem – I mean, you don't *look* like an alcoholic.' The onus is on you to explain yourself, not for them to shut the fuck up with their pissy questions. But you gamely carry on, Well, actually, I mean, it takes all sorts, ha ha, and anyway I wasn't one, really. If I'm feeling spiky and irritable, I might remind the interrogator that what they are talking about is a mental health problem with a physical component. So then I look like a po-faced bore. And then I become irritable, and I worry that I'm going to turn into one of those grimly snitty people who insist that it's 'anoretic' and not 'anorexic', who I've always wanted to attend to with a studded baseball bat.

What people want, I sadly conclude after many such conversations, is the addict version of an Uncle Tom. A poster girl for misery, like so-and-so who went on the telly coked up and then got sent to Arizona or wherever it was. Even cutting – *cutting*! – is seen as cooler than self-medicating due to depression. As long as there's a big, bright and beautiful physical manifestation of pain, you're OK.

society's message – get pissed or get lost

After sobering up, I noticed that bar staff, male or female, didn't really like me any more. I've encountered everything from polite whiffs of bemusement to downright attitude, and stuff added to the bill that I'd never ordered. To them I say this: cutie Armani washboard types, male and female, get those corks out of your arses. I don't drink alcohol, but I have the right to go out, don't I? The more shitty you are with me, the less likely I am to give you a tip, you dimwit gym-whore. Ahh, that's better. However, now that smoking's been given the boot, it may be that these attitudes will slowly fade away. One lot of giving up may cause a domino effect.

I am lucky. My sobering up came out of a life-or-death crisis. I had little choice. I could have done without all the humiliation, the consequent rock-bottom finances, and the suicide trip, but perhaps a Buddhist – ha! – might, in fact, look upon me with envy, and say that these painful events had bought me a lot of karma points. I've sometimes looked at the lines on my hand and wondered if they signify anything, that if I'd gone to a palm reader in 1999, I would have been given the grim news and taken action. The upper line on my left palm has a big break in it, but looking on the web hasn't enlightened me at all, since all the palmistry sites I look at say different things.

I once went on a press trip to Jordan, in the early nineties. As the journalists trudged up and down the rocky paths of the ancient city of Petra, we discussed weight loss and diets. As the vast pinkish red vista opened up to us, I mused aloud, my camera swinging, that if you really want to lose weight properly you need to change your whole life. There was a hiss from one woman, as if I had broken a cherished rule and ruined for her the idea that if you work hard enough at something, it'll happen. In an ideal world, it does. But, if anyone needed reminding, this is not an ideal world.

It's a mystery to me how anyone manages to give up smoking, drinking or over-eating – let alone heroin or crack – while remaining in the same house, doing the same work, and seeing the same people every day, even if they are submitting themselves to checklists on walls, the pinging of rubber bands, and mantras.

And the substitutes are often more unhealthy than the original problem – food for smoking, smoking for drinking, and ghastly low-fat substitutes, or semi-starvation, for food.

With hindsight, that same press trip afforded me a glimpse of what I would have to do, nine years later, to keep to my chosen path. As well as Petra, we visit the site of St Simeon Stylites' pillar. St Simeon Stylites was one of the early church fathers who chose to manifest his superior Christian tendencies by climbing to the top of a forty-foot stone pillar, and sitting there, in rags, in all weathers, and refusing to come down, enacting a kind of ongoing, self-imposed martyrdom. A bit like being sober, really, in the eyes of many. Presumably people passed water and crusts up to him now and again, and remembered to stand back when it all re-emerged, but his intention was to remain up there, according to Tennyson, 'Till all my limbs drop piecemeal from the stone.' We are shown what purports to be the Actual Pillar, and there is a picture of me leaning against it.

other people

On my 38th birthday, when I am two years sober, a friend turns up at the pub where I am celebrating and suggests getting me a glass of champagne. When I politely decline, she goes into a whole thing about it. 'But I didn't think there was a problem – I just thought you'd got tired of it and decided to stop. I'm only talking about just one!' I have been feeling terrible that day, and do not realise that I am spoiling for a nasty bout of flu, but I somehow manage to tell her, while remaining polite, that you never, ever ask a recently sober person to have 'just one'.

Mind, you, don't think people who actually are in AA or NA, who are supposed to know this stuff, are exempt from irritating behaviour. When I'd been sober for a year or so, I went to a party and ran into a man who put himself in the Priory – for cannabis, mind, not crack – and had been doing the full several-meetings-a-week for a heavily specified number of months, let's say twenty-six. I'd always known him as the opinionated type, but even then I was thrown when he patiently explained that my recovery 'wasn't real'. He adopted the smug, all-knowing look that some 12-steppers take on like a chocolate medal, and told me that if I hadn't been going to meetings, I couldn't have done it properly. Well, here I am, six years later.

Consumption in itself, and the capacity for it, makes people very competitive, and addiction makes them ten times more so. People love compulsion horror stories, about the vast amounts bought and swallowed, the MI5 levels of secrecy involved in hiding it from friends, family and colleagues, and, even more than the rest, the aura of romantic isolation that surrounds the addict to those observing from a distance. We're back to St Simeon and his pillar again. Celebrities get an extra wad of cred from their superior needs, and the whiff of The Outlaw their drink and drug use gives them. On an ordinary, civilian, level, the out-of-control drinker and drugger gets masses of attention because of the havoc their problems are causing. Nowadays, all attention seems equally valid and, just as a person who gets photographed a lot suddenly becomes important, the addict gets away with far more than the ordinary mortal. However, if you yourself declare the amount you were drinking and it proves not to be in the bottle-of-vodka-a-day category at the barest minimum, people's eyes will glaze over a bit. This is not interesting to them. People want to be amazed and wonder at both your superior needs, and your astonishing levels of tolerance, enabling them to feel that they have touched on a life more exciting and dangerous than theirs. It's a bit like them getting their photo taken standing next to a soap star, however accidentally. Your chosen audience for disclosure needs some validation for their own lives – hearing about the ordinariness of your decision will not give this to them. They may even talk over you, mentioning a friend of theirs who was a 'real' alcoholic or addict and starting up yet more tales of 'real' high jinks and 'real' madness. You could, of course, lie a bit and exaggerate the amount you were drinking, purely to make them feel better. After all, drinkers do it all the time.

FRIENDS

I'm lucky. I have three girlfriends who have sobered up as well. We don't always see each other, but I know they're around, and they know I am.

new friends

When I stopped drinking, I was amazed to discover that there is a whole world of people out there for whom alcohol is not their primary relationship. I must have been attracting them. They aren't necessarily teetotal, but they are happy with two glasses of wine, or a couple of pints, and that's it. What's more, they are equally happy to go without any alcohol at all, whatever time of night it is. This is a revelation. For years, I let drop people like that – people who actually make arrangements for weekend days, to do activities like sports or something else that needs co-ordination and remaining upright, and expect to stick to them.

old friends

Booze dampens your intuition. It's interesting that it should blunt your animal senses at the same time as making you behave like a child. It's been said many times that children are directly in touch with themselves, fully 'present', and speak their minds but, gradually, training to be an adult forces them to hide their feelings and ignore their intuition, their gut feeling, because it is too awkward for others to deal with, and damages the status quo. One newly sober woman I knew said that sobriety had enabled her to be much more frank with her friends and partner. Sometimes, though, if things have been going bad for too long, the situation goes beyond salvaging.

Thanks to the improved time delay in my reactions, sobriety has enabled me to see, with sometimes hideous clarity, what was wrong with some of my longer-term associations. The ambiguous nature of female friendships is well documented, as intimacy vies with competition, and 'ditch the bitch' is sometimes the only way to deal with it. If that sounds crude, there is nothing worse, and more dishonest, than continuing a friendship that has run its course. Perhaps, who knows, due to dealing with difficult mothers, some of us learned to tolerate personal relationships with other women that are, in fact, intolerable. And female friendships can become so enmeshed that the only way out of them is to destroy them. The same can be said of a marriage, except that at least in marriage the good and enduring old gender war means that there is at least some blurring of the interface between two humans. In other words, the mutual misunderstanding between the sexes gives some leeway for second-guessing, and making excuses for whatever's going on. Between women there is only the matter of trust. Female similarities are played out on an infinite number of levels. The concept of being unfaithful, somewhat cut and dried where romantic love and sex are concerned, becomes a kaleidoscopic haze among female friends. After all, you expect your friends to have other friends, who they meet up with, do things with, and tell secrets to. The two black holes in the pretty colour scheme are when you realise that a) despite your sharing with her, your girlfriend is telling other people stuff she's not telling you, and b) it's your stuff she's tattling about. And, as the old saying goes, it's the people closest to you that are in a position to do you the most harm.

foul weather friends

It stings when you realise that certain people are only hanging out with you because of your availability for partying. One couple in particular always seemed to enjoy my company. We shared party experiences and had long bitching sessions; he had done a lot of the same career things as me, albeit more successfully than me at the time. But I began to suspect that things were not what they seemed. In the safety of their flat, we were equal, but at parties we were not, and my heart would sink as he took the piss out of me briefly, before scuttling back to stand with his 'establishment' pals, who he bitched about at length when it was just the three of us together. Career-wise, perhaps I was seen as a Typhoid Mary, who knows? Perhaps my mere presence was seen as bad luck. It stung a little more when, at a party they gave for another writer, he confided to me, much later, and very coked up, that he was very glad I'd come, because 'it showed the literary crowd that he had different kinds of friends, and that he wasn't scared to have someone like me there.' Maverick me, the freak show?

Our chief topic of conversation was giving up things – drink, drugs and smoking. So when I finally did give up myself, I was baffled when my joyful 'Wagon update – three weeks now!' emails were not returned, given that there had been times when we had talked of little else, for literally hours on end. Everyone else I told, from close friends to colleagues to total strangers, was pleased for me even if they'd asked a bunch of nosy questions. So why not these two? I realised that the driving force behind what passed for friendship here was 'there but for the grace of God go we'; that while they saw me as a good time, they actually thought I was a bit sad. And now, here I was, spoiling their fun by turning my life around.

SUBSTITUTE HABITS

Every time I hear this word I think of the terrible seventies song 'I'll Be Your Substitute', screeched, as I remember, by a woman with an overweening frizzy perm who seemed to be telling some bloke that she was happy to play second fiddle to his full-time regular woman who'd gone off for a bit.

In the early days of my sobriety, I should perhaps have been kinder to myself, and expected very little of myself for a year, perhaps two. I was, really, still half mad but managed in my usual way to disguise it.

But I still needed a high.

coffee

Perhaps it was the Seroxat that helped me discover the delights of coffee and a cigarette before breakfast. I needed to stay awake in all the confusion of illness and staying alive. I usually avoided coffee during my partying life, as it made me too hyper. I remember once having a big one the morning after a night out, and panicking a little as my heart rate jumped. My boyfriend put his fingers against my neck to check my pulse and said 'I can't believe someone who's taken as many stimulants as you have is getting worried about a coffee.' Coffee was one of my first new friends. When a fellow recoverer told me she had seven different kinds in her fridge, I began experimenting, and decided that Continental Blend (5 strength) was the way to go. Out of the window the light suddenly seemed brighter, and the colours heightened, as if I'd had a quarter of an Ecstasy tablet. One morning I popped out to get a paper, but couldn't stop walking and ended up three miles away.

smoking

I'm not sure what set me off full-time chain smoking. I was only ever really a party smoker before, only doing it at home if a boyfriend was staying over. In my entire life, I had never, ever, smoked while working at the computer, a rule that I had, until 2002, never broken.

I was almost totally without funds, so I took up rollies. Luckily my affair with hand-rolled tobacco coincided with a nascent celebrity trend, and I wrote a piece about it eighteen months later for the late, much-lamented *Talk of the Town* magazine. A new distraction became an entrenchment, and a generation of filthy, compost-ridden computer keyboards was born.

I soon discovered that smoking has worse effects on the body than the equivalent wine habit. Alcohol, in large quantities, affects mental health, that's for sure, but for sheer physical effect, smoking takes the biscuit. Over a period of a few months, I gradually felt the circulation in my legs disappear. My skin and teeth did not thank me either. Coughing became a way of life.

But it was so, so enjoyable. For a writer, or anyone sitting in one place working, it's a time marker and a reward all in one. I did not award myself this 'vice' as a replacement addiction; it came upon me as a logical progression. I loved smoking, I really did, and it was four years before I dropped it.

sleeping
Between the first morning that I managed to get up and go to the clinic until I gave up smoking four years later, I had about ten full nights of sleep. Many report the opposite; that it is only when they gave up drinking or drugs that they understood what a proper night's sleep was.

Sleep was where my body seemed to be acting out its own detox, unbidden by me. I fell asleep like a potato sack thumping onto straw, and remained in the same position until I woke up, sometimes with half my body drenched in sweat. However hot I got, I never moved in my sleep. I begin to wake earlier and earlier, sometimes as early as 4 a.m., with the result that by the afternoon I was done for, and had to go to bed for three hours or so. This was not as bad as it sounds. The early morning is my best time and this is how I started my first steps towards my new addiction – work.

work
From my earliest sober days, I realised that the only way I could get back to work was by being freelance. I was probably unemployable, if I was truthful about my health situation, and I simply could not handle anyone in my face for more than ten minutes without wanting to run, screaming.

chanting
Just kidding.

hobbies
Pre-sobriety, I was never entirely sure what a hobby was. To me, the word always conjured up stamp collecting or competitive

cycling, and that was about it. For most of my adult life, my main pastime was seeing friends and getting drunk, period. Charity rock-climbing weekends, for example, are really going to be out of the question when you can barely stand, and are transfixed by light trails. After meeting and embracing my inner nerd, to the point where friends would ask me how to fix their computers, I took up photography. The world of ones and zeroes was far more welcoming to me than the pub – and I've always asserted that I cannot hear my biological clock, because it is digital.

cannabis

A bit misleading, this, because I have barely touched it in my life, and never in the last six years. This is just a reminder that it's a rubbish idea to replace one substance with another. No one will ever hear a passionate defence of spliff from me, because I found it a horrible drug, which made me sicker and more paranoid than any other substance I've ever tried. Some people smoke it so much that they may as well be on a mixture of smack and acid. They throw whiteys in clubs, or lock themselves in the toilet, having forgotten where the door is, or having become rigid with terror at the concept of touching the handle. A friend was smoking it with her boyfriend one night, and then went upstairs to bed. She came down in the morning to find him on the sofa in exactly the same position she'd left him in, with a burned-down dog-end and a line of drool running from his mouth to his trousers. And then there are the secondary effects – it makes people paranoid, selfish, lazy and resentful. Someone didn't replace the teabags and Mother's Pride? Phone messages not taken? Dopehead in the house! My dope phase lasted about a year. Despite its charms as a creative or sexual catalyst, in the end it usually puts people in touch with their inner loser quicker than anything. I definitely think it should be legalised, just so that everyone shuts up about it.

politics

For a year or so after I sobered up, I burned inside with a campaigning fervour. I really, really wanted to do something about the state of the mental health services in this country. I looked at the job ads, and vowed to start applying for advocacy jobs, when I barely had the strength. A Sunday paper published regular features about the system, and how it was failing the vulnerable. I wrote out long lists of article ideas, eager to speak out for people like me. But, somehow, I never sent them in. And after a while I realised that I wanted to leave it all behind. I didn't want to be reminded of what I'd gone through.

SOBER RELATIONSHIPS

Recovery experts suggest that you don't have any relationships in the early days. Sometimes it's suggested that you get a houseplant, and if it is still alive after two years you graduate to a dog or cat, and then, some time after that, maybe you could start a relationship with another human. Actually, celibacy isn't really hard when intimacy of any kind feels like a bomb about to go off, and your body feels as if it is crawling with maggots at the idea of getting close to anyone, even fully dressed. Almost overnight, I went from sexually generous to Scrooge-like levels of withholding. I couldn't exactly call it a vow, but it was close.

sober dating

Perhaps too much clarity isn't good for you. I can see now why the older men get, the more likely they are to pick younger women. As women age, we know too much, and younger women spend far more on their appearances than my contemporaries ever did. Anal bleaching may have caused a gross-out stir when Vanessa Feltz first showed it to us on the telly, but someone, somewhere on this isle, will already be selling this service.

And a sober woman is scary too. On disclosing, I've picked up an occasional 'no thanks' vibe from men, which is bordering on the logical. As the evening progresses, the sober woman will not laugh louder and louder at decreasingly funny jokes, and she will not disclose personal data – and take it from me, in date-land this stuff is just that – either about her past or her predilections. She will not, as she once did after a given number of vodka tonics, suddenly become up-for-it in a way that she wasn't at 7.30 p.m. Sober, she is less likely to take drugs and become ever more available. There is a loss of spontaneity when you stay in control, and perhaps, on the face of it, it's not always a good thing.

There is an entire book to be written about sober dating. It took me a long time to get there. This wasn't some newly discovered deep detestation of the opposite sex, but a sense of the utter precipice that I found myself on. I can't deny a residual cynicism, born out of experience, that made me very mean with my sweetness. But I had to rebuild myself from scratch and dealing with another person was impossible. I had already given away too much.

Sober or not, as a single woman you are, even among your closest friends, caught in a double bind. Traditionally, or at least according to a lot of women's novels and magazine articles, the woman who is without a man must walk through life veiled in pathos, dragging her misery and penitence behind her like a dead horse, eager to atone for her blatant inadequacies through exquisite, and relentless, suffering. She must bore her friends, male and female, to death with her self-examination, which is matched only by her eagerness to change, and be pathetically grateful to be set up with anyone – anyone – that they might think could save her from this shame. However, if she reveals herself to be contented with the situation, and is not crying for days on end or begging for help, she is seen as a bit of a freak. After a certain age, and her friends having known her for a certain number of years, it's unlikely that anyone will actually suggest that she is secretly a lesbian. What is left, therefore, is the suspicion that there is something very, very wrong with her. I used the 'I nearly died and I'm putting myself back together at my own pace' line with a few people, but, in fact, most people were too polite to dig, and for that I must thank them.

The good old British way of mating – to get blind drunk and fall into bed together, after which, unless it was a cruel disaster, you end up in a relationship by default, because it was such a relief to get that bit over with – was still going strong, but was now unavailable to me. Until I dipped my toe in again, all I could see was the American way of dating, a clipboard cattle market of multiple choice, a cold perusal of the socio-economic CV, that resembles the contractual dressage trials of a Jane Austen novel rather than the enlightened exchange of personalities and pheromones that you might expect in a supposedly advanced society such as ours.

A friend of mine internet dated for two years. She reported that, despite the shocking amount of lying she witnessed, the exes-that-weren't-exes, and the declarations of availability followed by total disappearance, topped up much later with opportunistic follow-ups by email, she actually ended up liking men more than she had previously, because it all laid bare the insecurity behind so much of the blather. After two years of this, though, it stopped being amusing. So it was fittingly charming that, with only two days of her online subscription left, she met a man who she was still with three years later. Sadly he turned out to be the biggest liar of the lot.

Despite still reeling from events I have yet to describe, I finally took the plunge and stuck myself on a couple of websites. The first man I met seemed familiar from his picture and description. We met up during a heatwave, on one of the hottest evenings of a blasting tar pit of a summer that left me gasping and vowing to give up smoking. Even before I'd set eyes on him I began to suspect we'd met before, and having got his full name (I withheld mine – the combination of a unique name, contributing to sex media, and Google means that you can run but you can't hide), I knew where. He was the bloke who I bought my first crack from back in 1995, in the attic room of a dilapidated arts centre in Soho. I remembered fancying him even then. He was now a recovering addict of five years' standing. We'd met loads of people in common, and used to go to the same drinking places. It was easy to talk about all that, for hours. I fancied him and wanted to jump on him in an alleyway. But he wasn't interested. I actually cried when he dumped me, post second date which was pretty pathetic really, especially as he'd behaved appallingly.

Over the next nine months I continued to date, and met a selection of perfectly nice, attractive men, most of whom I would have taken home after a bottle or two of wine. Wine-free, I quickly learned to spot the warning signs – once they knew a little about what I've done, some of them thought this entitled them to tell me stories with just a little bit too much information, signing off with the words, 'Whoops! Oh, but I can say that kind of thing to *you*, can't I?' For a tiny minute, Germaine Greer's 'ambulant spittoon' popped into my head. Really, I should not have been dating now. Some of them felt a sense of entitlement to ask me in great detail about my life. To keep on asking personal questions is a sign of naivety, that you've stayed pretty much in the same pond all your life. 'So you're basically a *sex journalist*, aren't you,' said one guy, desperate to pigeonhole me. He was also eager to tell me how different I was in person from on the radio. Not for the first time, the words, 'Can't you get the hell out of my face!' echoed through my mind unsaid. It wasn't the first time my work in sex media had got me labelled, and wouldn't be the last.

sex

At one point, a concerned friend, who I've only known since being sober, noted my ongoing singleness and told me that everyone she knew who was sober was at it like knives, because sex was the only form of intoxication left to them. Then I met Joe, who didn't ask me too many questions, and who accepted me along with my post-smoking weight. Actually, who wouldn't? I flourished to a magisterial 32F, and, at eleven and a half stone, weighed more than I have ever done. As they say, if you want the tits, you have to pay the arse tax. Real tits, please note. Joe didn't mind paying the arse tax, and helped me remember what my body is supposed to do. Sexually, I spent many, many years, frankly, as a bit of a rag doll, complete with – it has to be said – miniature sand pit. Now, I remembered. Some people say cocaine helps their sex life. All I remember was a mysterious urge to watch porn and masturbate, but I was too dried up, and my mind skipping off at tangents, to be of any real use to anyone, and I almost never had an orgasm. Not that this stopped me doing it, or anyone in the vicinity. Booze and drugs made me a bit of a heifer, really. Now it all works properly.

DANGER ZONES

emotions

It now takes me, on average, between two days and two weeks to react to something that upsets or disturbs me. This is progress, because it used to take me between two years and a decade. Those, anyway, are my natural responses. I have taught myself to react quicker than that, but it is generally through method acting. In my twenties, I never knew how to react to anything. I would leaf through friends or colleagues in my head, as if going through a photo album, thinking, 'What would so-and-so do if this happened to them?' and act the way I thought a particular person might have done. To others, I must have seemed very odd and inconsistent, as I varied constantly between charm and aggression, making a joke of things and then going stone cold. But then, I had spent my whole life not expressing how I felt, because I truly believed that the world would have ended if I had.

I consider myself fortunate that my sobriety was born out of such fire, because it let me go back to ground zero and start again. I am not surprised, then, that one of my newly discovered emotions was what I took to be numbness. I was so used to living with a sense of either apocalyptic doom or puppy-like expectation, that any other feelings just seemed grey. Oddly, perhaps, at the beginning I did not find parties terrifying. After Day Zero, for a long time I was buoyed up by the knowledge that I had escaped death by a whisker, and that was my armour. It didn't matter if nobody else actually knew that. It gave me an inner confidence, which got me through the seething crowds with what must have seemed like serenity.

The hard bit is learning about myself, such as how to cope with relationships, both starting and ending them, and finally ramming the point home to myself that new experiences are not necessarily going to be transformative. And just because I have taken up ecstatic dancing, and running, and given up smoking, doesn't automatically mean that in fifteen years' time there is going to be a huge retrospective interview with me in a newspaper, in which I describe the moment I decided to take up ecstatic dancing, or running, or give up smoking, and how my entire life changed forthwith, and I became the successful, respected, and rich, person that the whole world can see now.

Sober, I have taken on the burden of the hitherto ludicrous and taboo notion of actually getting my own emotional needs met, in friendships and relationships. I also have to learn this from scratch. Sometimes the world just makes me cross. I am given to understand that this is part of the female ageing process, and that there is something called the 'peri-menopause' that causes women to get angry, stay angry, and revel in it because, having got to the age we are, we just know we're right. And the trouble is, I quite like my inner grumpy old cow.

loneliness

Lots of people won't admit to being lonely, even though they feel like the single peanut on a floor that never gets swept up. The warmth of one drink can make you feel as if you belong. The warmth of a whole bottle can, if you shut your eyes, bring a whole person to you. I was so busy being glad to be alive that loneliness didn't get to me too much, until, when I was about to turn forty, I read a news story about a woman who, after bailiffs kicked her door in, was found dead, surrounded by Christmas presents. From the vast pile of mail in her hallway, they worked out that she had been there for three years, without anyone noticing she'd gone. Her age? Not ninety – but forty. Once upon a time I might have cracked open a bottle just reading about it.

time, aka boredom

The reason most musicians drink and take drugs is to pass the time – the hours spent in the tour bus, the hours waiting during soundchecks and rehearsals, and the yet more hours spent waiting for the last band member to turn up at the studio so that they can start. Musicians are just not very likely to pass these hours playing Scrabble, or improving their language skills quietly in a corner with an iPod and a set of headphones. It may be waiting with a specific reason in mind, but it's still waiting, and intoxication does your waiting for you very effectively. Most people are not musicians, and their lives don't consist of big chunks of between-time, alternating with the adrenalin-stoked reward of a session or gig at the end of it. And most musicians have their day organised for them by other people so, as long as they turn up eventually, they will be fed, watered, and given a place to sleep. For band members this is the incentive, as they are often so badly paid.

Sober, I don't have the option to pass the time intoxicated any more. A summer bank holiday Sunday, when I might previously have spent the day in a gorgeous haze, was a Sunday like any other, and lasted about eighteen hours of awake time – like every other day, in fact. Once I'd got over the boredom threshold of being sober in general, I then had to face up to other drunk people: the gurning mouths, the eyes lined with smudged make-up and the residue of cigarette smoke, the red-wine-encrusted lips and the endless, endless repetition of the same thing, over and over again.

When all else fails, for sheer joy in other peoples' imaginations, there's the web. I've lost count of the number of times I've stopped what I was doing to coo over someone's grainy little movie of their baby cats doing something furry and cute, or screamed with laughter at the Touretteaphone, Cats That Look Like Hitler, b3ta. com or Cute Overload. Thinking about it, I suppose kitten videos are substitutes for children. And I suppose in turn that that might seem really sad – but it's not. They're a lot cheaper for a start.

evil little voices

The tough part was when I'd managed to stay sober for long enough to be able to look back over my life since giving it all up, and wonder why I hadn't got my own TV series, my own company, a bestseller written, my screenplay made, or my own extraordinary new life-partner, oh, and some lovely children – possibly all six. This is where the haggling comes in. I feel as if I have made a massive deal with life, the universe, or whatever, but I gave all this up – for what? An agent once told me that he would have enormous problems selling this book. 'The trouble is,' he said, 'you don't have a *profile*.' 'But I'm still alive!' I wanted to shout. 'What more do you need?' I felt sick for a week. I didn't think that great wealth and fame would attach itself to me as soon as I got sober, but a little part of me had fantasised that miracles would happen; that, after all this time, I deserved them. Actually, good things did happen, but there weren't any miracles, unless you count me still being alive. Every time I heard a little voice asking what was the point of me being sober, all I had to think about was the hangover, the downsliding, the not paying bills, the days lost to pain and self-recrimination, and it was enough.

accidents

A few times since sobering up, I've been at a party and drunk from the wrong glass. The first time, I couldn't believe what was in my mouth and I shrieked a bit and spat it out, but not before some of the wine had gone down, and I could feel its warmth. Another time it was some revolting red wine that I'd mistaken for fruit juice. I felt it burn all the way down and I wanted to throw up. After the first time, I told my counsellor, who said that this could be interpreted by purists as a lapse. In fact, it's amazing how quickly my body forgot the temptation of wine. One Christmas Day, I overdid the brandy butter and couldn't work out why I had to lie down for a while, and then walk it off. I have only truly *gagged* for a drink about three times in the six years since I stopped, and I managed to keep a hold of myself. In all that time, I have not had anything stronger than Nurofen Plus and beta blockers.

16. trials

When sailing on the sea, you can be in terrible terror and on the point of capsizing, while just a few hundred yards away, there is a shaft of sunlight on a quiet patch of water, where another boat sits happily and quietly, without a care.

Life was good at thirty-nine. I had been sober for three years. I had a book deal and our sex podcast was climbing up the charts and I had decided to try internet dating and people were offering me work and I had enough money in the bank and Christmas was coming. Two months previously I had decided to come off the Seroxat. I didn't need drugs any more. For fun, I used to be able to call myself a 'legalised drug addict', but that was all over now. No more crutches necessary. I am healed. I am fine. I have plans, big plans, for a website, lots of journalism, lots of online, lots of radio, lots of readings, lots of me getting out there, lots of me being, finally, the New Me.

Actually, it's not so easy to come off Seroxat. I had already tried a secret cold turkey as an experiment, and after three days I was lying on the floor feeling so strange and hot and frightened that I gave up and took my GP's advice to cut down by missing a tablet every few days, then three days, then two, then going for two days without, until the space between doses was so large that the dose I was getting was sub-clinical and simply of psychological value. I was very proud of myself for doing this.

Two days after Christmas, which I spent in a state of relaxational bliss, I arranged to meet a friend for supper. I got out of the bath and went into the living room, naked. The blind was up and it was dark outside, so I ran to the window and let the blind down and went into my bedroom to dry my hair. A couple of minutes later, I sensed something out of the ordinary, so I went into the living room and before me was a wall of flame. I had let the blind down on top of a lighted candle. Naked, I stood there saying 'fuck' for a moment or two. Then I realised I had to rescue my brand new camera and my computer. I took another moment or two to decide whether to take a picture of the now spectacular flames, and decided not to. I yanked my desk out of the way. I pulled up the blind, thinking to compress the burning cloth. Then I performed the ill-advised action of opening the window to try and push the burning blind outside. Wind gusted in and it briefly flared up worse. I was still naked. Then I remembered that you have to actually put fires out. Secretly wishing that someone outside had noticed and called the fire brigade, I got a jug and threw water at the remaining flames. The strings burned through and the red hot metal cross-pole fell down, hissing. The window panes cracked with the cold water. There was a stink of burning plastic from the singed television and aerial sockets and the back of my computer. Smoke still issued from a remaining bit of burning wood, still attached to the top of the window frame. I hurled more water upwards. It was over.

My flat was full of acrid smoke, with a terrible smell, and the ceiling was blackened. I opened the window fully and faced down the minus one degree winds outside. Forlornly, I cancelled my friend. I hung an old sheet in the window, and another friend took me out for a drink in Soho. My warm festive mood was, unsurprisingly, killed. For several weeks afterwards, I jumped every time I smelt burning, in the market or in the street. It took a full day to clean up the mess. It took another nine months to get round to repainting the room.

Three weeks later, I walked to my dance class. I decided to

dance in white. My knickers were also white. On the way, I worried that I was becoming incontinent, and it was only when I got there that I saw that my period had come, three days early. Five days after that, I got back from work and there was a message from an editor at a national newspaper, telling me that she had just spoken to my mother, and that I was to call my mother as soon as possible, about my father.

Instantly I went into a spin. I found myself wondering what on earth the newspaper editor must have thought, but I knew what it must be about. I called a friend. He was mystified by my hesitancy in calling and said that I must find out what was going on. I chain-smoked for three hours in my blue leather armchair. I first left a message with my aunt and uncle, who I had also not seen for twelve years. I called my mother and she told me that my father had died five days previously. Actually, the first thing I noticed was that she sounded like the Queen, and totally artificial. I asked over and over why she had waited till he was dead to tell me, and she repeated and repeated that they could not get hold of me. This I knew to be nonsense. It is very hard to disappear nowadays, especially if you are involved in any kind of media. I had been around on the web for quite a few years by this time, and I would soon discover that my father, who was a very technical person, had a wide-ranging secret life on the internet that my mother was not allowed to come anywhere near. Fantasies flashed past, of us all reconciling around my father's deathbed, but it was too late. In nonplussed fury I hung up on her.

Everything had fallen down. I felt a rope around my neck. I was not totally, totally on the floor because I always knew something like this would happen. I could not be totally, totally high-horse about her waiting the five days, as I did make myself scarce for a very long time. But still.

I spoke to my aunt and uncle, who told me that my cousin was dying too and that I should come and see him soon. In the intervening decade my other cousin's young teenage son had also died, of an illness he had had since childhood. For the next few days I threw myself into work. Unbelievably I was writing about alcoholism, mental illness, drug addiction and suicide attempts. I could hardly bear it, but I kept on going.

I took a train to the south coast. My aunt and uncle were much greyer than when I had last seen them. We hugged. It came out that they had very little information about my father dying, and what there was, was gleaned from secret calls to him and emails that had to be hidden from my mother, even in the last months. We drove to see my cousin, his wife who had nursed him for years, and their four small boys. They warned me that he had a fifteen-minute memory. He was blown up from years of steroids but still had the same handsome, sardonic look, which he gave me in spades. We hugged. He was bright as a button and totally on the ball throughout my visit. The children played on the computer and the dogs ran around, and we ate his wife's carrot cake. The boys had only ever known their dad ill. At one point I went outside for a smoke. My cousin followed me outside. He looked at me and said something about my mother. 'I understand totally about all that,' he added, with knowing, gloomy sympathy. Two weeks later he was dead.

I managed to phone my mother one more time, for three-quarters of an hour. It was only after I'd hung up that I realised I had reverted entirely to childhood – acting and sounding totally normal and fine; not expressing anything of what I was really feeling. Feeling patronised and bullied. She had read my novels. 'What was all this about a bad childhood?' she said.

As the weeks passed she kept trying to call me but I did not pick up. I started to feel more and more like a hunted animal. I tried beta blockers but they barely touched the sides, and I had to go back on the Seroxat. 'If you go back on it now you'll probably be on it forever,' warned my GP. At that point I did not care. Whenever my mother left a message, my entire flat felt tainted and I had to leave. One day I thought I was going to have a stroke or just go mad, but I well knew by then that there was no point going to a hospital, so I wrote letters instead – to my mother to stop phoning, and to my aunt who seemed to have become a message service for my mother. I wondered if anyone wondered how I was. Did I deserve to have people wonder how I was? Two years previously, a therapist had told me that I had internalised all my mother's criticisms of me. My head was full of fear and hatred and envy all swirling round together. I felt eruptions of hatred and envy for any woman who had done better than me, or was younger than me, or richer than me, or anyone else, really. It was just yet more fear. I was in freefall again. This time, though, without alcohol to hand I was feeling it and living it because I really had no choice.

It took me four months to actually stay on the line long enough to get through to a bereavement counsellor on the phone, who recommended I see someone in person. I wanted to run away to Australia; somewhere as far away as possible. If I had had enough spare funds I would have gone. I ran off to Egypt for a week to get brown and take photos. I only cried once, when one of the pain-in-the-neck beach masseurs – who gave me a bit of extra hassle because I was the only woman holidaying alone in the whole 800-room hotel complex – commented on my chain smoking when I told him for the nth time that I did not want his services, and asked me why I was 'so nervous'. I retired to my room and cried.

I turned forty, quietly. I didn't tell any of my guests at the restaurant that I had reached this age. They were a mixture of old friends and new friends, and those that knew, knew, and those that didn't, didn't. I felt too sick and panicked about my life to make a proper speech.

Back home when the sun got too bright and I could not breathe with fear, I realised I had to drop everything but the most basic survival. I decided to dump all career aspirations and live like a normal person. In other words, work for money, and play the rest of the time. Instantly I felt better, but I still spent the next six months fighting depression and fear; feeling on show, feeling yet again that everything I did was wrong. I softened it to friends by telling them that I was having a 'mid-life crisis'. Yet again I was making things easier for others. I didn't want to scare everyone away by telling them how apocalyptically terrified I felt as if some official entity was going to appear and force me to live with my mother, and take away my life, so that people who once knew me would say, 'The poor thing. We always knew she would fail.' You cannot, in all honesty, go on like that on a daily basis, but it was ringing in my head from the moment I woke up from the moment I went to sleep. I was hunted. I was trapped.

In the autumn I took a week off to resume writing, but was unable to do more than lie on my bed and read a lengthy account of the Yorkshire Ripper case. I applied for a grant to help finish my book. I was utterly convinced that I would get something, that the assessors would all understand my pain by osmosis, but early in December, my application was rejected. Then, just before New Year, a friend died. Despite his great physical disability, he had been a raging party animal, and it was astonishing that he managed to survive until his thirties, but even so. It was a sad end to a sad year.

I write these personal things here to underline the fact that all these things happened but I remained sober. All these things happened but I did not once turn back to drink or street drugs, or the old stash of Valium and Temazepam that – still – remains in my flat. Not even once.

17. twelve benefits of giving up alcohol – a final entreaty

When I tell them, people say to me 'Good for you. I wish I could do that.' This, incidentally, is exactly what people say when you've written a novel, or slept with more than three men in a week. But they don't always mean it, and I sometimes get the sense of a continuing protest. 'Why shouldn't I drink? You gave up because you were obviously the one with the problem.' But, dare I ask, is this you?

You're tired. Tired of the hangovers, tired of the blackouts, tired of wondering where it all went wrong; even if it hasn't, yet. You feel like death every morning. You've got a mouth like a gravedigger's flip-flop, and judging by the paranoid chatter going round in your head, the Naked Mole Rats Of Doom are close by, taunting you with your inadequacies. You're tired of your clothes not fitting properly any more after the relentless post-party carb attacks. Looking four months pregnant is fine if you actually are. You're tired of minor health problems and worrying about major ones. You're tired of catching your own face in the mirror when you're out for the evening and seeing a desperate banshee, a snapshot of you in twenty years' time, whatever your age today. You've lost four phones in the past year, and cancelled five credit cards, two of which turned out to be under the chopping board all the time. Your life might not even be a disaster, and may look quite the opposite to others, but you're starting to feel that something's not quite right.

Well, is it?

1 weight loss

I lost about twenty pounds when I gave up drinking. That wasn't really surprising, as a bottle of red wine is about 500–600 calories. A pint of beer is about 180–200.[15] If you're doing a bottle of wine a night, it's going to add many pounds over a couple of years, and don't forget that weight gain is gently exponential as you get older. Once you've given up hangover food like fry-ups and cakes, the lard melts away like snow. (I suppose I should mention that, after a few years, my metabolism has re-set itself, so that if I want to lose weight now, especially after giving up smoking, I'll have to eat only steamed mushrooms and the occasional sprout if I want to get anywhere.)

2 money saved – or more money to buy other stuff

If you're a working person with a reasonable salary, if you are drinking a bottle of wine a night, let's say at £7 a go, and then add in two bottles of vodka a week at, say, £13 each, and then you stop for just six months, that's £1,950 saved already. That's an ISA. Or a holiday. Or a nice wad of shopping. Or, of course, a very reasonable donation to charity.

3 health improved

When you aren't feeling as if Satan is taunting your entire being with sizeable electrified tweezers, the world looks a bit nicer. Your body has not been dehydrated and stripped of vitamins, and your face looks less like a death mask.

4 weight loss

OK, your cup size will drop, but they were booze tits anyway.

5 your energy doubled
You get way more work done, or the same done in half the time. Times of day when you were previously white-knuckling it and trying not to fall asleep are now oceans of possibility.

6 your time is yours, not your throbbing head's
How much more of your life do you want to waste tossing up between aspirin and paracetamol?

7 your time is yours, and not other people's
Take alcohol out of the equation and the reality hits you that not everyone you know is good for you. You knew that, of course, but they were fun, even if they were kind of annoying or hurtful, or could treat you any way they felt like. You can ditch them and get more time to yourelf.

8 increased quality control
You will be in a position to exercise some quality control that was previously lacking in your social life, not to mention your relationships. You will find it easier to dump two-faced friends, and duplicitous lovers.

9 happiness
In the morning – remember that?

10 you stop talking about giving up
A good 50 per cent of my conversations with others, women and men, and not always started by me, by any means, used to consist of a) how bad I felt that day, and b) how great it would be to give it all up. Now, my oxygen supply can fly free of the taint of dullness. However, this could be a double-edged sword. Subtract lengthy declared intentions to give up smoking, drinking or drugs from any given conversation, and there might not be a lot left.

11 better sex

Kiss goodbye to horrible drunken lunges, sticky saliva from
dehydration, him ending up in the 'wrong hole' – or no hole
at all – embarrassing dryness, semen in the eyes, forgotten
or damaged contraception, falling asleep on the job, heavy
snoring, evil breath the next morning. And, of course,
exercising rather more discernment over who you are doing
all this with in the first place.

12 weight loss

Did I mention this before? Before you go into the 'It doesn't
matter what size you are!' rant, the one we all come out with,
even when it's someone else who is the object of criticism, let's
get real. When you're having a bad time, thinking you look
like crap is an extra slap in the face. *Knowing* you look like
crap is even worse. Weight isn't about size per se. We're all
different body types. Whatever build you are, there's flesh,
and then there's booze bloat.

Some of you will shout, 'I'm already thin, I've got a well-
paid job so I'm already saving money, I take vitamins and go
to the gym, I exercise total control over my relationships and
my social life, and I don't take any shit from anyone. My life
couldn't be improved in any way whatsoever. So I don't need
to stop drinking.'

OK then. Fine. You don't need me, or my book. But *I* know
they're booze tits, honey.

18. what society could do if it really felt like it

dump the war on drugs

What would this book be without a word on the government (any government, really) and its role in the promotion of alcohol? In the last ten years or so,[16] we've heard a lot about cannabis, and how it should be either legalised or criminalised further. However, I well remember the first time I read the phrase 'gateway drug' in a newspaper. There's a thing, I thought. The government, or some mouthpiece of theirs, was luridly describing cannabis as an infernal portal to the slime pits that are cocaine, heroin and crack. While I don't discount this – I moved to harder stuff myself very quickly, just because I thought cannabis was so crap – I have to point out that, as gateways go, cannabis is a small serving hatch compared to the gaping seaport represented by alcohol.

During the whole national debate on binge drinking, I haven't heard alcohol being called a gateway to anything, apart from increased tax revenues. Alcohol, legal, available and openly advertised, is a gateway to every drug you can think of. Most people try their first street drugs and sex during a night's drinking. The two are inextricably linked.

try actually celebrating something

Humans need intoxication, but we also need a reason to do it

– otherwise it just becomes a waste. How about getting caned a few times a year, on certain significant days, like some other cultures do? On Christmas, solstices and equinoxes? Hell, even once a month, when the moon is fat. Don't call me an old hippy – are you trying to tell me the average person has something to celebrate every night of the week? OK, OK, aside from the fact that we're all unique and beautiful snowflakes, of course. (I would have put a ':-)' here, but this is a book.) If confining benders to monthly is too awful a propect, there's a case to be made for a three-day weekend, so that we could all recover properly.

listen to wise people

Listen to wise people, like the writer and psychologist Oliver James, who has done more than most to highlight the connection between a society run on comparisons and depression. Look to the connection between depression and heavy drinking.[17] Look at the fact that between 40 per cent and 60 per cent of injuries in the European region are caused by alcohol.[18] Even though the numbers of working hours lost to alcohol misuse are now costing the UK economy nearly £2 billion,[19] no one is really addressing the immediate issues that divide and rule us all.

Actually, even though I look at the news online every day, and keep an eye on what's happening, there are days when I feel as if I've turned away briefly to make a cup of tea, and come back to find that the whole world has changed in my absence. Breast implants for sixteenth birthdays, violence in schools, property prices – everything seems like a catalogue of increasing madness and exclusion. A person famous only for being photographed has another picture taken of them, and the rich get richer. This keeps on happening, faster and faster, in one great manic looping groundhog moment.

I must admit, though, that sometimes I still feel that maybe it really would be easier just to sit and drink rather than bother about the world's problems. I watch a *Grumpy Old Women* Christmas special, and end up having to leave the room in frustration, after listening to these successful, prosperous ladies, most of them at the top of their game – or they wouldn't be on the show in the first place – whinge on about their Christmas preparations, and all the lists they feel obliged to make, and the military campaigns they make out of this annual festival, pushing themselves to the limits of domestic control-freakery, with the marshalling of the internet and the credit cards and the saucepans, and how one of them starts planning it, and actually buying presents in *February* – and I wonder why the hell anyone bothers with anything.

But it's just a passing thought. Thank God for kitten videos. And sex.

19. what I miss

Unpredictable evenings. Not knowing where I'm going to end up. Meeting lots of new people who are doing the same thing. The wonderful, precious, loss of whole chunks of time. Getting paid in vodka. Cackling. (You can cackle when you're sober, obviously, but it just doesn't have that same endless, breathless quality.) Intoxication in general. Mini Rolls. Competitive smoking. Churning through vast numbers of people around town and staying friends with some of them. Being out in a noisy place somewhere and just knowing there's a little bit of something waiting for me at home. Not minding going out and spending all evening in high heels because the drink numbs the pain after a bit. Spending whole days in the pub, shouting.

And I know full well, even now, that one of the best, no, hell, *the* best, way to spend the weekend, *ever*, is just the two of you, the place to yourselves, red wine, vodka, and a pile of your drug of choice. Talking, sex, shouting, sleeping, drinking, snorting, smoking, and then doing it all again, all on our little island. I miss that.

what I don't miss
Hangovers. Screaming, spinning head on the bus the next day. Party panic when no drink is forthcoming. Hunting for the missing twenty quid. Rubbish attempts at designing hangover

'cures'. Hangovers. Tolerating people that others consider to be mad, and putting up with them because I think I have some sort of deeper understanding of them. Pulling crispy bacon bits out of my nose. Being able to judge how drunk I am from how early I start to undress: removal of my jewellery while still in a bar is not a good sign. Sex not quite working properly. Feeling obliged to perform but probably not fooling anyone and knowing full well this is the case. Paranoia. Line, drink, line, drink, and hearing voices chattering out of the taps and being too afraid to leave the house. Being so miserable that I cannot listen to music, for months on end. Churning through endless life experiences just to feel human. Exhaustion from always trying to seem OK to others. Suicidal depressions. Hangovers.

20. 101 (OK, seven) things to do with a Saturday morning

1. Get up.
2. Breathe.
3. Wash.
4. Eat.
5. Go out.
6. Talk to people.
7. Do things.

The list is endless, really. Hmmm. I've never had a facial. Maybe I'll get one of those. I suppose I ought to plan some sort of ascent of Everest as well.

sources

page 34
1. Public Accounts Committee, April 2006
2. Foreign and Commonwealth Office (FCO), August 2005
3. FCO, August 2007
4. Home Office (via *Daily Mail*), May 2006
5. BBC *Panorama* (via *Daily Mail*), February 2007

page 35
6. Information Centre for Health and Social Care, Statistics on Alcohol England, June 2006
7. *Emergency Medicine Journal* (via BBC website), July 2007

page 118
8. Home Office, Research, Development and Statistics Directorate (via *Guardian* leader), March 2006

page 123
9. Home Office consent campaign, March 2006
10. BBC website, 21 December 2005
11. *Daily Telegraph*, 11 November 2003

page 129
12. BBC Website, 11 February 2005
13. *Guardian*, 26 May 2005

page 134

[14] Amnesty International 'Sexual Assault Research',
21 November 2005, part of the 'Stop Violence Against
Women' campaign.

Page 226

[15] There are many, many sources, such as
www.weightlossresources.co.uk/calories/calorie_counter.
htm

Page 229

[16] www.ukcia.org/library/pastevents/sindy.htm, for example.

Page 230

[17] Mental Health Foundation report 'Cheers?' 18 April 2006
[18] WHO 'Injuries and Violence in Europe. Why They Matter
and What Can Be Done' (via *The Globe*, published by the
Global Alcohol Policy Alliance)
[19] Health and Safety Executive, 16 September 2007

books and websites that I found helpful

about drink/drugs

Drinking, A Love Story Caroline Knapp
The Broken Cord Michael Dorris
A Head Full Of Blue Nick Johnstone
Heroin – How To Stop Time Ann Marlowe
More, Now, Again Elizabeth Wurtzel
Molly's Unofficial Alcoholics Anonymous UK Homepage
(aamolly.org.uk)

about depression

They F*** You Up Oliver James
The Noonday Demon Andrew Solomon
A Bright Red Scream Marya Hornbacher
Walkers in Darkness (walkers.org)

people

Urban Tribes Ethan Watters
Only Child – How to Survive Being One Jill Pitkeathley and David
Emerson
The Language of Letting Go Melodie Beattie

acknowledgements

A big thank you to Pete and everyone at Serpent's Tail and Profile for their patience, after life events caused me to deliver a year late; the Society of Authors for all their help; Michael for the great editing; Suzanne for helping spread the word; Alex for the really useful comments, among many other things; Paul at Frith Street; Sharon at Kentish Town; and M, G and C, for staying on the wagon with me. Thanks to all the people from my drinking days who are still around, and to all the many and wonderful new friends I've made since 12 September 2002.

www.taniaglyde.com